Make Your Contacts Count

Networking Know-How for Cash, Clients, and Career Success

Anne Baber

Lynne Waymon

AMACOM

American Management Association

New York • Atlanta • Brussels • Buenas Aires • Chicago • London • Mexico City
San Francisco • Shanghai • Tokyo • Toronto • Washington, D.C.

*This publication is designed to provide accurate and authoritative informa-
tion in regard to the subject matter covered. It is sold with the understanding
that the publisher is not engaged in rendering legal, accounting, or other professional service. If legal advice or other expert assistance is required, the
services of a competent professional person should be sought.*

*Library of Congress Cataloging-in-Publication Data
Baber, Anne, 1938–
Make your contacts count : networking know-how for cash, clients,
  and career success / Anne Baber, Lynne Waymon
      p. cm.
Includes bibliographical references and index.
ISBN 0-8144-7093-9 (pbk.)
  1. Career development. 2. Business networks. 3. Social networks. 4. Interpersonal
  relations. 5. Business etiquette. 6. Success in business. I. Waymon, Lynne.
  II. Title.*

*HF5381 .B143 2002
650.1'3—dc21*   *2001053558*

*Printing number
10 9 8 7 6 5 4 3 2*

Contents

PART I

How's Your Networking Know-How?

Networking—you're expected to just know how to do it. As you go through life, from graduation to the grave, you'll have thousands of encounters with people in business and social settings. Aren't you supposed to know automatically how to remember names, turn small talk toward business topics, exchange business cards so that they won't end up in "the round file," quickly build the kind of trust that results in sales and satisfied customers, follow up without making a pest of yourself, and find a new job or change careers?

What do you know about this vital business skill? Do you want to find out how you stack up as a networker? Do you want to see if you understand the subtleties, if you know the strategies, if you are using state-of-the-art skills? The self-assessment in Chapter 1 will help you determine where you are. You'll be able to decide whether you need to read every word of this book or just selected sections or chapters. Your results will help you prioritize your learning. Then you'll be able to use your time—and this book—in the most effective way. That's why we wrote this book: So that you can make networking an art . . . not an accident.

CHAPTER 1

Assess Your Mastery

Taking the self-assessment will give you an overview of the specific behaviors, attitudes, and strategies that make up the skill of networking.

It will help you to:

▶ Test your current level of mastery of state-of-the-art networking behaviors and beliefs.

▶ Increase your awareness of the vast repertoire of skills and strategies available to you as you build business relationships.

▶ Remind yourself of some techniques that you know but don't use as much as you could.

▶ Pinpoint topics that you want to focus on in order to increase your impact, professionalism, and comfort.

▶ Chart your increasing skill when you take the quiz again after perusing this book.

Instructions

As you go through the self-assessment, you should know how we define some of the terms we've used. Then, you'll need to know how to select your answers. Finally, after you are finished with the self-assessment, you'll need to know how to assess your mastery and decide what to do next.

Defining Some Terms

Networking event: A business, quasi-business, or social situation in which you have opportunities to develop valuable connections.

Organization: Any group you join for the purpose of making business connections (professional association, chamber of commerce, alumni group, business referral group, board, etc.).

Company: Who you work for (your firm, your agency, etc.).

Selecting Your Answers

Below, you'll find eight sections: Observing the "Netiquette," Assessing Your Comfort Level, Being Strategic, Meeting People, Using Networking Organizations, Making the Most of Events, Achieving Bottom-Line Results, and Following Up. Each section concentrates on a specific area of the networking experience. The statements in each section focus on what you believe about networking and what you do and say when you are networking.

For each statement, check one of the following as your response:

Rarely	0 to 20 percent of the time
Sometimes	20 to 50 percent of the time
Frequently	50 to 80 percent of the time
Almost always	80 to 100 percent of the time

At the end of each section, you'll find a commentary that will help you in your self-assessment.

Observing the "Netiquette"

If you've ever had an awkward moment as you engaged in a networking activity, you know how daunting it is to feel as if you don't

Observing the "Netiquette"

I talk to discover reasons to hand out my business card.

Rarely _____ Sometimes _____ Frequently _____ Almost Always _____

As I talk with someone, I'm trying to figure out a reason to give him my business card and get his.

Rarely _____ Sometimes _____ Frequently _____ Almost Always _____

I sense when I can begin talking about what I can offer or what my company provides.

Rarely _____ Sometimes _____ Frequently _____ Almost Always _____

I'm comfortable joining a group of people who are already talking.

Rarely _____ Sometimes _____ Frequently _____ Almost Always _____

I consciously work at talking only about 50 percent of the time.

Rarely _____ Sometimes _____ Frequently _____ Almost Always _____

I find interesting ways to say thank you when someone gives me a resource or referral.

Rarely _____ Sometimes _____ Frequently _____ Almost Always _____

If a contact doesn't reciprocate, I skillfully and tactfully point out how she can help me.

Rarely _____ Sometimes _____ Frequently _____ Almost Always _____

know what to do. However, as you learn the skills and techniques—and the rationales behind them—you'll find that you rarely find yourself in a situation that you can't handle with aplomb and confidence.

Handing out lots of business cards isn't networking. And do you know what actually happens to those cards? See Chapter 14 for the rest of the story.

Do you worry about seeming too pushy? Too passive? If you're too pushy, you'll turn people off. If you're too passive, you won't get much out of networking.

When you approach a group, are you mentally back at the eighth-grade dance, wondering if people will snub you? If you know the steps for joining (not breaking into) a group, you'll be able to do it with ease. The process appears in Chapter 10.

Do you, out of nervousness, find yourself chattering away, dominating the conversation? Or do you have a hard time holding up your end of the conversation with Success Stories and other important things to talk about? Give and take is basic to networking. Besides, you have to listen in order to learn what your contact needs. Talking too much is a turn-off. Chapter 9 will help you avoid all of the top twenty turn-offs.

Do you say, "Thanks!" in ways that make you memorable, yet are appropriate? Corporate cultures differ. Appropriate ways to say thank you at IBM are bound to be different from what's done at the dot-coms.

Do you sometimes feel that you are the only one in the relationship who is giving? Do you know what to do about that?

> **Never underestimate the power of networking to enhance your life, both professionally and personally.**

Great connectors observe and learn the "netiquette" in a particular organization from the members of that organization. You can always ask the advice of a mentor at work when deciding how to say thanks. Or, you can watch the pros in your association to figure out how quickly it's appropriate to talk business with potential clients at the meetings.

Smart networkers use their connections to learn the art of connecting as well as to find resources and opportunities.

Assessing Your Comfort Level

Networking has become a respected business and career skill. Why, then, does it sometimes feel uncomfortable?

Assessing Your Comfort Level

I feel professional and comfortable when I'm networking.
Rarely _____ Sometimes _____ Frequently _____ Almost Always _____

I become energized and excited as I enter a room full of people.
Rarely _____ Sometimes _____ Frequently _____ Almost Always _____

Networking is something I want to do, not just something I have to do.
Rarely _____ Sometimes _____ Frequently _____ Almost Always _____

I can talk easily about my successes.
Rarely _____ Sometimes _____ Frequently _____ Almost Always _____

When I talk with people, I find out something of interest to me.
Rarely _____ Sometimes _____ Frequently _____ Almost Always _____

At networking events, I can think of plenty of meaningful topics to talk about.
Rarely _____ Sometimes _____ Frequently _____ Almost Always _____

Few families today sit down to a long Sunday dinner where Uncle Charlie tells stories and Grandma chimes in with the morals. Good conversational skills are learned. Contrary to popular opinion, nobody's born with the gift of gab. But anybody can learn how to use conversation to build networking relationships.

Often, the ground rules for networking are unclear. Because it's a hidden career and business skill that you're just expected to know, many people are unsure about what's considered professional.

In some circles, networking is mistakenly equated with hot-dogging, tooting your own horn, or grandstanding. Some people say, "I shouldn't have to network. My good work should stand on its own without my having to promote myself." But who will know what you do well and what you need if you don't develop ease in talking about those things? For tips on constructing and telling Success Stories, see Chapter 12.

After years of looking down their noses at anything that smacks of selling, professionals of all stripes are realizing that they must network. Do they love it? Probably not. But they can master the skills and begin to incorporate it as an integral and valuable part of their professional lives. Eventually, they may even be able to stride into a networking event feeling upbeat. Every skill you stuff into your bag of tricks, every tip you try, will add to your ability to enjoy networking.

What happens in the conversation is this: After you exchange names and ask, "What do you do?" there is a pause. It's the pause that comes right before the conversation about the weather. Here's the rule: Never—and we mean never—talk about the weather or the ball scores. Instead, see Chapter 12 to learn how to carry around with you a pocketful of topics that you really want to talk about, topics that will convince others of your expertise, build your credibility, teach others to trust you, lead you to resources, and ensure that opportunities drop into your lap.

Being Strategic

Are you surprised that "being strategic" didn't turn out to be one of your strong points? In this sped-up world, it's all too easy to run from activity to event (whatever's available this week will do) and then wonder why networking doesn't work!

So slow down! Make a long-range plan about which Arenas you want to become known in and for what reason. Which organizations should you join? Test drive them before you plunk down the membership dues. There's a quiz in Chapter 16 that will help you make smart choices. Want to do Olympic-level networking? Design a project for yourself that will make you the natural and only choice when opportunity comes knocking.

If you find yourself resisting being strategic, you may be thinking that deciding on a networking goal and going after it is just too calculating. You want things to "just happen" without their being so programmed. Tell yourself that managing your networking contacts is okay; manipulating them is not. When you know the difference, you'll feel more comfortable making a strategic networking plan. Tell

---

Being Strategic

I have a long-range, strategic plan for my networking efforts in each organization I belong to.

Rarely _____ Sometimes _____ Frequently _____ Almost Always _____

I join organizations because of my strategic business/career development plan.

Rarely _____ Sometimes _____ Frequently _____ Almost Always _____

Before I go to an event, I make a list of specific resources/tips/trends I have to offer to the people I'm likely to see there.

Rarely _____ Sometimes _____ Frequently _____ Almost Always _____

I initiate at least one networking meeting (breakfast, lunch, etc.) a week.

Rarely _____ Sometimes _____ Frequently _____ Almost Always _____

I let people know the types of problems I can solve, so that they refer exactly the right kinds of opportunities to me.

Rarely _____ Sometimes _____ Frequently _____ Almost Always _____

I'm comfortable telling my contacts what I want or need.

Rarely _____ Sometimes _____ Frequently _____ Almost Always _____

---

yourself that planning for visibility and credibility is just like any other planning you do for your business or your career: It makes sense. You have limited hours and dollars to spend in the marketplace, and without a plan, you'll sink down into aimless activity that doesn't amount to anything.

Meeting People

Are you surprised to be told that giving your job title isn't the right thing to do? It's of more value to you for people to know your talent than your title. When people meet you for the first time, they don't care (yet!) that you're with Smith, Jones, Miller, Barnes, and Blarney or that you work for Lucent. To craft answers to the inevitable "What do

Meeting People

When someone asks, "What do you do?" I avoid giving my job title
(executive vice president of administrative services, for example).
Rarely _____ Sometimes ____ Frequently ____ Almost Always ____

I use several methods to learn people's names.
Rarely _____ Sometimes ____ Frequently ____ Almost Always ____

I've figured out a way to teach others my name and make it memorable.
Rarely _____ Sometimes ____ Frequently ____ Almost Always ____

When I've forgotten someone's name, I reintroduce myself.
Rarely _____ Sometimes ____ Frequently ____ Almost Always ____

When someone asks, "What do you do?" I avoid saying, "I'm with . . ."
and giving the name of the organization I work for.
Rarely _____ Sometimes ____ Frequently ____ Almost Always ____

When people ask what I do for a living, my answer paints a vivid picture.
Rarely _____ Sometimes ____ Frequently ____ Almost Always ____

When someone asks, "What do you do?" I avoid leading with my occupation or job category (accountant, lawyer, systems analyst, architect).
Rarely _____ Sometimes ____ Frequently ____ Almost Always ____

you do?" question without telling your title, naming your company,
or providing your occupation, consult Chapter 11. Hint: Your answers
should make it easy for people to talk with you and should begin to
teach people about your Character and Competence.

Have you given up on remembering names? Don't despair. In
Chapter 10 you'll find three ways to remember somebody's name
and three ways to make your own memorable. That's important too.
You'll be pleased to know that there are several things you can do
when you forget someone's name other than saying, "Oh, no. I've
forgotten your name." Isn't that sort of insulting?

To be a successful networker, you'll have to shed the rituals for meeting and greeting people that we know so well and do so mindlessly. These rituals restrict, rather than enhance, your ability to build relationships.

Using Networking Organizations

Are you making the most of your memberships? What are the worst mistakes members make? See Chapter 16. Too often, when it comes to joining organizations, people say, "I'm too busy!" or "I'm too bashful!" or "I'm too broke!" If you're in the midst of a job search or starting a business or professional practice, you may wonder whether joining is worth the time and money. Well, it isn't if you just join and hang around on the fringes. It isn't if you spend all your time sitting with and talking to coworkers you see every day. It isn't if you fail to find ways to exhibit

---

Using Networking Organizations

The first year I'm a member of an organization, I take an active role by serving on a committee or doing some job.
Rarely _____ Sometimes _____ Frequently _____ Almost Always _____

When I join an organization, I attend at least 75 percent of its events.
Rarely _____ Sometimes _____ Frequently _____ Almost Always _____

I know whether my company supports business development/networking with time and money.
Rarely _____ Sometimes _____ Frequently _____ Almost Always _____

I introduce myself to the leader or speaker when I go to an event.
Rarely _____ Sometimes _____ Frequently _____ Almost Always _____

At networking events, I avoid spending time with people from my own organization.
Rarely _____ Sometimes _____ Frequently _____ Almost Always _____

I know how to increase my visibility in any organization I belong to.
Rarely _____ Sometimes _____ Frequently _____ Almost Always _____

your Character and Competence. It isn't if you overlook teaching people to trust you, so that you never become part of the inner circle.

Do you know how to connect at conventions? If you really want to get your money's worth, see Chapter 17.

Visibility is valuable. You'll find some great ideas about increasing yours in organizations and at work in Chapters 6 and 7.

Making the Most of Events

Have you ever left a networking event grumping, "I don't know why I come to these things. I don't get a thing out of them"? If you learn the skills in this book, you'll never have that experience again.

Do you want to meet the movers and shakers? Arrive early.

Do you sometimes feel stuck talking to the same person long after you've exhausted topics of mutual interest? Most people do. Did you ever say, in leave-taking, "I think I'll go freshen my drink," and head in the opposite direction from the bar? Tsk! Tsk! You need our easy *LEAVE NOW Formula*, so that you know how to end conversations professionally and comfortably. Then you'll be able to move on and meet a dozen people in a two-hour event.

> A good networking relationship means that somebody (besides you!) is looking out for your best interests while you are looking out for theirs.

Are you confused about how to get down to business at networking events? Learn how and when to start talking about your company or your product or service.

People want to do business with people they trust. Do your contacts trust you? Do you trust them? What's the key to developing trust? See Chapter 5 for some surprising thoughts on the topic.

Do you wonder why you should bother to introduce one of your contacts to another? Find out the benefits of becoming a great connector, someone known for bringing people together.

Making the Most of Events

I know how to end a conversation comfortably and professionally and move on to the next person.

Rarely _____ Sometimes _____ Frequently _____ Almost Always _____

I avoid "ho-hum" conversations about topics like the weather or the ball scores.

Rarely _____ Sometimes _____ Frequently _____ Almost Always _____

I find it easy to turn the conversation toward what I do or what my company does.

Rarely _____ Sometimes _____ Frequently _____ Almost Always _____

At a typical networking event (two hours), I introduce myself to ten to twelve people.

Rarely _____ Sometimes _____ Frequently _____ Almost Always _____

What I say at networking events is consciously designed to teach people to trust me.

Rarely _____ Sometimes _____ Frequently _____ Almost Always _____

I arrive early at networking events.

Rarely _____ Sometimes _____ Frequently _____ Almost Always _____

When I'm listening to people, I try to think of someone they'd like to meet, and then I introduce them to that person.

Rarely _____ Sometimes _____ Frequently _____ Almost Always _____

Achieving Bottom-Line Results

This is where the rubber meets the road. The questions in this section will reveal whether your network is working.

How about networking at work? Have you detected a resistance to networking inside your corporation, government agency, or institution? Why? How can you decide if your organization (whether you're a sole proprietor or part of a huge corporation) values and

Achieving Bottom-Line Results

After an event, I can name at least three valuable pieces of information that I've learned from others.

Rarely _____ Sometimes _____ Frequently _____ Almost Always _____

At work, I hear stories about how people have developed business and enhanced their careers through networking.

Rarely _____ Sometimes _____ Frequently _____ Almost Always _____

I can cite examples of how my networking activities have paid off for my company.

Rarely _____ Sometimes _____ Frequently _____ Almost Always _____

I can say exactly how my networking activities have paid off for my own career.

Rarely _____ Sometimes _____ Frequently _____ Almost Always _____

I can point out examples of assistance or resources I've given to my contacts.

Rarely _____ Sometimes _____ Frequently _____ Almost Always _____

When I need something, I know whom to call.

Rarely _____ Sometimes _____ Frequently _____ Almost Always _____

When my key contacts talk about me, I notice that they can describe what I do vividly and accurately.

Rarely _____ Sometimes _____ Frequently _____ Almost Always _____

supports relationship building? If you don't know how to read the culture, look at the quiz in Chapter 19. What if networking became "the right thing to do" in your corporate culture? You could help make that happen.

How about you personally? Is your network ready to tap into? Can you point to bottom-line results from specific contacts you've cultivated? When you need a resource, a referral, or an idea (or maybe just a pat on the back), do you know exactly whom to call?

How vibrant are your networking relationships? Have you been able to develop a cadre of people out there who are promoting you and actively looking for ways to contribute to your success?

Have you ever listened to a contact describe you, your capabilities, and your successes to someone else? What a revelation! Use every encounter to teach your contacts something else about you.

Following Up

Wouldn't it be great to follow up creatively and consistently? Sure, we recommend that you use an electronic database. But, technology isn't the whole answer to keeping in touch. The real key to following up is having something to follow up about. So, be sure that, in addition to talking about yourself, you also find out what's on the other person's agenda. What are her challenges, interests, needs, enthusiasms, dilemmas? Then you can follow up based on her needs, not your need for a new client or your interest in getting a better job. The best

---

Following Up

When I get a business card, I put the information in my Rolodex™ or database.
Rarely _____ Sometimes _____ Frequently _____ Almost Always

I follow up within three to five days.
Rarely _____ Sometimes _____ Frequently _____ Almost Always

Soon after a networking event, I reconnect with two or three people I talked with.
Rarely _____ Sometimes _____ Frequently _____ Almost Always

After an event, I have several requests to fulfill from people I talked with.
Rarely _____ Sometimes _____ Frequently _____ Almost Always

I am able to fit staying in touch with key contacts into my daily/weekly/ monthly routine.
Rarely _____ Sometimes _____ Frequently _____ Almost Always

relationships are built on giving. When you Listen Generously and focus on being more of a go-giver than a go-getter, following up becomes a whole lot easier.

Check Your Results

Throughout the self-assessment, the best answers are "Frequently" and "Almost Always." Look at your array of answers. If most of them are "Frequently" or "Almost Always," you probably have mastered the networking concepts behind the statements. As you go through this book, you will get a kick out of delving deeper into what makes networking work, and you'll pick up some new tips and techniques along the way. If most of your answers are "Sometimes" or "Rarely," you will be saying, "Aha!" a lot as you read this book. You'll discover new ideas, new concepts, and, of course, skill-building tips and techniques. Soon you'll be able to put the new ideas to work for you as you build your network.

Next Steps

After you've checked your results in the eight skill areas, take a look at the big picture. Maybe you're doing well at meeting people, but you need to focus on being strategic. Or maybe you find that your comfort level is high, but you fall down on following up. Use this self-assessment to set your priorities. Should you go straight to a specific topic or chapter? If you give attention to specific areas, you'll see results quickly. For instance, if the self-assessment indicates that you need more skill in meeting people, then you'll want to pay special attention to Chapters 10, 11, and 12. If you find that you were stymied by a majority of the statements, you may decide to start at the beginning of this book and read straight through to the end.

Take out your day timer or Palm Pilot. Make a note to retake the self-assessment in six months. That way, you'll have time to read this book and to put many of the tips and techniques to work. Go ahead. Experiment. Making a small change or adding a new behavior can have a dramatic effect on your ability to connect with people. We predict you'll be pleasantly surprised at how easily you've made your new-found, state-of-the-art networking skills a way of life.

PART 2

Why—and How—Contacts Count

Everybody has contacts. Not everybody has contacts that count. How about you?

The chapters in Part 2 will help you rid your mind of self-defeating ideas so that you can put more purpose, profit, and pleasure into your networking. You'll find that the benefits will boomerang right back to you when you help others find what they need. You'll relish the abundance your network brings you—a constant flow of business, career, and life opportunities. You'll find out how to tailor your network to your life and your goals. There's no such thing as a one-size-fits-all, ready-made, off-the-rack network. Your custom network will bring you into contact with the very people you need to meet. You'll understand that all relationships go through six very natural stages, and you'll know how to move toward more active relationships with your contacts. You'll discover the two essential components of trust, Character and Competence, and see how to demonstrate them.

CHAPTER 2

Unmuddle Your Mindset

What is networking, anyhow? The term has been around since the 1960s, but many people still don't have a clear idea of its meaning. Here's our official definition:

Networking is the deliberate process of exchanging information, resources, support, and access in such a way as to create mutually beneficial relationships for personal and professional success.

More informally, it's making contacts for business and career purposes.

What about your mindset? Could it be that you have some misconceptions about making connections?

The Ten Biggest Misconceptions About Networking

1. "Networking is manipulative," says Teresa, who owns a nanny agency. "I don't like the idea of twisting someone's arm to get that person to do something for me."

It's true, you can't exploit others and expect to build long-term relationships. The way to avoid manipulation, though, is to give more than you receive. And, when you want something, be up-front and overt about it. Saying, "To build my business, I give free workshops for young parents to show them how to find and manage a nanny. Do you know anyone who'd like an invitation?" will prompt a better response than a "hidden agenda" question, such as, "So, do you know anyone with kids under five?"

2. "I tried networking last Thursday," says Mel, a franchise owner. "It doesn't work."

To cultivate a bountiful network takes months—maybe even years. Mel has a microwave mentality. You can't zap a relationship for thirty seconds. Networking is a long-term process.

3. "I just do my job," says Brad, an engineer. "I don't need to network at work. What's the point?"

Smart employees use networking to stay in touch with internal customers and suppliers. Their networks alert them to problems before those problems get out of hand and help them spot emerging needs. These employees break through bureaucratic bottlenecks. They use their personal contacts to get things moving and speed things up. They build constituencies and gain support for projects and proposals. They collaborate and cooperate. They create ad-hoc, cross-functional, problem-solving teams. When somebody says, "I need it yesterday," they come though. If Brad networked at work, he could serve his organization better and develop his reputation as a person who can get things done—fast.

There are no fast-food networks.

4. "Networking is fine for the junior folks who are still struggling to climb the ladder," says Richard, a vice president of human resources. "But I don't need to network anymore."

No matter what your title, you never outgrow the need to network. Richard could be using networking to his company's—and his—advantage. He could ensure that his company remains competitive by networking with people who have similar jobs at other companies. That's the best way to benchmark, to check out the best practices and compare yourself with people one rung above you on the corporate ladder. And the higher up in the hierarchy someone is, the more vulnerable he is. Middle management and staff positions disappear daily. Richard had better get cracking to create his personal safety net.

5. "Networking is just schmoozing," says Karla, a manager of administrative services. "It's boring and . . . uncomfortable."

If Karla's conversations skitter over the surface, she needs to find out how to sidestep those superficialities and get down to business. She can learn how to go beyond the chit-chat into conversations that can help her solve problems, come up with new ideas, and access valuable resources.

6. "I'm not looking for a job," says Diana, a purchasing manager. "I don't need to network."

Absolutely the worst time to begin networking is when you need to—after you decide to change jobs or lose your job. If you expect to be job hunting anytime in the future—and in today's economy, you should expect

> **You never outgrow the need to network.**

to be a job seeker at some point—you should be networking now. How long you'll have to search before you find a job depends on how strong your network is. By increasing her visibility among her peers and superiors, Diana can achieve top-of-the-mind awareness. When these people think "dynamite purchasing manager," her name will pop up. Not only can networking protect her if her job goes away, it also can lead to new job opportunities—even when she isn't looking.

7. "Networking has never done a thing for me or my career," says Kyle, a director of corporate planning.

That's hard to believe. People can provide access to vital information—

> **A single conversation can change your life.**

news of a job opening before it's advertised, insights into industry trends, great ideas for a business of your own. Sometimes, people can put a bottom-line figure on the value of a single conversation. Sometimes a single conversation can change your life.

8. "Sure," says Carmen, who owns an art gallery, "I know how to network. You just hand out your business card."

Handing out cards isn't networking. Most cards end up in the wastepaper basket. To make contact, you must create a real, human connection.

9. "I wasn't born with the gift of gab," says Morton, a CPA. "I'll never be any good at networking."

Only about 10 percent of the people we've interviewed say that they come by their conversational skills naturally. The rest of us need networking know-how. Luckily, networking skills aren't brain surgery. Morton can easily learn how to become better and better at connecting with people effectively and comfortably.

> **Networkers are made, not born.**

10. "Networking is a waste of time," says Henri, an attorney. "I leave networking events asking myself, 'Why did I come?'"

More than 85 percent of people who attend networking events tell us that they haven't figured out what they want to achieve. If you aim at nothing, you'll hit it, as the saying goes. Henri needs to go to networking events with goals in mind. That way, he'll find what he's looking for.

Come In from the Cold

Albert Einstein, the physicist who changed the way we think about the world, once was asked, "What is the most important question to ask?" Without hesitating, he replied, "Is this a friendly universe?" Building relationships with people creates a world of abundance—a friendly universe—for all.

Yet, people say:

▶ "He gave me the cold shoulder."

▶ "What can I say to break the ice?"

▶ "I hate to make cold calls."

▶ "I got cold feet when I thought about going to the meeting alone."

▶ "I just froze up."

It's hard to feel excited about making contact when your mind is full of associations like that.

If you think of other people—people you might network with—as cold and rejecting, it will be hard for you to enjoy the moment, exchange information, or explore future opportunities.

Believe the Best About Yourself and Others

There are two kinds of truth about you. There are objective truths, or facts about yourself: I am thirty-six years old; I was born in Omaha; I'm a lawyer. And then there are subjective "truths," or beliefs—positive and negative—that you hold about yourself: I'm too skinny; I'm not very interesting; I'm a good manager. You can't change the objective truths, but you can change the way you think about yourself—the subjective "truths."

Your beliefs about yourself and other people may get in the way of comfortable networking. Take Paul, for example. He used to be apprehensive about entertaining out-of-town clients at dinner. But to cope with his hesitancy about meeting new people, he's gotten into the habit of giving himself a pep talk before he goes out. "I go into it saying, 'These guys don't know any more about what I do than I know about what they do. They've got kids and hobbies and hopes and dreams.' I think about all the things we have in common. If I prepare, I'm okay."

Paul discovered through experience what psychologists have verified by studying the conversational patterns of strangers. These researchers have found that if strangers believe that they have a lot in common, they act very much as if they were old friends. They pay attention to subtle conversational clues and match each other's progress through the conversation. If one of them brings up a lighter, more informal topic, the other will match that topic with a light topic of his own. If one says something of a self-revealing nature, the other follows.

On the other hand, if the strangers are told that they have nothing in common, conversation limps along, and both parties feel as if they have not connected. This research reinforces the idea that your attitude toward others has a great deal to do with your success as a networker.

Successful networkers believe that they can enjoy talking with other people, that they can make satisfying contact with other people, that other people can provide resources, and that other people can open up opportunities.

You may see the value in making contact. You may know that people are excellent sources of information and ideas. You may be able to enjoy someone through conversation. You may even believe that people will open opportunities for you. But you still may not have reached your potential as a networker. There's another part of your mind you must master.

Catch Your Critic

You climb into your car after a long day at work. You put your key in the ignition. You turn out of the parking lot. . . . All of a sudden, you're at home, turning into your driveway. You have no recollection of the route you took, the traffic you coped with, or the signs and houses and businesses you passed.

You've been on autopilot. But if you think about it, you'll remember that something has been going on in your mind. Your Critic has been talking to you all the way home. It has said a lot of things:

▶ "Tomorrow is going to be awful because I didn't check with Stan about the meeting."

▶ "I'm too tired to go to the store. Why can't I ever remember to take something out of the freezer?"

▶ "I ate too much again at lunch. When will I ever learn! I'll never lose this weight."

▶ "I should have just told Becky I couldn't help her move on Saturday. I'm such a pushover. . . . I never can say, 'No.'"

You'll notice that the Critic comments on what you have done (or haven't done) in the past and what you probably will do (or won't do) in the future. The reviews are always bad. So are the previews. The chorus repeats and repeats: "I didn't do it right yesterday; I won't do it right tomorrow."

You couldn't think of just the right retort in an argument? Your Critic will hash over what you did say and supply a dozen versions of what you should have said. The voice in your head is prosecuting attorney, judge, and jury, and the verdict is always "Guilty."

> **Bad reviews and bad previews are the Critic's stock in trade.**

The Critic is talkative as you drive your car, but it really gets going in stressful situations like networking. Because the Critic focuses on the past and the future, not the present, the voice makes it very hard—sometimes impossible—for you to connect easily with others.

Notice How Your Critic Sabotages You

The Critic in your mind whispers to you during introductions. Just when the person you're talking with is saying his name, the Critic says, "You never can remember people's names." Sure enough, while the Critic is whispering at you, the other person's name is blotted out.

The Critic mutters when there is a silence in the middle of a conversation. In your head, the Critic says, "You never can think of anything to talk about." Because you're listening to the Critic, guess what . . . it's a self-fulfilling prophecy; you aren't able to think of anything to say.

The Critic mumbles, after you've been talking with someone for several minutes, "You're not interesting or important. You know, don't you, that this person wants to get away?" And

> **Anybody can learn to make small talk and to use small talk to create valuable networking relationships.**

you fade out of the conversation, stammering something about needing to freshen your drink.

The Critic is bad news. Your brain believes what you tell it about yourself. You create your own subjective "truths" about yourself. Often these are negative "truths." If you give yourself—or allow your Critic to give you—negative messages, you will act as if those messages are true. That's pretty self-defeating.

The good news is that you can transform your Critic into a Coach. You can reprogram that voice in your head to give you positive and supportive messages instead of negative and defeating ones.

Convert Your Critic Into Your Coach

Who writes all the Critic's scripts? You do! Taking responsibility for what the voice in your head is saying isn't easy. It's been with you for a long time. It's always there. It's so automatic that it seems to be firmly entrenched. You forget to listen for it, but it slips in. It's hard to be conscious of the Critic. And you may have gotten so used to letting the Critic beat up on you that you've started to believe that what it says is true.

There are many theories about why the Critic appears and where the critical voice in your head comes from. Often, people remember that their parents or teachers put a label on them. "He's shy," they might have said. Or, "She's clumsy." Even well-meaning adults can give children plenty of critical comments that are replayed through the years by their Critics.

When you're grown up, bosses tend to focus on and comment on the mistakes you make. One researcher found that only 8 percent of a boss's comments were compliments. When you goof up, you hear a lot more about it than when you do something right.

So the Critic mimics all the voices in our lives that criticize us. By the way, your Critic's voice—or voices—can be male, female, neither, or both. We learn to criticize ourselves, and we do it well and constantly. The Critic reveals our fears about talking with other people and our feelings of inadequacy about connecting with people. Here are some things people say their Critics have said to them:

▶ "I never can think of anything to say."

▶ "I just know I'll say something stupid."

▶ "If I give something—like information—I won't get as much back."

▶ "If I talk with him, he'll think I'm flirting."

▶ "I'm not good at figuring out what people are thinking."

▶ "I don't have much to offer because I'm new in my field."

▶ "They won't accept me or like me."

▶ "It's a sign of weakness to need anything."

▶ "It's rude to ask for what I want."

▶ "I have nothing to contribute."

▶ "Everyone else but me is at ease."

▶ "I'll be stuck and won't know how to end the conversation."

The trick is to tune in to your Critic, listen to what that voice says, and write it down. Analyze the topics. On the topic of making contact, most people's Critics focus on two areas:

> The value of networking: "It's a waste of time, phony, and manipulative."

> Their ability to do it: "I'm no good at this."

Write Down Your Critic's Comments

Write down some of the things your Critic has said to you in networking situations recently.

The next step is to transform each criticism into an encouraging statement. Some people call these positive comments *affirmations*. Your affirmations may not be true yet. You may not even believe them yet. It doesn't matter. Say them over and over until they unmuddle your mind.

Take some comments that your Critic has made to you in networking situations and transform those comments into positive statements.

Knowing how to turn your Critic into a Coach can help you in many areas of your life. Changing the way you talk to yourself about your ability to network and combining that new mindset with the specific skills in this book will help you become a better networker.

Creating your own Coach isn't accomplished overnight. But practice makes permanent. There's no magic formula, but these instructions will help you begin to experience the power of positive self-talk.

How to Create Your Coach

Use one index card for each Coaching (positive) statement.

Write your statement three times. The first two times, use the word *I*. The last time, use the word *you*. The word *you* blocks out the critical comments others may have made to you that your Critic replays. It's like a person outside yourself complimenting you and giving you support.

Here's an example:

▶ "I always know just what to say."

▶ "I always know just what to say."

▶ "You always know just what to say."

Read your index cards aloud several times a day. Repetition is essential. Some experts advise repeating your statements a dozen times a day.

To save time, tape record your statements and play them when you're riding in the car or getting ready for work in the morning or preparing for bed at night.

Practice your positive statements faithfully every day for a month.

Read your statements before you go to a networking event.

You'll find positive Coach's statements throughout this book as we lead you through the networking skills. At every step, it's important that you work on your mindset as well as learn the skills.

CHAPTER 3

Customize Your Network

People ask, "Where do I begin? How can I expand my network and build new alliances?" Start with strategy. Before you leap into action, joining organizations or calling people for lunch, stop and develop a plan. Your strategic plan will help you make networking a way of life, not another task to put on your "to do" list.

Put Yourself in Charge

You are CEO, president, and chairperson of the board of your own network. Create that network and customize it to fit your own needs. It won't be a carbon copy of anybody else's network. It will include only those contacts that you develop for your own reasons. For example, you might focus your network to deal with a specific situation, like job hunting (Chapter 23) or generating clients (Chapters 20 and 21).

> **Make strategic choices about where to network.**

Ask yourself, "What are my goals for the next six to nine months?" Given today's volatile business climate, it's hard to plan much further ahead than that. Focusing on a six- to nine-month time frame gives you enough time to have the six to eight meetings you'll need to create strong, long-lasting, mutually beneficial networking relationships.

Make your goals as specific as possible. You may focus on organizational goals or personal goals—or both. Here are some examples:

29

Marie, a health care educator at a hospital, says, "To gain higher visibility—for the hospital in the community, and for my own career protection in an industry that's in turmoil."

Randy, who works in financial services, says, "To double the number of referrals to qualified prospects that I'm receiving."

Sheila, an interior designer, says, "To stay in touch with past clients and generate repeat business from at least half of them."

Wayne, a banker, says, "To improve the bank's access to information on local business trends and real estate development."

Now, with business goals in mind, these people are ready to design a proactive plan for building strategic business relationships.

Link Up One-on-One

There are two ways to create your network: to link up with people individually and to join organizations. Some of your best networking contacts will come from one-on-one relationships: your next door neighbor, your accountant, your cousin in Tulsa. You find these people (or they find you) outside of any formal organization.

Your personal network will include people from many different sources. You may forge strong business alliances with:

▶ Coworkers, past and current

▶ Bosses, past and current

▶ People you went to school with

▶ Neighbors

▶ Volunteers you've worked with (at church, in political groups, in the Boy Scouts, in the United Way)

▶ Past college professors or continuing education instructors

▶ Leisure time acquaintances from activities (sports, the neighborhood pool, hobbies, etc.)

▶ Relatives

▶ People who provide services to you (your doctor, dentist, office supply store proprietor, etc.)

However, to expand your network quickly and target people with similar interests, it makes sense to join groups of people.

Keep in mind, however, that not all groups are equally useful for networking.

Choose Groups Strategically

Use the list that follows as you make strategic choices about where to network. These Arenas are arranged with the most highly structured and intentional networking groups at the top of the list and the most "accidental" and serendipitous at the bottom. The groups at the top focus on bringing people together to do business; the groups farther down the list have different goals. The groups at the top will actually teach you how to network and guide you in the behaviors that are appropriate as you cultivate business contacts. The groups farther down the list may be useful networking Arenas, but only for the most skilled, savvy, and sophisticated networkers.

Customer common groups. These groups (we call them Constellations) are made up of businesses that have customers in common. Owners of businesses that beautify and maintain the home might band together to refer work to one another. For example, an interior designer, a real estate agent, a home remodeler, a lawn care professional, and a chimney sweep might form a group. Sometimes these customer common groups are subgroups of business referral groups. Sometimes people start them just because the benefits are so obvious. (See Chapter 20 for more information on creating and profiting from these groups.)

Special-purpose networks. Occasionally, networks are created with only a single purpose. In one midwestern city, for example, entrepreneurs created a special network to attract venture financing.

Job-hunting support and career change groups are other typical special-purpose networks. Finding a job or changing careers is hard work. The people who do it most successfully, most quickly, with the least damage to their self-esteem and finances are usually those who join support and strategy groups. Often these groups are found in churches, at women's centers, through private career coaches, and as offshoots of community college or open university courses.

Business referral groups. Owners of small or home-based businesses, sales professionals, and people in professional services benefit from these groups. The groups' missions are tightly focused on getting business and generating referrals. Only one business in each "category" may join. For example, the group will include only one divorce lawyer, one electrician, one alterations shop. At weekly or bimonthly meetings, members become familiar with one another's products and services through a variety of activities. A commitment to attend and generate leads is essential to the success of the group. (See Chapter 20 for more information on starting and participating effectively in these groups.)

Networking organizations. These groups often have the word *networking* in their names. Yet their missions may go way beyond generating leads. Their goals may include professional development for members, or they may be special-interest groups (such as book clubs, investment groups, groups devoted to dining out, etc.). One women's networking group, the Central Exchange in Kansas City, has as its motto "The thing that sets us apart is the people we bring together." All of its activities are designed to do just that: bring people together.

Professional associations. Whatever your job type, whatever your industry or profession, there is a professional association for you—probably several. Ask more experienced people in your chosen field for information to help you decide which one, or ones, would be right for you. Watch the business section of your newspaper for announcements of meetings. Check the *Encyclopedia of Associations* at your local library, then call or write to a group or go to the group's

Web site for membership information and the name of a local contact or the local chapter. These organizations usually offer their members a wide range of benefits, including:

▶State-of-the-art professional development at local, regional, national, and even international events

▶Help in finding a job

▶Mentor-mentee programs

▶A place to meet and get to know peers, potential customers, and clients

▶Opportunities to hone your leadership skills

▶Online activities that link you with people who have similar interests or expertise

▶Visibility in your industry

(See Chapter 16 for additional information on making the most of your memberships.)

Industry-specific organizations. These organizations can put you in touch with people in other companies. A telecommunications association, for example, brings together people from a variety of communications companies and long distance companies, as well as related businesses. As they face similar problems, these people can be the source of good ideas. Also, visibility in such groups may help your upward mobility, since there is usually a lot of opportunity for job movement among similar organizations. Within these industry-specific groups, there often are subgroups for people with various kinds of jobs—a public relations group, for example. These subgroups provide access to your peers and superiors across the industry.

Workplace task forces/committees. Don't forget opportunities to network at work. Get out of your cubicle and mix with others by serving on the Run for Fun Committee, or the Interagency Quality Team, or the Diversity Task Force. These are good ways to increase your visibility at work and to discover new opportunities for yourself in other areas of your organization. (See Chapter 19 for tips on inside networking.)

Chambers of commerce. Whether you're self-employed or work for an organization, the chamber of commerce will welcome you. This group's mission focuses on civic improvement, economic development, and legislative efforts to favor business. At a chamber meeting, you'll come in contact with people from a wide variety of workplaces with a wide variety of interests. Networking is certainly part of the picture, but not the total picture.

Civic and service organizations. These groups include such organizations as Rotary International, Lions Clubs, and many others. They focus on service to the community and civic improvement. The conversations you have in these relaxed, informal groups help others trust you and, in the long term, can lead to job opportunities, new customers, and previously undiscovered resources.

Volunteer groups. When Jon agreed to help build new play equipment in the community park, little did he know hammering nails with Martin would lead to a contract to videotape every corporate presentation made at Martin's company for the next five years. Volunteering is a way to blend a passion for giving back to the community with the chance to establish long-term business relationships as you demonstrate your Character and Competence.

Hobby groups. When Patti was suddenly laid off and began a home-based graphic design business, some of her first customers were the people she'd met while singing in a barbershop quartet. As you enjoy leisure-time activities, remember to see yourself as connecting with others, teaching them about your skills and talents, and Listening Generously for ways in which you can contribute to the quality of their personal and professional lives.

Health clubs and sports activities. Sondra and Marilyn noticed that they both kept showing up at the health club at 6 A.M. on Mondays, Wednesdays, and Fridays. They could have simply continued to exchange pleasantries, but instead they eventually used their exercise time together to explore ideas about "life after the corporation." After three years, they quit their jobs and started an interior painting and wallpapering business.

Alumni groups. A special kind of camaraderie arises from having attended the same school. Alumni clubs put you in touch with people of a variety of ages and from many walks of life. Their mission focuses on promoting the school, raising scholarship funds, or supporting the school's teams.

> Every chance meeting is an appointment. When you meet someone, try to find out why you have an "appointment" with that person.

Religious organizations. While business may not be the first thing you talk about at your church or synagogue, it's undeniably true that by being active in a religious community, you establish relationships from which businesses and careers may eventually grow. Watch carefully to see what's appropriate behavior in your group.

Kid connections. Your son plays on a soccer team. Or a basketball team. Or takes swimming lessons. How many times have you waited impatiently for the coach to end practice when you could have been developing your relationships with other parents? Kudos go to Amy, whose sideline conversations with Amera resulted in Amy's providing some management training for Amera's organization— even though their daughters were on rival teams!

Seatmates. There you are in the airplane for three hours, elbow to elbow with your seatmate. Sure, you might want to read a book or take a nap, but remember that a lot of business flyers have made a business contact with someone they met on an airplane. On a trip to Chicago, Bob sat next to David, a sales rep for a box manufacturing company. Bob told David he was looking for a heart-shaped box for his company's new specialty food product. David faxed him the specs the next day and got the contract.

Wild cards. Networking with people whose perspective is completely different from yours broadens your horizon in unexpected ways. To seek out contact with people with whom you seem to have nothing in common makes each conversation an adventure. These wild card contacts can sometimes be winners.

Where will you be thrown together with a couple of strangers for enough time to begin a business relationship? Marilyn got a $50,000 training contract after saying hello to a fellow passenger in the van from the airport to the hotel. Roberto met a potential client standing in line at the License Bureau waiting to renew his driver's license.

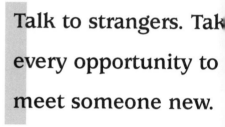

Talk to strangers. Take every opportunity to meet someone new.

Sometimes the payoff is personal enjoyment, not business. When Leah was visiting her daughter in Florida, she met a neighbor of her daughter's in the supermarket. The neighbor had his own shrimp boat. As they talked, the fisherman said that both his crew members had come down with the flu, and he didn't know what he was going to do for a crew the next day. After they discussed what a shrimp boat crew does, Leah thought that she and her husband could handle the job. She volunteered them. Being shrimpers for a day was a memorable experience. After the net dumped the catch on deck, Leah and her husband sat on overturned plastic buckets and, using sticks the size and shape of twelve-inch rulers, shoved everything that wasn't shrimp overboard. They enjoyed the scenery along the Intracoastal Waterway and the amazing variety of marine life spread before their eyes. Their "pay" at the end of the twelve-hour workday was a sack of shrimp.

Any place people are is a networking opportunity . . . if you have the know-how.

Pinpoint Your Arenas

Your Arenas are the groups you belong to, the circles you are known in. To maximize your opportunities for building your network, we recommend that you be involved in about six different Arenas.

Start with the most obvious (but most often overlooked) Arenas: your family. In some families, providing business and career help is taken for granted; in others, it's taboo to talk about money or work. But does Uncle Joe really know what you do? What kind of clients you're looking for? The next move you'd like to make in your career? Probably not. Tell him, and everyone else in your family tree, about your goals and capabilities. Ask them to keep an eye out for opportunities for you.

As you begin to analyze your network, write down the Arenas you're already a part of because of who you are and what you already do. I'm a parent who knows the parents of the other kids in my daughter's ballet class. Or, I sing tenor in the community chorus.

Then list organizations that you're involved with. Make a note about the nature of your participation—what role you play. Be honest. If you attended only two events last year, put that down. If you aspire to be president of the group one day, list that. Then list the benefits of each involvement. Finally, list your goal for belonging to that organization.

Notice the amount of time and money you're spending on these memberships. Are you getting what you want? If not, are these the wrong organizations for you, or do you need to find more strategic ways to participate? Does being involved contribute to your business and career goals, or have you outgrown your need for and interest in the group?

Adele is a lawyer who specializes in serving clients in the high-tech industry. In addition to being responsible for gaining "key player" status in that industry for her firm, she's in charge of her firm's new hire program and has initiated a plan to increase by 25 percent the number of women associates hired over the next three years. Figure 3-1 shows the chart she made of her involvement in six different Arenas.

Adele decided that she liked the idea of being involved in her alumni association, but that its importance had diminished in the eleven years since she'd graduated. She realized she would rather spend her time developing contacts at the Board of Trade and at the Technology Council, where she was in line to be president year after next.

As you assess your Arenas, ask yourself, "Where have I developed the most profitable contacts in the past?" Don't start joining new Are-

FIGURE 3-1. Adele's involvements.

Organization	Role	Benefit	Goal
University of Maryland Alumni Association	Member (rarely attend)	See people from all walks of life. Service to alma mater.	Clients. Look for new hires.
Northern Virginia Technology Council	Long-Range Planning Committee chair	Hot information. A chance to show problem-solving and leadership skills.	President.
Greater Washington Board of Trade	Vice President	Wide visibility with 1,200 member companies.	Collaboration with and referrals from CPA firms. New clients.
Women in Technology	Member	Updates on current trends.	Look for new hires.
Dingman Center for Entrepreneurship at the University of Maryland	Lecturer	Visibility, prestige.	Refine public speaking skills.
Maryland Bar Association	Member	Professional development.	Referrals; update credentials.

nas if you have not taken advantage of the opportunities in groups that you're already a part of.

When it is time to choose a new Arena, ask yourself, "Whom would I like to meet, and where can I find that type of person?" We recommend choosing at least one group that will contribute to your professional development and provide you with peer relationships. Also choose one that your potential customers or clients frequent. Joan, a CPA, wanted to cultivate business with associations, so she joined the Greater Washington Society of Association Executives. Sure, she felt like a fish out of water sometimes, but being active was a great way to tune into the challenges and trends her potential clients were experiencing. And as one of the few CPAs there, she was extremely visible to her marketplace.

Size Your Network to Fit Your Needs

There is no magic number for the size of your network. If fifty people think of you when they need a certain kind of expertise, speak well of you to their colleagues, and consider you someone who can give them advice and information, you have an excellent network.

If, however, you fear being laid off, want to start your own business someday, have a business that could profit from referrals by current customers or clients, or are facing a major life change (such as moving across the country, leaving the military, or retiring), then you need to think big.

Access Anybody

No matter who you need to know, somebody you know knows somebody who knows that person. A man who studied this small-world phenomenon is the late Stanley Milgram, a psychologist. What he discovered proves that it's possible for you to make contact with just about anyone you wish—because you have friends who have friends who have friends.

Milgram wondered if it would be possible for a package to be passed from a specific, randomly selected person in Omaha to a specific, randomly selected person in Boston using "friends" as the conduits. Milgram defined "friends" as people you know by their first names. He discovered not only that it was possible, but that it took surprisingly few people to make the exchange. It typically took only five or six people for two individuals half a continent apart to make contact through a chain of acquaintances.

As Milgram explains it, if you know just 50 people on a first-name basis, and they each know 50 people, you have access to 2,500 contacts. If each member of that group knows 50 people, you can potentially reach 125,000 people. And if each of them knows 50 people, you can reach more than 6 million contacts. If you remember seeing the movie *Six Degrees of Separation*, you'll recognize that its concept came from the idea that you're only five or six people away from anyone you'd like to meet.

Of course, the range and quality of the contacts that your contacts have will dramatically affect your ability to use the small-world phenomenon to find resources and opportunities. Great networkers know people who know people who know people in a variety of Arenas—organizations, subcultures, marketplaces, groups, and niches.

Take MaryLou in Philadelphia, for instance. Her new boss, Shelia, moved to town from Seattle. Shelia's hobby is collecting antique inkwells. "How obscure," thinks MaryLou, who knows nothing about inkwells or antiques. But using her network she discovers that a friend of a friend is immersed in the antiques subculture of Pennsylvania. MaryLou is able to connect Shelia with the people who know the best shows, the best appraisers, and the best dealers in Pennsylvania. Shelia is thrilled and sees that MaryLou is resourceful and creative.

You may hear people talk about various networking "generations." Your "first-generation" network includes the people you know directly. Your "second-generation" network includes the people who are known by the people you know. The "third generation" includes those people's contacts. And the "fourth generation"—the pool of more than 6 million—includes their contacts. It is possible to relate to "fourth-generation" contacts, but only if you've been passed along by people who have established a great deal of trust.

When Ardys, who lives in Washington, D.C., was looking for a family in Taos, New Mexico, to swap houses with for a month, she told everybody she knew. It took a couple of months, but she finally made contact with her husband's college roommate's mother's friend and her husband! They wanted to go to Washington to see the museums. The two families arranged a successful house, car, and cat swap.

Continue to customize your network by being on the lookout for chance encounters. See every accidental meeting as an opportunity to explore a new subculture, find out about a new marketplace, or just enjoy the serendipitous connections that life sends your way.

CHAPTER 4

Move Through the Six Stages

Understanding that networking relationships offer the possibility of growth through six stages of development will help you figure out what behaviors are professional—that is, not too pushy and not too passive.

When you understand these stages, you can assess your current network, determine where you need to put your energies in order to widen and strengthen your network, and take the necessary steps to move your relationships forward. Networks are always becoming. They are never complete or static. They are always dynamic, expanding or contracting to meet the needs of the people involved.

You can do more than hope that your networking efforts will pay off. You can make it happen.

Make a list of ten people you know. Include a variety of people: a few people from work; somebody you know really well; someone you just met; a client, customer, or vendor; someone in a professional association or community group you belong to; someone you sing in the choir with or play racquetball with. Keep these people in mind as you read about the six stages.

41

Picture these stages as a target, as shown in Figure 4-1. On the outside of the outer circle are all the people you run into, however casually. They are called *Accidents*. At the center are those few people with whom you have very active relationships. They are your *Allies*.

FIGURE 4-1. Targeted networking.

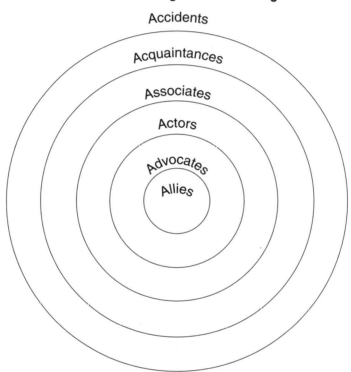

Accidents
Acquaintances
Associates
Actors
Advocates
Allies

Accidents. In your lifetime, you will bump into thousands of people. These casual, unplanned, random encounters are Accidents. They probably will never be repeated. They are one-time-only meetings. You are thrown together for some period of time—in line for tickets to the hit play, in the emergency room waiting area, when you are 14C and she is 14B on the plane. So you talk to each other. Any person you meet outside a common context is an Accident. Networking relationships can sometimes grow out of Accidents if you can find a reason to stay in touch.

Acquaintances. People that you run into because of who you are and what you do are Acquaintances. They have something in common with you. An Acquaintance may be a person who is a friend of a friend. You meet at your neighbor's daughter's wedding, for instance. You *might* see an Acquaintance again. Then again, you might not. However, there's enough of a connection there that, if you *had* to, you could probably find an Acquaintance again.

> **Give first; give freely.**

When someone mentions Ramon Sanchez to you, you're likely to say, "Ramon Sanchez? Sounds familiar. I think I've met him. Isn't he a lawyer or a CPA or something like that?" He'd probably be just as vague about you. You may be able to recall an Acquaintance's name, but you haven't really begun to learn about each other.

Associates. People you come in contact with on some regular basis for some period of time are Associates. You are both part of the same system. Both of you have chosen to belong to Rotary or both of you have joined the alumni association or both of you attend First Christian Church. Because you meet Associates with some regularity, you are in a much better position to begin a networking relationship. Relying on your common bond, you can develop a trusting relationship. Because you see each other every week or every month—at choir or at a professional association meeting—you have the chance to learn each other's names and to reconnect often enough to learn a bit about each other. But unless both of you work at the relationship, it will never develop. You will continue to see each other, chat briefly, and part, without providing any assistance to each other. Associates can and do network, but often it's a one-time trade or one person provides help to the other, who has yet to reciprocate.

If Ramon has become an Associate, you may say something like this about him: "Ramon is a attorney. He's a member of the chamber of commerce I belong to. I think he specializes in estates. I could find him in the membership directory."

Actors. People with whom you exchange valuable information, resources, or leads are Actors. Sometimes you are the giver in the exchange; sometimes you are the receiver. Whether you realize it or not, you are checking out two things about each other: Character and Competence. If each of you finds these two things, you'll want more activity with each other; if you don't find them, you won't pursue the relationship. (See Chapter 5.)

You gather data about each other and have each other's phone numbers and e-mail addresses. You know enough about this person, and he knows enough about you, to be useful to each other.

When you need to find someone to advise you on setting up a trust, you say, "Oh, Ramon. I met him at the chamber of commerce. I think Sally used him. I could call her." Once you make an appointment with Ramon, he becomes an Actor. You make a note of his phone number and his addresses. When you meet with him, you look for evidence of his Character and Competence and begin to demonstrate yours.

Advocates. People who promote you and whom you promote are Advocates. You know that your Advocates will come through, and they know that you will help them. You believe in their Character and appreciate and understand their Competence. You have developed a high level of trust in each other. Your antenna is up for information and resources for these people. And they, likewise, feed you opportunities. You speak well of them.

When Ramon becomes an Advocate, you look for ways to assist him. When someone mentions that she is having to spend more time with her mother and is concerned about how well organized her financial situation is, you recommend Ramon, saying, "I worked with an excellent attorney, Ramon Sanchez, who helped my mother set up a trust. Why don't you give him a call? His first consultation is free. You can reach him at 555-0101. I recommend him highly."

Allies. People who are experts on you, your business, your career, your needs, your aspirations, and your vision are allies. They can talk about you in detail. They know where you've been and where you're headed—and they want to help you get there! They are your senior advisers, and you are theirs. Because you talk about core life and business issues, you have established confidentiality as a ground rule of your relationship. You both are so committed to your mutual success that you serve on each other's unofficial board of directors. They are the people you turn to for sage advice—on a new marketing approach, on whether it's time to open a branch office in Denver, on how to deal with a difficult client. Allies commiserate with you when the going gets rough and celebrate with you when success is sweet.

When Ramon becomes an Ally, you might call him and say, "Hey, Ramon, I know of a board opening that might be a good career move for you. Do you want me to give your name to the chairman? Also, let's get together next week: I'm thinking of making some big changes, and I'd like your thoughts."

Go back to that list of ten people you made. Decide what stage you are in with each person on your list. Assuming that your list of ten is fairly representative of all the people you know, what does it tell you about how you need to expand and develop your network? What does it tell you about the appropriate next steps with these ten people? If you made an even broader list of people you know, would there be a good mix of people from a variety of Arenas? Would it include people from your workplace, your profession, your industry, your friendship and leisure-time circle, your family?

Don't repeat the mistake that Allison made when rumors of downsizing and mergers swept through her organization. She began working seventy-five-hour weeks in an effort to make herself "irreplaceable." By the time layoffs were announced and she found that her name was on the list, she had so neglected her friends, family, and professional contacts outside of her company that she virtually had to start her job hunting network from scratch.

The Next Move Is Up to You

If you understand the stages, you can see what you need to do to bring contacts into more meaningful and useful relationships with you. Once you figure out whether someone is an Associate, an Actor, an Advocate, or an Ally, what you can do to extend the relationship becomes much clearer (see Figure 4-2).

If you and Jim are Associates, your number one job is to Listen Generously so that you can find out what he needs. When you find

FIGURE 4-2. Move people along.

If you want more Associates	Make strategic decisions about which organizations to join based on your career, business, and life goals.
If you want to move from Associate to Actor	Listen Generously so that you can give ideas, resources, and referrals.
If you want to move from Actor to Advocate	Show your Character and Competence in everything you do and say.
If you want to be a strong Ally	Respect confidentiality, tell the truth with caring, and support your Ally's success in life and business.

something that you can give, you will just naturally move to the Actor stage of exchanging.

If you and Monica are Actors, your number one job is to show her your Character and Competence through everything you do and say.

If you and Horatio are Advocates, your number one job is to promote him and to keep your antenna up for opportunities and possibilities to pass along to him.

If you and Svetlana are Allies, your number one job is to tell the truth, provide support for all she does, and help her to succeed in any way you can.

You'll probably have hundreds, or maybe even thousands, of Accidents, Acquaintances, and Associates in your lifetime. You'll enter into an Actor relationship with fewer people, and even fewer will become Advocates and Allies. You can't make anyone move to the next stage with you, of course, but you can say and do things that will make it more likely that the relationship will grow.

Rate Your Relationships

Networking is a process of teaching and learning. Choose someone on your list of ten and use this quiz to figure out where you are with that person. When you hit a no, that will give you a clue as to what you want to be sure to tell—and ask—that person the next time you meet.

1. Does this person recognize my name instantly when I call?

2. Does this person know me well enough to recognize me out of context (at the store, in a new group)?

3. Does this person know my face and my name well enough to come up to me in a crowd and introduce me accurately to others?

4. Has this person found a reason to have my phone number or e-mail in her system?

5. Does this person know the name of my company or organization?

6. Can this person accurately describe what I do?

7. Can this person give vivid examples of what I do?

8. Does this person know that I am good at what I do, and can he cite reasons why my service, product, or skills are superior?

9. Does this person know of some independent verification of my expertise, such as an award, a certification, or a third-party endorsement?

10. Does this person regularly send me valuable information and respond to requests from me?

11. Does this person know what kind of customers, clients, or job opportunities will appeal to me, and does she send them my way?

12. Does this person always speak well of me to other people and pass my name around?

13. Does this person regularly refer qualified customers, clients, or job opportunities to me?

14. Does this person consistently create opportunities to stay in touch with me?

15. Does this person treat the business, career, and life issues we talk about with confidentiality and caring?

Imagine that you meet Mitchell at an association meeting. If during that first encounter you learn his name and teach him your name using some of the techniques in Chapter 10, you might be comfortable answering yes to question 1. It may take two or three conversations before you can answer yes to questions 2 and 3. When you Listen Generously and find a reason to exchange business cards, you're working on questions 4 and 5.

Next, give your attention to questions 6 and 7 by asking him good questions, by telling Success Stories, and by talking from your Agenda. Use conversation to keep your contact up to date on your projects, interests, challenges, and successes. Questions 8 through 12 have to do with continuing to let him know about your Character and Competence through a series of exchanges and interactions. Our studies show that it often takes six or eight contacts with someone before he knows who you are, has learned your marketplace niche, and begins to trust you enough to become an Advocate. Once that trust is established, you may be in touch once a week or once a year, depending on the relationship. You'll probably establish the caring and intensity referred to in question 15 with only a few people—those are the hallmarks of Allies.

If your contact does not reciprocate and do his share toward building the relationship, it's probable that she doesn't understand the networking protocol. Gently teach your contact how to hold up her end of the conversation. Say, for example, "I'd like to hear more about your background. Tell me how you developed your expertise in this field." That question will help you learn about your contact's credentials.

In networking, the ball is always in your court. It's up to you to take the next step to cultivate the relationship.

CHAPTER 5

Teach Trust

Everybody says, "People want to do business with people they trust."

Have you ever been at a networking event where someone came up to you and introduced himself saying, "Hi, I'm George. I sell long-term care insurance. Do you need any?"

It's this kind of "going for the jugular" that gives networking a bad name. You don't know or trust George enough to do business with him.

Trust is the outcome of several (we estimate six to eight) interactions and conversations in which you provide examples of your trustworthiness and observe your contact's behavior (among other things) to determine if she can be trusted. People teach people to trust them.

If Peter, a career coach, takes sloppy minutes at the committee meeting, or forgets to return JoAnn's phone call, or has a couple of typos in his marketing brochure, JoAnn probably won't hire him. Nor will she recommend him to her friends and acquaintances.

Your contacts won't help you until they trust you.

On the other hand, if he handles his committee responsibilities carefully, promptly returns calls, and has professional-looking marketing materials, then JoAnn will probably think of him when she decides to make a career change and needs some help.

After JoAnn becomes Peter's client, if she cancels sessions at the last minute, fails to follow through on the "homework" that will help him guide her job hunt, and looks as if she came straight from her workout at the health club, Peter will be reluctant to recommend her for a job he's heard about.

If JoAnn arrives on time, dresses in a professional way, completes all of the assessments Peter has provided, and speaks positively about her expertise and her current employer, then Peter probably will pass along the job lead.

Move from Taking to Trusting

As people begin to network, they typically focus on trying to get something for themselves. There's nothing wrong with wanting your efforts to bear fruit, but that's only part of the story. Networking is not just about *taking*.

The *taking* mindset works when you happen to connect with somebody who has what you want or needs what you're offering.

George, the guy who sells long-term care insurance, is focusing on *taking*. He's interested in you only if, at that very moment, in the middle of the chamber of commerce's Business After Hours event, you happen to need long-term care insurance and are willing (remarkably!) to buy it from him on the spot. His approach is no more than a face-to-face cold call. Chances are he'll grump after the event, "This networking is a bunch of hooey!"

Charlene went to that same chamber of commerce event thinking about a problem: how to ship a fragile antique desk to her daughter in London. When she asked Bart, whom she'd just met, what he did, he said, "I ship anything anywhere, especially valuable things. I just sent a baby grand to the Philippines." Bingo!

But if that's the only kind of networking you are ready to do, you are not going to be very satisfied. During that networking event, which lasted two hours and involved more than eight hundred people, how many serendipitous meetings like Charlene's and Bart's do you think there were? Probably not very many.

When you begin to see networking as the exchange something of value, you've begun to think of networking as *trading*.

Trading is exciting. It makes you feel that your networking efforts are worthwhile. Clarice, who has her own training company, went to a networking breakfast and met the college-age son of a member who has a window-washing business. She was delighted to meet Howie because she needed that service—right away. She took Howie's card so that she could call him and get an estimate. When Howie found out what Clarice did, he suggested that she talk with his dad because he knew his father's company was looking for someone to write a training manual. That's a great trade. But it's a one-time trade. Clarice will need her windows washed only occasionally. Howie's business may not last beyond the summer, and he may not know anyone else who might need her training services.

What happens for people who are thinking of networking as taking or trading is single-sale networking. Though this may result in instant gratification, it's time-consuming, and you miss out on the long-term benefits. Unfortunately, many people feel that when they have achieved a trade, they have reached the epitome of networking.

Long-term networking relationships are built by *teaching* people what you need and what they can count on you for, and by learning the same about them. When you meet someone, take the time to be interested in that person and his business. Put your antenna up for resources, ideas, tips, information, or access that you could give to that contact. Look for ways to become known to that person and to educate that person about yourself and your capabilities. We call this kind of networking relationship networking.

Remember the old line: "It's not *what* you know, it's *who* you know?" That's only partly true. Sure, *what* you know is important. It's your expertise, your knowledge, what you are paid for. *Who* you know is important, too. Those are the people you call when you are looking for an idea, a resource, a referral.

But just as important as *what* you know and *who* you know is *who knows you*. Does Fred know you so well that when something comes into his life, you pop into his head and he says to himself, "Oh, I've got to send this to Sean"? Who knows you that well?

The big networking challenge, then, is how to teach your contacts who you are and what you are looking for, so that they can send good things your way. An equally big challenge is how to learn about your contacts and what they are looking for, so that you can send good things their way. Make sure you spend as much time learning your contact's business as you do teaching him what you do.

When put your emphasis on developing *trust*, then relationships become mutually beneficial.

Teach That You Can Be Trusted

Your contacts will begin to trust you as you teach them about your Character and Competence. To teach your contacts about your Character:

▶ Be unfailingly reliable.

▶ Meet deadlines.

▶ Go for the win/win solution.

▶ Treat everyone you meet fairly.

▶ Speak well of people even when they are not present.

▶ Collaborate rather than compete.

▶ When something goes wrong, ostentatiously make it right.

▶ Compensate generously for your failure.

▶ Go the extra mile.

▶ Respect other people's time and possessions.

To believe in your Character, your contacts must either see you in action (observe your behavior) or hear about you (listen to stories you tell about yourself that provide vivid examples of your Character).

If you promise your contact that you'll call her on Tuesday, do it. That's how you teach someone that you will do what you say you will do.

If you promise that you'll come up with ten items for the public television fund-raising auction by December 5, provide a dozen. That's how you teach someone that you meet deadlines, are reliable, and go the extra mile.

Suppose you want to teach someone that when something goes wrong, you'll do more than just make it right. You could tell about the time you inadvertently charged a customer more than you should have for a job. And how, when you discovered the mistake, you not only called to apologize and to ask if he would like his money returned or credited to his account, but also sent him a bouquet of cookies as an additional apology.

Networking isn't about taking, it's about teaching.

Suppose you want to teach someone that you're a stickler for details. Talk about the newsletter you edit for your professional association. Tell how you go to great lengths to be sure that every name is spelled correctly and all details in the articles are correct.

Suppose you want to teach someone that you are innovative, tell about your work on the program committee that's resulted in an award-winning lineup of programs for the association. If you want to teach someone that you are a good organizer. Tell about the time you compiled information to submit to national to enter the Chapter of the Year contest. To teach your contacts about your Competence, you will need to reveal that you:

▶ Have earned the proper credentials.

▶ Stay at the leading edge of your profession.

▶ Have won praise and awards from your peers.

▶ Take lifelong learning seriously.

▶ Are cited as an expert in the trade press or in the mass media.

▶ Teach or mentor others.

▶ Consult with others to share your expertise.

▶ Do the job right the first time.

▶ Handle "the little stuff" with care.

▶Follow through to be sure that your work meets or exceeds expectations.

Here are some suggestions for ways to show your Competence. Frame diplomas, accreditation certificates, and customer kudos and hang them on the wall of your office. Invite your contact to lunch and give her the "grand tour." Send your contacts articles that quote you and newspaper clippings or conference programs that show you speaking. Tell Success Stories about consulting with others. Protect the confidentiality of the organization or person you consulted with. Tell other Success Stories about doing the job right and handling the little stuff with care. Provide your contact with a sample of your work or a tour of your work site.

To build a strong network, make sure your contacts know your capabilities and are confident of your ability to perform. It's unreasonable to expect that people who don't know you will be comfortable giving you referrals or suggesting you for jobs. They have no idea of your special areas of expertise and have not known you long enough to be sure you will come through.

Use a similar process to learn about your contact's Character and Competence: Look for the same behaviors and ask for Success Stories.

The Trust Matrix

The Trust Matrix graphically depicts the process of developing trust. When you first meet someone, you probably have little knowledge of her Competence and Character. Your contact probably doesn't know how you would rate in those areas either. That's why most relationships begin in the lower left quadrant of the Trust Matrix, with Competence and Character still to be determined. You are acquaintances.

If a contact has a bad experience with you, or if you have a bad experience with a contact, your relationship will derail into the upper left quadrant or the lower right quadrant.

If your relationship moves to the upper left quadrant, your contact trusts your Character, but questions your Competence. He thinks that you are admirable but not able. This situation can be remedied. It

FIGURE 5-1. The Trust Matrix.

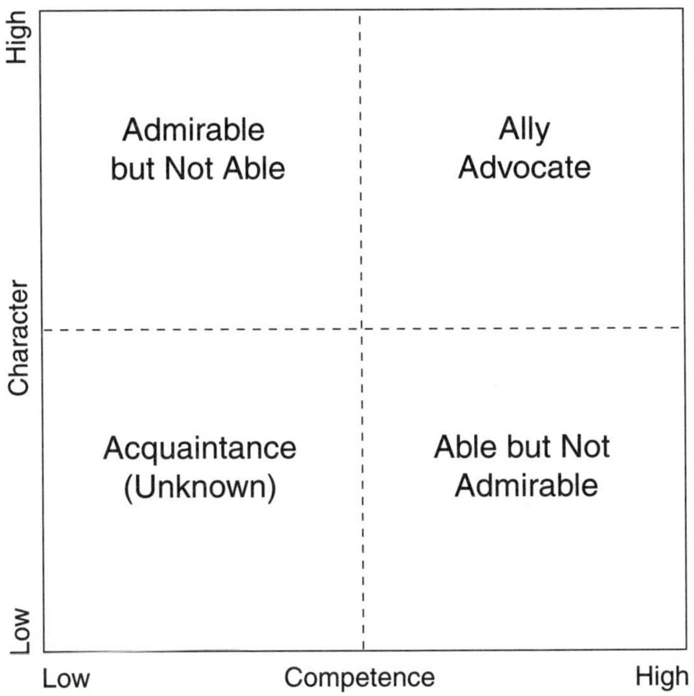

	Low ← Competence → High
High Character	Admirable but Not Able Ally Advocate
Low Character	Acquaintance (Unknown) Able but Not Admirable

could be that you have just changed jobs or just graduated and are in your first job or have moved into a new career field. Think about how you can teach your contact that you are able (or competent) as well as admirable. Tell Success Stories as you talk with people, or send out a newsletter or press release to let contacts know about your increasing expertise. Take a visible role in organizations, so that contacts can experience your Competence firsthand.

If your relationship moves to the lower right quadrant, your contact trusts your Competence, but questions your Character. Your contact believes that you are able but not admirable. Everybody makes mistakes that contribute to concern about Character or Competence. Can you repair the mistake and your reputation? If you were late to an event, show over time that that lateness was a one-time aberration, not a habit. You will have to demonstrate repeatedly that your Character is admirable.

If you and your contact have positive experiences with each other, your networking relationship will move to the top right quadrant, Advocate or Ally. Advocates speak well of you and your business, refer qualified customers or clients to you, and create opportunities for you. Allies are trusted advisers. Your trust in the confidentiality of the relationship and the value of the relationship is so high that you feel comfortable sharing frustrations and trade secrets, and celebrating successes. Developing that level of trust takes time.

It's also possible that one of you—or both of you—may have established a reputation in the community. Ideally, you want contacts to hear good things *about* you before they hear *from* you. If your good reputation precedes you, your relationship may start off in the upper right-hand quadrant. If so, you've jump-started the process and can begin your relationship with your Character and Competence assumed. That doesn't mean that you can relax and forget about trust. As your relationship continues, you need to continue to reaffirm both your Character and your Competence.

Avoid Manipulation

Networking is not about manipulating other people. If you are absolutely honest about what you want to establish—a mutually beneficial, long-term, trusting business relationship—you will not be manipulating your contacts. It's only when you connive to get something for yourself through misdirection, subterfuge, or telling only part of the truth that you are being manipulative. Don't do it. (See Chapter 12 for a more detailed discussion of the dangers of manipulation.) To build trust, you must convince your contact of your Character as well as your Competence. Nothing destroys relationships more quickly than one party feeling manipulated by the other. So, be totally up-front about your motives.

PART 3

Hone Your Networking Know-How

You say you weren't born with the gift of gab? That's okay. Anyone can learn how to turn small talk into smart talk. Whether you think of yourself as outgoing and gregarious or as shy and retiring, you'll be able to enter a roomful of strangers enthusiastically, comfortably, and professionally. Do you want people to notice you and hear your voice above the din of the marketplace? You'll get hundreds of tips on presenting yourself, achieving more visibility, and becoming memorable. You'll find out about the quiet side of networking, too, and learn how to Listen Generously. Are you worried that you don't know the no-nos? Take a look at the top twenty turn-offs, things that no savvy networker would ever be caught dead doing.

CHAPTER 6

Present Yourself

Presenting yourself means taking charge of all your nonverbal communications—your energy level, your carriage, your tone of voice, your facial expression, your eye contact, and more.

That's both good news and bad news for networkers. The good news is that sheer energy is just as important as content. The bad news is that most people are unaware of how they are presenting themselves. So, no matter what words you choose, don't let your presentation of yourself send the larger message, "I'm not comfortable being here. Talking to me will be a chore!"

Think of the nonverbal part of a conversation as the music supporting your words, the lyrics. You can gain more control over the nonverbal part of your communication. The first step is awareness.

Enter Enthusiastically

For many people, the hardest part of networking isn't talking at all; it's entering a room full of strangers. Your Critic may be saying, "Everybody here but me knows each other. Everybody's better at this than I am. Everybody's looking at me." Nonsense. That's just not so. You'll be in the spotlight only if you are a celebrity or the guest of honor. If you are the star, relax and enjoy the attention. If you're that special, people will make the first move and initiate contact with you. They'll take care of you.

"I enter a room in an upbeat way with a smile," says Martha. "That way people want to talk with me. Sometimes people coming into a room look so serious and forbidding that they give signals that say, 'Don't talk to me!' I like to let my body language show that I'm glad I'm here."

That's good advice. Often, people spend a lot of time before an event fussing with their hair, their clothes, their makeup. Of course you want to look your best. But be sure, also, to put on a smile and energize yourself.

The way you relate to space sends a message. The pace of your entry and the amount of space you take up indicate your level of confidence. If you move slowly, edge into the room keeping your back to the wall, and make little or no eye contact with people, you will look uncomfortable. Relax. To energize yourself, listen to your Coach's encouragement. (For more about your Coach, see Chapter 2.) Talk to yourself. Use positive statements like:

▶ "This is going to be interesting."

▶ "I'm ready and eager to talk to people today."

▶ "I wonder what great ideas and opportunities I can discover as I talk with these people."

Engage Your Partner

You have the power to use your body language to reward and encourage your partner in conversation. On the classic TV show *Star Trek* (all the versions), the captain of the *Enterprise* always ends the show by saying, "Engage." That word indicates that the Starship is underway again, off to new adventures. The letters in that word can help you remember how to give a positive message through your body language as you engage in conversation.

E = establishing eye contact. You don't actually have to look at the other person's eyes. If you're looking at any part of your partner's face, she will feel that you are looking at her. In our culture, it feels comfortable to break eye contact every seven or eight seconds or so. Glance away and then back. It's more flattering to your partner to glance down to the side and then move your eyes back to your partner's face rather than glancing over your partner's shoulder, as if you are looking for someone else to talk with.

N = nodding. Nodding is nonverbal encouragement. It shows that you're following and enjoying the conversation.

G = geniality. Be cheerful and cordial. Your geniality tells your partner that you're having fun in the conversation. Smile often, but do it appropriately. Nervousness can lead to smiling at serious or even sad topics. Women who are concerned about being perceived as assertive should be careful to smile only when the occasion or topic warrants.

A = aiming your attention. Take your attention away from your Critic and aim it at your partner. Notice that person's unique and special qualities. Let your body language acknowledge that your full attention is concentrated on that person. To aim your attention at your partner, lean slightly forward. Keep your arms at your sides; don't fold them across your chest.

G = gesturing appropriately. To enhance your message, use your hands as you talk. Watch other people to expand your use of gestures. The people who are the most comfortable will use more expansive motions. But small gestures also work well in close-up conversation. If you're giving a speech in front of a big crowd, you'll need to exaggerate a bit more. When you're talking, one-on-one or in a small group, you don't have to look as if you're an orchestra conductor. Just use gestures to emphasize key words or concepts.

E = Easing your posture. Your posture indicates how comfortable you are. Learn to stand with your feet slightly apart and your back straight. Center your weight so that you don't sway or feel off balance. Keep your arms uncrossed and lean into the conversation just slightly. In a crowded, noisy room, it's especially important to create a "bubble" around you and your conversational partner with your eye contact, your gestures, and your forward-leaning posture.

Ask your spouse or friend to help you become aware of how well you are following the ENGAGE Formula.

Consider Closeness

Every culture has different rules about how close together people should stand when they talk to one another. In the United States, we prefer to stand about three feet apart when we are having social conversations. If the room is very noisy or if the conversation becomes more personal, we move in, closing the range to perhaps eighteen inches. If we move closer than that, we are usually having an intimate conversation. If the people you are talking to typically move away from you, you may be violating this rule. On the other hand, if you talk from farther away than three feet or if you move away during a conversation, your partner may think of you as stand-offish or distant.

Sometimes a person moves away from her partner in conversation for other reasons. Television commercials for products like deodorants and mouthwash have created anxiety about being close to other people. The most sensible thing to do is to take reasonable precautions and then don't worry about these problems.

Watch What You Put in Your Mouth

Of course, you won't smoke in close proximity to others without their permission. People who drink too much are equally obnoxious. In business or social situations, neither smoking nor excessive drinking is acceptable behavior.

If the event involves eating, use your best manners. At a stand-up networking meeting, choose foods that are easy to eat: grapes, crackers, bits of cheese. Steer clear of the chewy, dripping, garlic-laced, hard-to-eat items at the hors d'oeuvres table. If you are unsure about your ability to eat and talk, and if you worry about a piece of spinach attaching itself to your front tooth or about dripping shrimp sauce on your tie, don't eat.

If the etiquette of eating concerns you, read a book or two on manners, find a course on etiquette in your community, or encourage your company or organization to offer such a course. Many companies are offering such training. There's no point in letting concerns about manners sabotage your ability to be at ease with people.

Treat Touching as Taboo

Except for shaking hands, it's usually inappropriate in business settings to touch your partner. Two people of the same gender and rank may find it comfortable to touch during a conversation. In general, though, it's either the female or the more powerful person who initiates touching during a conversation. If a woman touches, it may be interpreted as flirting. If a person of higher rank touches, it may appear to be an indication to his partner that he is pulling rank, trying to establish control, or even engaging in sexual harassment.

Unless you have established a special relationship with someone in which touching is acceptable, don't do it. And even if you have a warm relationship with someone, it's better to err on the side of formality in public—especially with someone of the opposite sex.

Forgo Flirting

Marilyn says, "As a woman, I'm concerned that people will misinterpret my friendliness. I don't want them to think that I'm a featherhead or that I'm flirting."

Jorge says, "I worry about the do's and don'ts of networking with women in business and social situations."

Worries of this kind are unnecessary if you're clear about the difference between flirting and networking and if you practice reading the unwritten ground rules in different organizational cultures. For example, two past presidents of one professional organization, one male and one female, who have known each other for nearly two decades, hug when they meet. In other groups, that behavior might be off limits.

In business situations, you'll want to avoid a sexual come-on. If you know how to flirt, then you can figure out how not to. But just in case you do it unconsciously, take a look at some common flirting behaviors.

Men flirt by extending eye contact beyond the normal length of time (more than eight seconds or so) that signals attention and interest. A man may also indicate a romantic interest by inappropriate or extended touching—a handshake that turns into hand holding, for example. Or he may sit closer than necessary. Or he may assume responsibility for a woman's comfort through excessively solicitous hovering. It is not appropriate in a business setting for a man to open doors or help remove a woman's coat or pull out her chair. Or, rather, it's not appropriate if the behavior is unilateral. If one person helpfully opens a door for another person who is encumbered, that's fine. A man doesn't need to offer to carry packages or suitcases. He shouldn't use a diminutive nickname—saying Katie for Kathryn, for example. If a man introduces himself as William, you'll *never* hear a woman say, "Hi, Billy." That's a put-down in business. So are overenthusiastic comments about a woman's dress or hair or other personal compliments beyond, "You're looking well."

Women use many of the same tactics in flirting. Women may "serve" men, offering to bring them coffee, for example. Eye contact, especially lowering the head and looking up through the lashes, can be flirtatious. So can touching in a proprietary manner—fingering a man's tie, for example, or brushing lint off his shoulder. Women also flirt by touching their own hair or twisting a curl. They may stand closer than normal. Inappropriate laughter is another clue. So is calling a man "honey" or "love." Most comments about a man's clothing or hair are also off limits.

None of these behaviors is appropriate in a business context. If business colleagues have been friends for years, some of these rather arbitrary rules may be relaxed, but only if the person breaking the rules is sure that his behavior will not cause comment among other associates. If you're unsure, take the more formal approach in public.

Exchange Cards Effectively

Handing a business card to someone does not constitute a networking relationship. Strangely enough, the biggest mistake people make with business cards is giving them out too freely, too soon. When you do that, your contact will go back to the office, look at the card, say to himself, "I wonder who this is?" and throw the card in the wastebasket.

Challenge yourself not to give out your card until you've found some connection, some reason for exchanging names and phone numbers. Approach conversations by asking yourself, "I wonder what she needs that I can provide? Let's see if I can figure it out." Or, "I know what I'm looking for today. I wonder if I can find someone who has the information I need."

> ## Wait! Don't hand out your card too soon.

With this approach, you have to work to make a conversation lead to an exchange of cards. When you hit upon a reason to trade cards, you have accomplished something very important: You have extended the relationship beyond the event at which you met.

Jewell mentioned her aerobics class to Tess, a woman she met at a seminar. Tess seemed very interested in finding a low-cost exercise program, so Jewell asked for her card and said she'd send some information. The next time Jewell went to her aerobics class, she picked up the catalog put out by the Parks and Recreation Department, took it home, and mailed it to Tess.

When you find a conversational connection and you need to exchange cards, take a moment right then and there—or as soon as you leave the event—to note on the back of the card anything you want to remember about the person, the conversation, or what you agreed to do: "Has twins." "Went to Duke University." "Wants to know more about the chamber of commerce networking night." "Needs speaker." "Looking for software to make certificates."

> ## Create a reason to exchange cards. Your reason may be, "I'd like to put you in my database."

If you have promised to do something, follow through.

The next time you see your contact, you don't have to start all over again; you can build on the information that you provided. You might update your contact on how you are using the information he sent you: "Thanks so much for sending me Tom's phone number. He sounds like just the speaker we need for our sales meeting. We plan to meet next week."

If someone gives you a card the moment you meet, don't just stuff the card in your pocket. Read it carefully. Use it as a way to learn the person's name. Discuss his title. Notice the organization. Clarify the organization's focus. If it's an engineering firm, ask what kinds of engineering projects it specializes in. Talk about the location.

Then, give this person your card and use it as an aid to teach him about you. "My card says Robert James Hensy, but everybody calls me 'R.J.' My office is about five blocks from yours, at Tenth and Broad. I've listed some of the health-care management services my firm provides on the back of my card. Our new facility is for patients with Alzheimer's. Did you see the story about it in the *Kansas City Star* last Sunday?"

Join Groups Comfortably

In any roomful of people, most of the people will be talking in groups. You certainly can look around to find someone else who is not attached to a group and make a beeline for that person. Barbara, who seems comfortable wherever she goes, says, "When I feel nervous about joining a group, I form my own. I look for someone standing alone and start a conversation with that person."

Or you can join a group. In our workshops, people ask, "How can I break into a group?" We tease them a bit: "Well, first, you find a big sledgehammer . . ." We have chosen not to use the term *break into* a group. Breaking in implies that you must force yourself on the group, a violent act; joining implies that the group was incomplete without you.

To join a group, use body language to signal that you're committed to becoming part of the conversation. Gently but firmly touch the arm of one person. Almost always, the circle will open up to allow you to come in. Don't be tentative; show commitment by making eye contact with the speaker or smiling at one of the listeners. Take a few seconds to tune in to what's going on. You can start participating any time you feel tuned in. Don't worry about interrupting the flow of the conversation to introduce yourself or to find out people's names. When the conversation slows, you can turn to a person next to you and introduce yourself. Often, someone else in the group will initiate introductions. If the people in the group seem to be acquainted, ask, "How do you all know each other?" as a way to prompt introductions.

If someone quickly introduces everyone in the group to you, don't despair. Simply go back to each individual later and say, "Let's introduce ourselves again. It's hard to catch everyone's name in a group."

If you are uncomfortable joining a group, analyze why. Are you remembering high school? Most of us have vivid memories of feeling excluded—even people who were members of an "in group." As grown-ups, we still carry some of those adolescent feelings around with us. Analyze what your Critic says when you are thinking about joining a group. You may find that when you bring the Critic's comments out into the light of day and examine them, they are quite ridiculous and based on old ideas that are left over from your teenage years:

▶ "They don't want to talk to me."

▶ "They are talking about me."

▶ "They don't want to include me."

▶ "They will laugh at me or tell me to go away."

Imagine that someone just joined your conversation group. What were you thinking about when that newcomer walked up? Certainly you'd rarely be thinking that you didn't want to include that person in the group. When a new person joins your group, smile, nod, and make eye contact. When whoever is talking comes to a stopping point, fill the newcomer in. Say, "Jack was just telling us about his new job." Then look back at Jack so that he can continue.

Sometimes people worry that they might be joining a private or intimate conversation. Trust your powers of observation. You will be able to tell when a private conversation is taking place. Here are some clues to look for: People may be touching; there may be visible emotion; voices may be very low or higher than normal; the people will have moved closer to each other.

If you enter a conversation that's too intimate, or if you don't like the topic, you can leave comfortably. If the conversation is too personal, just say, "Looks like I've interrupted something. I'll talk with you later" or, "This feels like a private conversation. I'll catch you later." If the topic is not something you want to talk about, you can just say, "Hey, I'll talk with you later. It looks like you're really getting into this topic." You may find that one of the people who is involved in the intimate conversation or is talking about the topic you're trying to avoid will regard you as a savior and grab you into the group as an excuse to reduce the level of intimacy or change the topic.

If you're still unsure about how to present yourself with greater confidence, ask yourself, "How would I act if I had just 10 percent more confidence? Or 25 percent more? Or 50 percent more?" Then act that way.

CHAPTER 7

Be Visible

Have you ever noticed how some people stick in your mind and others fade away into oblivion? Great networkers work on becoming visible and, as a consequence, memorable. The strength and expanse of your network depends on how many people know you so well that when resources or opportunities drop into their lives, you pop into their minds as the person to call.

This chapter is full of ideas that will help you enhance your reputation, establish your credibility, and raise your visibility.

Shelve Your Shyness

Do you think of yourself as shy? You're not alone. Many people think of themselves that way. In 1999, Dr. Philip Zimbardo and B. J. Carducci wrote *Shyness: A Bold New Approach*. In this book, Zimbardo reports that in his first studies in 1972, he found that 40 percent of all Americans labeled themselves as shy. But that figure, he notes has steadily increased, year by year, to 50 percent. He blames this rapidly growing fear of being with people on a variety of phenomena, from ATMs to video games to TVs, that reduce day-to-day informal contact with others. And, he says, children aren't seeing their parents relating in a natural, easy, friendly way. Families are smaller and often are too busy to spend time honing conversation skills at the dinner table.

Zimbardo and Carducci define shyness as reticence and self-consciousness, not just occasionally in stressful social situations, but overall. They found that shy people are less popular, have fewer friends, exhibit lower self-esteem, make less money, more often say that their lives are boring, demonstrate fewer leadership skills, are more likely to be depressed, have less social support, and are more likely to be lonely.

"Shyness will cost you," say these experts. "You won't be as successful as someone who is networking, making a good appearance, socializing on the job, and just generally making people feel comfortable in his presence."

Unfortunately, if people aren't outgoing, don't smile, and hesitate to start conversations, then others assume that they are dumb, unmotivated, boring, not interested, snobbish, or condescending.

Whether you always feel shy or just feel shy in certain situations, you can learn to be more comfortable.

Recognize that others feel the same way. Half of us feel shy all the time; the rest of us feel shy sometimes. Say to yourself, "For the next thirty minutes, I'm going to show my

Networking is not just appearing, it's interacting.

energy and enjoy talking with people." Anyone can become more comfortable reaching out to people and become an excellent networker. Work on your body language by using the suggestions in Chapter 7. Transform your overactive Critic into a Coach who can support you and give you more confidence (see Chapter 2). Remember that many confident, easygoing networkers (including us!) once were shy and uncomfortable. They've just learned new behaviors.

Often, people who believe they are shy try to be invisible. Shy people use few gestures. They are very quiet. They avoid eye contact. They control their facial expressions very carefully. All these behaviors are an effort to give people as few clues as possible to what's going on in their minds.

The shy person's message is, "I'll have a low profile; I'll be indefinite, so you can fill in what you would like to see." They create an ambiguous facade, hoping to be all things to all people and trying not to offend anyone. This ambiguity, however, creates anxiety in the people they are with. Anxious people leave the source of their anxiety and thus reinforce the shy person's assessment of himself as someone that people don't want to be with. A shy person's body language alone can isolate her.

Instead of giving into feelings of shyness, find a role model, someone whose presentation of himself you admire. Choose one thing that he does and make it part of your repertoire—a confident handshake, a ready smile, an energetic walk.

Raise Your Profile

The best way to come in contact with the same people again and again is to join organizations. Your memberships will help you develop and nurture long-term relationships. However, also think of organizations as places to become visible—to expand the number of people *who know you.*

Build your reputation among people who can assist your career. Take a high-profile role in organizations you belong to. Be active in professional associations, community and neighborhood groups, your alumni association, or volunteer and service organizations. Organizations give you opportunities for recognition and for affiliation, a place to stick out and a place to belong. Organizations provide proving grounds for new skills, especially leadership skills.

Showcase your skills to the people who count.

When you are visible, there are lots of people *who know you.* That's essential. When opportunities arise, you want to be the person that others think of first.

Use the organizations you join to:

▶ Learn new skills and expand your expertise

▶ Find out more about yourself—what you like and what you don't like

▶ Demonstrate your skills and expertise

▶ Provide a low-risk environment for trying out new things

▶ Gain recognition for your accomplishments and successes

▶ Grow personally and professionally

▶ Find new resources

▶ Discover new directions

▶ Add to your résumé

▶ Make a career change

▶ Get feedback about yourself and your activities

▶ Create career options and opportunities for yourself

▶ Establish your reputation with people you might want to network with

▶ Give back and contribute to your profession and community

Write an article for the organization's newsletter. Provide a program. Staff the registration table at the monthly meeting. Get elected to the board of directors. Set up a job bank if your group doesn't have one. Enter your work in the annual awards program. Winning awards for your work from your own peers is an excellent way to become known for your abilities. Demonstrate your speaking skills, your budgetary wizardry, your organizing expertise, your ability to manage the membership campaign.

Ten Ways to Stand Out in a Crowd

1. *Act like a host, not a guest.* You are president of your own network, even when you are attending an organization's event. Take responsibility for the success of the meeting. Greet newcomers, even if you aren't yet an old hand yourself. Make others comfortable. Be helpful.

2. *Showcase your capabilities.* Take on only those roles that you can and will do well. If you do a great job as treasurer, people will assume that you are an excellent computer programmer or an outstanding real estate salesperson. Conversely, if you've promised to do something, but you don't come through, people will assume that you are not a competent attorney or public relations practitioner. We call it the All or Nothing Principle: If you do *one* thing well, people will assume that you do *everything* well. If you do *one* thing poorly, people will assume that you do *nothing* well.

3. *Show off your wares or your services.* Provide a demonstration or a sample. Contribute door prizes. Do a display.

4. *Show up.* Come early and stay late. Be there, and be present in the moment. Leave behind all your thoughts about the phone calls you have to return back at the office. Pay attention to the here and now.

5. *Listen carefully with a bias toward action.* What do people need that you can offer? Always be ready to give information, resources, or help to others. If someone says, "Boy, I'm ready for a vacation!" respond by saying, "I have a terrific travel agent. Would you like her name?"

> Don't small talk, smart talk. That's small talk with a point.

6. *Help others connect.* Introduce people to each other and build your reputation as an expert networker. Say, for example, "Oh, Sarah, I just met Ona, who has also just started her own business. Let me introduce you to her."

7. *Tell Success Stories.* What picture do you want to pop up in people's minds when they hear your name? They will remember what you last told them. Have something important to tell them when they ask you, "What's new?" See Chapter 12 for ideas on how to create Success Stories.

8. *Talk to and sit with people you don't know.* View every chance meeting as an appointment. By chance, you sit next to Dorothy. She later introduces you to her boss. He invites you to speak at a conference. An attendee likes your approach and hires you to design a training program. That's how networking can work, if you move out of your comfort zone and meet new people.

9. *Find a reason to exchange business cards.* Jot a note on the back of the card so that you can remember what you intend to do to further your relationship with that person: "Send information on how to exhibit at November trade show"; "Call for lunch."

10. *Follow up quickly.* After the meeting, send a note, card, or postcard. Give your contact the information you promised (the name of a consultant, for example). All your effort will be for naught if you don't follow up quickly.

> **Raise your visibility. If you introduce yourself to the speaker, he often will mention you from the podium.**

Be Memorable

At networking events, be memorable. Stick out like a giraffe, don't blend in like a zebra! Here are a lot of ideas that will spark your thinking on ways to stand out.

Say Something

Introduce yourself to the speaker before the program begins. Explain why the topic is important to you. If you do this, the speaker may mention you. It's a great way to become visible to those in the audience.

Renee, the president of a temporary services firm, chatted with Peter, a change management expert, before his speech to a CEOs roundtable group. In his presentation, Peter mentioned her firm and its services as an example of the shift toward hiring part-time and temporary employees.

Introduce yourself to the emcee, the president, the program chair, or anyone in a leadership position with the organization. That person is likely to announce that you are a new member or to repeat news that you've shared.

Wear Something

▶ Patricia, a dynamic professional speaker, makes her appearance memorable by wearing fantastic hats. Referring to networking events, she says, "There's no point in going if no one remembers you were there!"

▶ Louise always wears purple. People marvel at her purple suits. "Oh, you know Louise," people say. "She's the one in purple."

▶ Harriet always pins a jeweled bee on the top of her shoulder. The bee doesn't relate to her job, but it always acts as an ice-breaker.

> **Stand out. Remember, at a networking event it's better to be a giraffe than a zebra!**

▶ Ron, who owns a MotoPhoto franchise, always wears a tie with cameras or other photo motifs on it.

▶ Ken, a golf pro, always carries a golf club along to meetings of his breakfast networking group.

▶ Mickey, whose company provides party decorations, always wears ties covered with cartoon characters.

▶ Maureen, a travel agent, dons a pith helmet to promote her African safaris.

Do Something

▶ Joanne, who owns a chocolate shop, hands out sample goodies to people she talks with.

▶ Lavonne, who has a beauty shop, occasionally gives away a free haircut as a door prize.

▶ Gayle, who sells fine leather products, carries a briefcase that shows off her wares.

▶ Harrison, a masseuse, brings his special chair and provides on-the-spot neck rubs.

▶ Libby, who has a frozen yogurt shop, provided dessert for the networking group's annual picnic.

▶ Harry, who has a pest control business, sprayed the picnic area for bugs to make sure nobody would be bothered by mosquitoes and chiggers.

Manage the Media

Visibility through the media allows you to become known to great numbers of people. So, consider how print, TV, and radio can amplify and complement your face-to-face networking efforts.

One nationally prominent CPA firm offered a syndicated public relations program for selected CPA firms around the United States entitled Growth Through Visibility. This program assisted firms with marketing and client development by helping them to become more visible in their communities. For example, participants received training from media pros on how to:

▶ Work with the media

▶ Promote themselves to talk show producers

▶ Create events that the media wanted to cover

▶ Be lively radio and TV talk show guests

▶ Contact editors and become the "experts" quoted by reporters

▶ Turn contacts into clients with face-to-face marketing (i.e., networking)

Participants also received:

▶ Monthly articles that they could personalize and localize and submit under their names to their daily papers or weekly business publications

▶ Newsletter copy so that they could produce a newsletter for clients and prospects

Finally, participants had the opportunity to become contributing authors and editors of a paperback book that they could then provide to clients or prospects. The book was called *100 Ways You Can Save on Taxes*.

No matter what your business or career niche, you can learn to use the media to establish your credibility and increase your visibility.

Be Quoted

Send editors, reporters, and local freelancers a letter explaining your area of expertise and offering to be a resource if they are doing an article on that topic. Or, pitch a story angle with news value or human interest. That's even more likely to attract the media's attention. Once you are quoted, send a copy of the article to contacts to educate them about your expertise. Also send the article to prospective clients, past clients that you want to stay in touch with, or potential employers if you are job hunting.

Create an Event

Gloria, whose shop specialized in toy bears, held a Bring Your Teddy to Tea party for grandmothers and their granddaughters. She notified the media, and a TV station aired a short segment on the party.

Talk

Talk radio and TV talk shows are always looking for guests who can discuss interesting topics.

Caroline, the owner of an antiques store, became a frequent guest when she proposed a series of shows on decorating for holidays all year long with antiques. She showed milk-glass chickens and antique rabbit toys around Easter, flags and Americana around the Fourth of July, and angels at Christmas.

Speak Out

Judy, a financial planner, was just one of the crowd of financial planners before she created Beulah the Bag Lady and four other female characters that allowed her to dramatize the financial problems facing women. In costume, she spoke before many women's organizations and at trade shows and expos, and gained media coverage.

When she called attendees to discuss their financial needs, she had only to mention Beulah for her prospects to instantly remember her. Best of all, her prospects were willing to talk with her.

To be more comfortable with speaking as a visibility tool, take a speech class, hire a speech coach, join the National Speakers Association, or participate in a Toastmasters Club.

Publish

Write a book, booklet, or pamphlet that you can sell or give away. Create a quiz. Lon, who sells carpet, hands out a quiz entitled, "What do you know about carpet?"

Write an article for your daily newspaper, suburban newspaper, business journal, or other publication. Look carefully at the publication that you hope will print your article and notice how often businesspeople provide feature material. Work with a freelancer to maximize your chances of publication. Nothing establishes you as an expert faster than publishing.

Create a newsletter. You can hire a freelancer to actually put it together. E-mail it to networking contacts, current clients, and prospects. You can use it to bring people to your place of business. One owner of a day spa sent her customers a newsletter that contained this special offer: "Word of mouth is great advertising. To encourage more of this and to reward you for it, October is *Bring a Friend* month. Come in and enjoy one of our services with a friend who has not yet been to the day spa. You'll each receive a gift certificate for a thirty-minute massage at your next visit."

Pay close attention to the media in your city. Keep a file of good ideas and unique approaches. Then launch your own campaign.

CHAPTER 8

Listen Generously

Remember the old story about movie star Zsa Zsa Gabor? At a party, she was talking on and on about her very favorite subject: herself. Finally, she stopped short and turned to her companion. "But dahhh-ling," she purred, "we must talk about *you* for a change. How do you like my dress?"

Of course, *you're* not that self-centered. But chances are you aren't listening as well as you could. In school, we learn to read and write, and we may have a speech class, but we rarely receive much instruction in listening effectively. To network, you must listen—and Listen Generously.

Exercise Your Ears

Writer Fran Lebowitz quips, "The opposite of talking isn't listening. The opposite of talking is waiting." Unfortunately, many people act that way in conversations—they wait impatiently instead of listening. To build relationships, develop your ability to listen. Listening is the quiet side of networking. A talk radio station in Washington, D.C., had as its slogan, "You've got to listen to *talk*." All too often, however, people think that listening is merely *not* talking. Not so. There are ways to improve your listening skills and to make these skills a vital part of your networking conversations.

Listening is work. Don't think of it as a passive activity in which you just nod every once in a while as you wait for your turn to talk.

79

Listening is active. To be a good listener, you need to give your undivided attention and focus. You speak at a rate of about 150 words a minute. But you can think at more than 800 words a minute. That's one reason why you must train yourself to pay attention rather than allow your mind to wander off on tangents. Another challenge is that networking is often noisy. You'll probably be trying to listen in a room in which lots of other lively conversations are going on.

Think EARS

Use the EARS Formula to train yourself to listen better.

E = encourage your partner. Nod, ask questions, indicate with your body language that you are following what he is saying.

A = acknowledge your partner. Restate or repeat her point of view.

R = respond to your partner. Comment, ask questions to get more information, provide information or answers.

S = save what's being said. Mentally store important pieces of information for future reference.

The Benefits of Being Quiet

Jay Conrad Levinson, author of *Guerrilla Marketing Excellence*, advises, "Networking is not a time to toot your own trombone, but to ask questions, listen attentively to the answers, and keep your marketing radar attuned to the presence of problems."

He's right. Here are the benefits of listening carefully.

You'll stand out. Giving someone your true attention is so rare (especially at networking events, where people have a tendency to glance around the room to see who else is there) that you will make a positive impression. Sarah says, "I create an imaginary bubble around me and the person I'm talking with. Six elephants could dance through the room, and I probably wouldn't notice." You can bet people remember talking with her.

You'll find out how to follow up. Listen for what's on the other person's agenda. Listen for the other person's challenges, interests, and enthusiasms. Bill asked some questions about the move James was about to make from a downtown office to a home office. A few days later, Bill sent James an article about home office design. Bill isn't selling file cabinets. He's a computer coach who sees business value in building his network by giving first.

Remember, it takes six to eight contacts with someone before you know each other well enough to have established a long-term business relationship. So listen for reasons to stay in touch.

You'll develop a reputation as a great connector. Whom would your conversation partner like to meet? To find out, listen. When Carla introduced herself as an interior designer who focuses on the senior citizen market, Mitzi immediately said, "I've got to link you up with someone I know who shows businesses how to market to the fifty-plus generation." Listen for links, what people have in common: "You went to the University of Chicago? So did Dan. Let me take you over and introduce you." Or, "You have twins? So does Sherrie. I want you two to meet."

When you become known as somebody who knows everybody, people will call you and ask you if you know someone who . . . As you link people together, you give to them and plug into the Reciprocity Principle. They will try to give you something back.

You'll be able to bridge to what's on your agenda. Suppose you and your partner get into a conversation about the horrors of business travel. Without being abrupt, you'd like to bridge to your need to find a conference center for your sales meeting. Listen carefully, then make the transition: "Sounds like you've clocked a lot of miles to far-away places, Fred. You know, that reminds me. I'm looking for something close to home, and you might be able to help. I wonder if you know of any conference centers within about seventy-five miles of the city. I need to find a place for my upcoming meeting of two hundred salespeople."

You'll learn something. There's an old saying: "A good listener is not only popular, but after a while, he knows something." Learn how to ask good questions, questions that increase your understanding and knowledge of the topic under discussion.

Carlos, an architect, was visiting friends in San Francisco. At a dinner party they gave, he met Bill, who is in the import/export business. Carlos couldn't imagine what he and Bill could possibly have in common, but he asked a lot of questions about Bill's business and listened intently as Bill explained how he sought out artists around the world. Several months later, one of Carlos's clients wanted an unusual work of art for the lobby of his new building. Carlos remembered Bill and enlisted his help in finding just what the client wanted.

Take Turns

You learned about taking turns in kindergarten. In the best relationships, people share. Yet, have you noticed that some people handle their nervousness by talking too little, and others by talking too much? Monitor yourself and make a conscious effort to have your fair share of air time. But also learn how to encourage others to talk.

Try these ideas for getting other people to open up. As you explore a variety of topics, you'll find many opportunities for Listening Generously, developing trust, and encouraging relationships. Some of these ideas will help you as you begin a conversation with someone you have just met; others can be used as you follow up with contacts and learn more about them so that you can build your relationships.

Organize some openers. Do your brain a favor and think of several openers ahead of time. What can you say to start a conversation with the person sitting next to you at a workshop? How would you begin with someone standing alone next to the hors d'oeuvres table? Here are some possibilities:

▶ "What was it about this session's title that caught your attention?"

▶ "You seem to know lots of people here. How long have you been involved with this group?"

Notice other people. Noticing statements are excellent openers. When you say, "I noticed that you were on the edge of your seat during the speech," it's a compliment. When you take the time to notice people out loud, you'll find that the interaction deepens and the conversation becomes more personal. What has happened is that you've let the other person know that he is visible to you, that you are aware of him, that you are thinking about him or her. That's when a relationship begins.

Here are some examples of noticing statements.

▶ "I noticed you really enjoyed giving that presentation. Have you always liked talking in front of groups?"

▶ "I noticed your pin. It's very beautiful. Is there a story behind it?" (Often, people ask, "Where did you get it?" Avoid that question. It can sound envious or even predatory—as if you want to go right out and buy one just like it.)

Noticing another person means that you have made a commitment to the conversation and to getting to know her. It signals that you are willing to be involved. And it encourages the other person to notice something about you.

Appreciate other people. When was the last time someone told you something they appreciated about you, for no reason, out of the blue? Maybe you were a little embarrassed, but wasn't it wonderful? Didn't it brighten your day and give you a special connection to that person? The willingness to give appreciation to other people is a sign of confidence and strength. As your capacity for gratitude grows, your ability to give also grows. Unfortunately, most of us have the idea that if we tell someone about the positive impact he has had on us, then either we'll be "one down" or he will think we want something. Give up those outdated ideas and enjoy the glow that giving genuine appreciation can bring to you and the people you know. No phony baloney stuff here, please. Just ask yourself from time to time, when you're with people, "What do I appreciate about this person? What would feel good to acknowledge about this person?"

Here's what happened when Lindy appreciated one of the superstars in her field:

"At a business meeting recently, I realized I was sitting near one of the greats in my field," Lindy said. "I longed to meet him. Even to impress him. But I was a little in awe of him, so my Critic was saying things like, 'He doesn't want to talk to you. You'll probably say something dumb. He's busy talking to important people.' I noticed how my Critic was making me freeze up and was able to transform some of those negative comments into positive ones. I decided that one way to approach this 'great' would be to go back and let him know how he'd influenced my career. I reached out my hand to shake his and said, 'Hi, I'm Lindy Wilkerson. I noticed your name tag and wanted to be sure to meet you. You were one of my very first heroes when I was entering this field fifteen years ago!'

"He lit up and enthusiastically shook my hand. We explored how I'd heard about him back then. 'Don't I remember that you wrote some books?' I asked. (My Critic had tried to drag me over the coals because I didn't remember any exact titles. I didn't fall for that.) I felt fine about my questions because the energy in my voice showed how interested I was.

"I asked him what a typical day was like for him now. He asked about my work. I told him that my partner and I were writing a book and were just beginning to look for an agent. We got interrupted, but as I was about to leave, he came up and offered, 'Here's my card. Call me and we'll talk about agents. I'm warning you,' he said with a chuckle, 'I never give advice, just information!'

"I did call him the next day, and his information was very helpful. My willingness to overcome my fear and acknowledge him created a pleasant way for us to enjoy the meeting, engage in a real contact, exchange information, and explore future possibilities."

Take clichés seriously. Listen for clichés and know how to handle them. When someone says, "How are you?" and you reply, "Fine," you're embarking on a dead-end routine. Coping with these routines is one reason people hate to network. The question "How are you?" is too big, too open-ended. The possibilities are too enormous. That kind of question invites you to answer with a cliché. As a result, that predictable answer, that cliché in response to a cliché, feels like a turn-off or fencing. When the question is too big, people's minds go into overload. Other similar oversized questions are:

▶ "What have you been up to?"

▶ "Tell me about yourself."

▶ "What's new?"

When you're faced with this kind of opening ritual, you can move along to a more interesting conversation. Here are some tactics that will help you move from a ritual conversation into one that goes somewhere:

▶ If you're bored, bore in. Take the cliché one step further; explore it. Be seriously curious.

▶ Make the conversation more personal.

▶ Make your response unexpected, fun, and energetic.

If you ask, "How have you been?" and your partner replies, "Busy," how do you move the conversation along? Use the "bore in" technique. Intensify the question. Get serious about it. Take it apart. Get personal.

Here are some ideas.

▶ "What's a typical busy day like for you?"

▶ "What do you do on a busy weekend?"

▶ "If you decided tomorrow not to be busy any more, what would you quit doing?"

Be Seriously Curious

When you were four years old, you were curious about everything. Nothing escaped your interest. Everything got your undivided attention. But somewhere along the way, we learned to look cool, as if we've seen it all, as if nothing surprises us. To be a great connector, reconnect with some of that four-year-old curiosity. Find a role model. Anyone under the age of five will do. Notice the questions he asks, the energy he has for finding out.

When four-year-old Matt saw the fisherman bring his boat to the dock, he ran up to have a look at the catch. He had dozens of questions: "Why is that one striped, but this one is spotted?" "Will that one grow any bigger?" "Are all of these fish good to eat?" "Which one is best?" "Do you like to touch them?" "Can they make noise under water?"

Do something about the weather. Everybody talks about the weather, but nobody does anything about it. Weather is a safe topic because it's noncontroversial, it's harmless, and everybody experiences it. Here's how to do something with the weather when it comes up, as it inevitably does.

If your partner begins talking about the weather, how can you say something different or something personal about it? How can you move the conversation to a more businesslike topic? How can you begin to develop a relationship as you have a conversation about the weather?

> **Be seriously curious about other people.**

Like other ritual topics, the weather can become interesting if you are Seriously Curious. If someone says, "Terrible weather we're having," where do you go with that?

Ask:

▶ "Have you lived anywhere where it's more terrible?"

▶ "How does terrible weather affect you? Why do you suppose you feel that way?"

In the middle of a snowstorm, John says, "Boy, it's really snowing hard." Someone else replies, "Yep, it sure is."

Have the courage to really pursue the topic.

Ask:

▶ "What's the biggest snowstorm you've ever seen?"

▶ "Do you remember what it was like when you were a kid and you woke up and found that it had snowed?"

Suppose Dan says, "What a beautiful day!"
Ask

▶ "What's your favorite thing about spring?"

▶ "What are you doing now that it's warm outside?"

▶ "Are you a warm- or cold-weather person?"

Asking serious questions about a superficial topic turns your partner into an ordinary expert. Notice how these questions lead to more important topics. Your partner's answers provides clues to new topics for you to follow up on.

Don't forget your Agenda. You can steer even those conversations about the weather toward it. Eleanor says, "My interest in talking about the weather was zero until I realized that I can live anywhere when I retire in two years. Now, I direct the weather conversation to my Agenda, saying, 'You're so right. This humidity is a killer. It's recently hit me that when I retire, I can live anywhere on earth. Where do you suppose has the best weather? Have you ever lived anywhere you'd recommend?'" Directing a typically boring weather conversation in this way will prove to you that networking comes alive when you talk about your real interests or needs.

Encourage dialog. Martin, a tax specialist, says, "I go to professional meetings to meet as many other professionals as I can, since they might be sending work to me someday. Beforehand, I cram, like for an exam. I read the latest cases, and I have enough intelligent stuff up here in my head so that I can talk for half an hour, nonstop, about the latest and the greatest." Martin's going too far. After that kind of preparation, he's likely to dominate the conversation. Martin's monologue may be informative, but it could just as well be delivered in front of the mirror in his bedroom, rather than to his conversation partner. Good conversation is a dialog, not a monologue.

Explore the icebergs. Imagine that someone says to you, "I've been much too busy to go to any of the meetings." That's an iceberg statement. Only the tip is visible, begging for you to explore what's hidden under the water. Surprisingly enough, most people respond with, "Oh, me too." They ignore the obvious question waiting to be asked: "What's been keeping you so busy?"

As Jean and Chuck talked before the board meeting started, he said, "What a week! I've never seen anything like it." Instead of responding with the usual cliché, "I know what you mean," Jean went for the iceberg, saying, "Tell me more. What's going on in your life?"

Interview people. When Ari went to journalism school, the professor who taught feature writing would hand each student the city phone book, ask the student to open it anywhere, and tell the student to put his finger on a name. Then each student was sent out to interview the person he had selected at random from the phone book for a feature story for the newspaper. The assumption behind the assignment was this: Every person is a feature story. It's not a bad attitude to have about your networking partners.

To interview someone, think of some questions ahead of time. You're probably familiar with the journalist's five Ws: Who? What? When? Where? Why?

You'll normally cover the *who* with introductions. Asking the other questions will give you a formula for conversations that might come in handy. Here are some examples:

▶ "What brought you here today?"

▶ "What did you find particularly interesting about the CEO's speech?"

▶ "What's the best resource you've found lately?"

▶ "When did you begin working here?"

▶ "When did you start your own business?"

▶ "Where are you from?"

▶ "Where do you hope to go with your career? With your business?"

▶ "Why did you come to this meeting?"

▶ "Why did you decide to open your own business?"

Try using the five Ws in a networking situation and see how many questions you can formulate using those five words.

Avoid dead-end questions. These are questions that can be answered by yes or no. The following words provoke yes/no dead-end answers:

▶ *Are:* "Are you going to the Marketing Club meeting?"

▶ *Do:* "Do you know anything about the next speaker?"

For example, when you say, "Do you like our new advertising slogan?" and your partner answers, "No," he may seem abrupt and negative. It may be difficult for you to continue. Instead, ask open-ended questions. They provoke a more lengthy response. Here are some examples:

▶ *How:* "How do you spend your free time?"

▶ *In what way:* "In what way is this corporate reorganization different from the last one?"

▶ *Describe for me:* "Describe for me what you do all day."

▶ *Why:* "Why do you think that software is better?"

Ask about origins and history. Asking people about their origins is a good way to hear about how those people got where they are and to explore their Character and Competence. Ask:

▶ "How did you get started?"

▶ "How did that begin?"

▶ "What happened first?"

▶ "How did you meet your business partner?"

▶ "How did you become interested in this?"

▶ "Do you remember the first moment when you . . .?"

Richard Meryman photographed celebrities for *Life* magazine. When someone asked him how he always managed to capture their essence, he said, "There is always about a person, a single central question." Often, a question about a person's history or origins will reveal that "single central question" that Meryman based his portraits on.

Make other people talk. Do you want people to tell you more? Prompt them to continue the conversation. When you are listening, make encouraging your partner your goal.

Networking doesn't mean doing all the talking. The world abounds with free information if you take the time to be seriously curious, encourage others to talk, and Listen Generously.

CHAPTER 9

Avoid the Top Twenty Turn-Offs

It's easy to recognize other people's sins, the things that turn you off. The question is: Are you guilty of any of them? If so, how can you change your ways so that you are a more attractive conversation partner?

1. ***Don't tell all the details.*** The classic definition of a bore is someone who, when you ask him how he is, tells you. The person who insists on telling everything will soon lose her audience. We've all had the experience of being infuriated with people who wonder out loud, "Let's see, was that in October or November?" Don't include everything; sketch in the broad outlines.

Share the air. Talk only about 50 percent of the time. Make your "air time" count.

2. ***Don't do monologues.*** Encourage and invite others to participate. If other people don't leap in, ask them a question and wait for their answer.

3. ***Don't interrogate people.*** Persistence is usually counted as a virtue. However, you have to know when to stop probing. The inter-

rogator doesn't. He says, "You should . . ." It's one of his favorite phrases. "Why don't you . . . ?" runs a close second. "Surely you know that . . ." ranks right up there. Long after a topic has run out of steam, the interrogator is still battering his partner with it. The interrogator generally has strong feelings about the topic and pushes for her partner's agreement. Tone of voice has as much to do with interrogation as does the wording of a question. The interrogator uses a harsh tone of voice rather than a mild or curious one. Questions are delivered in an accusatory tone, often belittling or demeaning to her partner. If you are being put on the spot by an interrogator about something, say, "Why on earth would you ask me about that? I never talk about . . ." Or, "Are you comfortable talking about that? I'm not." Depersonalize the topic. Move the question from a topic that makes you uncomfortable to one that you'd like to discuss.

4. *Don't insist on one-upmanship.* The person who always has a better story than yours or a better deal to crow about is committing one-upmanship. This person can never merely accept a comment or story; she has to top it with one of her own. These people use conversation to make themselves look wonderful—sometimes at the expense of others. If you've closed a $1 million deal, they've got a $5 million one to tell about. If you went skiing at Keystone, they went to the Alps. Don't play Can You Top This?

5. *Don't seek free advice.* The person who does this wants something for nothing. Such people corner doctors to ask about physical symptoms, lawyers to ask about planning an estate, computer consultants for detailed advice on setting up a computer system. They abuse their conversational partners by asking questions that they should be asking in a more formal situation. They want free advice, when they should be paying for it.

6. *Don't interrupt.* This type of bore never lets you get a word in edgewise. He trounces your comments with nonstop verbiage. He insists on having the first, the middle, and the last word. If this bore is a man, he likes to interrupt subordinates and women to show who's more powerful. He ignores questions and insists on directing the conversation.

7. *Don't hide.* Some people, not wanting to appear self-centered, never tell you anything about themselves. You have to pry it out of them. Or they downplay what they have done, leaving you to feel quite foolish when you discover, through additional questions or other means, what it is that they are obliquely referring to. If you bring up a topic, be sure it's one that you feel comfortable discussing fully.

8. *Don't be dogmatic.* These people have all the answers and merely want to convert other people to their way of thinking. They want confirmation of what they've already decided. Compare them to listeners who keep an open mind in order to gain understanding and sometimes, as a result of talking with others, even change their point of view. People do expect to be comfortable as they network. They don't want to be harangued by someone who is trying to change their mind or force opinions down their throat.

9. *Don't give unsolicited advice.* If you evaluate your own life, you reveal yourself—not a bad thing to do in conversation. But if you evaluate others' lives, you may offend them. You need to know the difference. Never say, "Why don't you . . . ?" or, even worse, "You should . . ." or "You should have . . ." If you feel that your experience might be helpful to someone else, ask permission. Say, "Would you like to hear about what I did in that kind of situation?"

10. *Don't be a bigot.* Bigots are people who make ethnic, religious, or sexual comments in order to put down others. Unfortunately, they come in many varieties. Bigots insult various people in various ways. They stereotype, lumping people into groups and making comments about a group as if those comments apply equally to all its members. They generalize based on a single experience or a small number of experiences. If someone makes a bigoted remark, practice your assertive behavior. Force the bigot to examine his prejudices. Call attention to them. A hearty executive grabbed a woman's hand at a meeting, saying "You must be Marvin's secretary!" The woman calmly replied, "Why ever would you think I'm someone's secretary?" It may be necessary to keep the bigot's good will and to help him save face. If so, speak in a light tone of voice. Tact is the knack of making a point without making an enemy.

11. *Don't whine.* Whiners never have anything good to say. They go on and on about their health (dreadful!), the economy (dreadful!), today's teenagers (dreadful!). You know the type. What a downer!

12. *Don't do hard sells.* When Benny goes to a networking event, he thinks he should get somebody's name on a contract. He walks up to people and says, "Hi, I'm Benny. I sell disability insurance. Are you insured against disability? I can get you covered today." Contrary to what many people think, a networking event is not a place to sell. It's a place to make contact with people so that you can arrange to meet them later to do business. Benny isn't focusing on building trust; he's putting all his energy into finding a customer. He needs to back off and cultivate the relationship. That's when he'll make sales.

13. *Don't assume that you will get paid.* Gina gave Carlotta the name of a potential client to call. Carlotta followed up and contacted the prospect. She got the contract and wrote Gina a note of thanks for the lead, saying that she would be on the alert for something to send Gina's way. Gina's response was to bill Carlotta for a 10 percent "finder's fee." Most networking implies reciprocity. It is okay to charge a finder's fee only if that agreement is made up front. Expert networkers generally consider such arrangements to be self-defeating because they terminate the exchange abruptly and do not necessarily develop the relationship. These networkers would rather have someone looking out for an opportunity to give to them. If, however, someone does something for you that results in business, and you know that you'll never have an opportunity to pay that person back, then you might consider paying a finder's fee or sending a gift. Thea wrote a magazine article quoting Dorothy, who lived in the Midwest. Dorothy got a call from someone who read the article, and that person became a client of Dorothy's. In gratitude, Dorothy sent Thea a finder's fee.

14. *Don't make unreasonable requests.* Una, a part-time professor, told her class of eleven graduate students to call certain middle managers in her company and interview them. The next time one of the managers saw Una, he asked her, rather pointedly, to check with him before making that kind of assignment in the future because it was too time-consuming for him to talk to so many students during his busy workday. The professor apologized and was especially careful for several months to find information to give to all the managers to repay them for the inconvenience she had thoughtlessly caused them.

15. *Don't confuse contacts with friends.* "Networking, ugh!" says Yvonne. "I just want to be friends with people." You can develop friendships with networking contacts, but it takes time, something that many businesspeople don't have. It's possible to have many warm business contacts without turning them into friendships. Women are more likely than men to be confused by the invisible line that separates contacts from confidants. Don't worry about it. Be friendly with your contacts. If a friendship takes root, fine; if not, you still have a good contact.

16. *Don't abuse people's trust.* In many networking situations, you are dealing with sensitive information or business intelligence. Don't pass it on without permission. If you are a real estate agent who sold a house that was part of a divorce settlement, for instance, you would, of course, avoid using your clients' real names. As you tell stories to illustrate your Character and Competence, disguise real situations if they are sensitive. The world is a small place, and word gets around if you violate someone's confidence. Don't use one person's name to make contact with another person unless you ask permission. Always be trustworthy.

17. *Don't be so eager to provide resources that you pass along the names of people or organizations that you haven't thoroughly checked out.* Before you give your contact a name, be sure that person's or organization's performance will reflect well on you.

18. *Don't burden others with inappropriate or intimate information.* You have to know someone very well before it's appropriate to discuss your daughter's divorce or how much you spent on your last vacation.

19. *Don't expect to get without giving.* Absolutely the worst thing you can do is to take repeatedly from a person without reciprocating by sending information, referrals, or opportunities her way.

20. *Don't forget to enjoy the journey.* It's easy to keep your eyes on the horizon—on your business goals—and fail to enjoy the ride. Sure, you're looking for business or career benefits, but relax. Take time to appreciate people's unique gifts beyond their usefulness to you at the moment. Allow yourself to enjoy encountering the unexpected. Just as you might drive around a bend and discover a wonderful view, a conversation may veer off, and you'll find you're talking about something that you haven't even thought about for years or something that changes your view of the world. People who enjoy

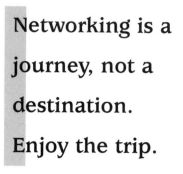

Networking is a journey, not a destination. Enjoy the trip.

window shopping or browsing through bookstores or antiques shops can get the same kick out of being with people. People take courses in art appreciation; networking can be a "course" in the appreciation of people and of life. Be ready to be delighted.

PART 4

Master the Million-Dollar Moments

What really happens when you meet someone? Do you muddle through those oh-so-important first few minutes? The chapters in Part 4 will help you rid yourself of the worn-out rituals that don't work. (How are you at remembering names?) And you'll find out exactly what to say and do to manage those three Million-Dollar Moments that happen over and over again every time you shake hands. You'll discover state-of-the-art skills and secrets that nobody ever told you about—the rules and tools that make networking easy. You'll find out how to get the most out of every conversation, from "Hello" to "Good-bye." (By the way, there's a new ritual for ending conversations, a ritual that removes all the awkwardness from leave-taking.) Want to know what to do next to enlist the people you meet in your network? You'll learn scads of ways to reconnect, stay in touch, and follow up.

CHAPTER 10

"Who Are You?"

There are three big questions that always come up in every networking encounter:

1. "Who are you?"

2. "What do you do?"

3. "What are we going to talk about?"

These questions are "Million-Dollar Moments." How you deal with them can make the difference between beginning a relationship that might be worth millions over a lifetime or blowing it.

Most people muddle through these moments, relying on the rituals for meeting and greeting that we all know so well. Instead, learn how to maximize these moments and make sure your business relationships start off in the best possible way.

This chapter will help you deal with the first question, "Who are you?" effectively.

Understand What Usually Happens

Okay. You're right. When people meet, they rarely say to one another, "Who are you?" What exactly do they actually do?

One person takes the initiative and sticks out her hand, saying, "Hi, I'm Jennifer Allsgood."

Shaking her hand, the other person responds, "Bob Schafer. Nice to meet you."

"You too," says Jennifer.

How long does that name exchange take, do you suppose? If you guessed three to four seconds, you'd be right. The next time you're around people who are introducing themselves, listen in. Count how many seconds it takes. Check out for yourself how much time people usually spend on this important moment.

No wonder people have trouble remembering names! We are asking the impossible when we try to learn someone's name—and teach that person our name—in only a few seconds.

What's the rush?

People say, "I just whiz through the name thing so I can move on to the good stuff." But in networking,

> # The average name exchange takes less than five seconds. No wonder we can't remember people's names!

names are "the good stuff." It will be mighty difficult for you to initiate a relationship with someone if you don't know that person's name.

So, slow down. Linger longer over the name exchange.

Learn Names

Avoid the "head-on name crash" in which you say your name at the same time someone else is saying his. When someone says his name, do not immediately reply with your own. Instead, focus initially on learning that person's name.

When someone introduces himself to you, here are three things you can do to learn that person's name. These ideas are so simple that you may be tempted to dismiss them. Don't do that! Train yourself to use them every time you meet someone. They work.

1. *Repeat the first name.* Say, "It's nice to meet you, Jennifer." You may think that you habitually do that, but our research indicates

that less than 25 percent of people involved in introductions repeat the name. Train yourself to do it every time. Hang on to the name in order to introduce Jennifer to at least one other person at that event. Whether you make that introduction thirty

> # To remember a name, say it immediately.

minutes later or three hours later, Jennifer will appreciate that you bothered to remember her name. Notice that you are focusing only on the first name. That's fine. It's the tried and true principle of "divide and conquer." Learn only the person's first name first.

2. *Ask for the last name again or confirm it.* Say, "And your last name was . . .?" or, "Tell me your last name again," or, "And your last name is Allsgood?" The person will repeat her last name, "It's Allsgood," or say, "Yes, it's Allsgood." Usually, people will say their last names very distinctly when you ask only for the surname. One problem with the old ritual is that people are so used to saying their names that they say them too quickly, running their first name and their last name together. By asking for the last name separately, you will encourage the person who is introducing himself to you to separate the names and to say them clearly.

3. *Ask a question or make a comment about the person's name.* Comment on either the first name or the last name. Here are some suggestions.

▶ "Do you like to be called Jenny or Jennifer?"

▶ "Allsgood is an interesting name—it sounds optimistic."

▶ "Allsgood sounds like it might be an English name. Do you know where it came from?"

Teach Your Name

Notice that you have not yet said your own name! Now is the time to do just that. Be ready to help someone learn your name. There are three things that you can do.

1. *Give 'em a double dip.* Say your first name twice: "I'm Bob, Bob . . . Shafer."

2. *Separate and articulate.* Say your first and your last name with a tiny pause in between and pronounce your last name crisply and distinctly: "I'm Bob, Bob (pause) Shafer."

3. *Make your name memorable.* Say something about your name to help the person you're talking with remember it. Here are some suggestions. Spelling your name is a good idea because a majority of us are visual learners. That means that we learn best when we can see the letters in our mind's eye. To help you learn her name, Jennifer might have spelled Allsgood when you asked her for it again. Nancy Mann says, "It's Mann with two *n*'s. I'm the only woman in real estate in Kansas City who's a Mann."

There are several concerns people have as they begin to use this system:

▶ *"It feels awkward at first."* Yes, it does. We are used to playing the name game like Ping-Pong: Your name to me; my name back to you. That's the ritual. You'll need to practice to be comfortable with the new system because the timing is different.

▶ *"What should I do when people are wearing name tags?"* You can still use this system. Use the name tag as a visual aid. While Bob is learning Jennifer's name, he can say, looking at the name tag, "I see your name is Jennifer. Do you ever go by a nickname?" When he is introducing himself, Bob can say, "My name tag says 'Robert,' but I prefer 'Bob.'"

▶ *"Sometimes the other person—who is still playing Ping-Pong—will interrupt. What do I do then?"* Go with the flow. Answer the other person's question. Then go back to ask something else or say something else about that person's name later. The point is to talk longer about the names.

▶ *"What if you're being introduced to someone, and he says, 'I never can remember names?'"* That's your cue to say, "You can remember mine. Here's how. It's Sherry Hunter. Sherry like the drink. You can remember Hunter because I hunt down computer problems and fix them." Use the suggestions in this chapter to help both of you learn each other's names this time.

Try These Twenty Tips

1. Continue to use the other person's name as the conversation moves along: "Are you a new member, Fred?"

2. Look for a personal connection, perhaps someone else you know who has the same name. Make the connection out loud. Tell your partner, "Hi Adam. Good to meet you. Adam was my college roommate's name. So it will be easy for me to remember you." Or, "Nice to meet you, Harriet. Wasn't your name mentioned as one of the new board members?"

3. Associate the name with a picture in your mind to help you remember the name. If you meet someone in a leadership position whose name is Arthur, visualize him as King Arthur with the knights of the Round Table. (Some people like this technique; others say it just confuses them. Use it if it's helpful.)

4. Ask the person to spell his name. "Is that Carl with a *C* or a *K*?" "Is that M-a-r-y or Merry as in Christmas?" If the person is wearing a name tag, you still may comment on the spelling, "I see that you spell Marsha with an *S*."

5. Ask how the person got her name. "Do you know why you were named Savannah? Were you named for the city?" We find that nearly half of our workshop participants can tell a story about how they got their names.

6. Tell the person what you have heard about him. Acknowledge his uniqueness: "I understand that this new orientation program was your idea, Kay."

7. If you notice that people often have trouble understanding your name, it may be because you run the two words together. This

sort of problem may be accentuated if your last name begins with a vowel. If your name is difficult for people to understand, separate the two names like this: "Hi; my first name is Helen, and my last name is Anderson."

8. If your name comes from a culture that is not very familiar to the people you are meeting, then you'll have to make a special effort to teach them your name. Barbara Rodvani says, "Rodvani, think of a van going down a road, Rodvani." Weng Po says, "If you want to remember my first name, just think of Winnie the Pooh."

9. If your last name is a hyphenated combination, say so. It's very difficult for people to understand a first name plus *two* last names. "Hi, I'm Maureen, Maureen . . . James-Martin. James is my maiden name, and Martin is my husband's last name."

10. Come up with several ways to help people remember your name. As you say your name, give your partner a little extra information so that you have a chance to repeat your name for her. This can be as simple as saying, "Jack's a nickname for Jackson."

11. Tell people where your name came from. "Stanton was my grandfather's name. I like having his name because he encouraged me to start my own business." "My first name is Andreal. My mother liked the name Andrea, but she wanted something unique, so she added an *L*."

12. Keep your energy level high—rev it up. Let your body language and tone of voice indicate that you're seriously trying to learn your partner's name and teach him your name. People say that this is very flattering.

13. Always say the person's name again as you leave him to reinforce your learning: "It was good to meet you, Ronda."

14. Give yourself a realistic goal. At a networking event, for example, vow to really learn the names of five people before you leave.

15. Decide whether you want to teach your conversation partner your first name or your last name. If you want your contact to be able to find you in his Rolodex or industry directory, concentrate on your last name. Professional speaker Maggie Bedrosian says, "Hi, I'm Maggie, Maggie Bedrosian. Bedrosian, like bed of roses."

16. Design a way to teach your partner your name and what you do at the same time. Debbie, a new franchise owner does just that. She says, "Hi, I'm Debbie Danforth with Decorating Den. Just remember: *D* for Debbie and *D* for Decorating Den."

17. If you don't like the association that people often make when they hear your name, say something to redirect their attention. Even though the TV show is long gone, Mindy found that people were always asking her, "Where's Mork?" So, she decided to say, "Hi, I'm Mindy, Mindy . . . Jones. Mindy, like Lindy, but with an *M*."

18. Set up a positive association. Don't use a memory hook that links you with a negative impression. Annabel Lector used to say, "Hi, I'm Annabel Lector, like the killer in *Silence of the Lambs*."

19. Don't assume that people with foreign-sounding names are not native-born Americans. When Ying-Chie introduces herself, she often is asked, "Where are you from?" She replies, with some irritation, "San Francisco."

20. If your name is memorable or connects easily to some idea, you may become bored or irritated with what people say about it. "People always say, 'Just like the bird,' when I say my name," complains Bob White. Find a way to use that connection. Bob, a realtor, might say, "Yes! And, when I find just the right home for people, they sing!"

Break Up Bunches of Introductions

You've joined a group of people, and one of them is quickly introducing each member of the group to you. You're thinking, "I'll never remember all these names!" What can you do?

Smile. Say "Hello" as each person is introduced. After a while, when the group breaks up, go back to each individual and introduce yourself one-on-one, using the new system.

Deal Skillfully with Forgotten Names

Have you ever seen someone across the room and said to yourself, "I know that person. What is her name?" This is not an age-related problem; it's a brain overload problem. Let's face it, you know hundreds of people—coworkers, customers, colleagues, cousins—so expecting that you will never forget a name is unrealistic.

At all costs, however, avoid the following scenario. Erase it from your repertoire.

You see someone across the room whose name you think you should remember. You make eye contact, then hang your head, shuffle over with a discouraged look on your face, limply put out your hand, and apologetically announce, "Ooooh, no! I've forgotten your name." If the person wants to make you feel better, she'll say, "Oh, I've forgotten your name too," even if she remembers it!

This low-energy start has no place to go but down as you stand around mutually beating yourselves up with a duet of "I'm so bad with names"; "No, I'm much worse." After you commiserate about how dumb you are, you finally reintroduce yourselves, all the while protesting that you'll probably forget each other again.

What should you do instead? You have several options. Try one of these ways to reconnect, even if you can't remember the person's name:

▶ Walk up to the person, stick out your hand, and say your name. You're banking on the ritual. The other person will most likely say his name back.

▶ If you recall the situation in which the two of you met or a topic you discussed, refer to that. "I remember meeting you at the conference, and we talked about job opportunities in Denver. Tell me your name again!" Or, "As I remember, we talked about the seminar you'd just attended. I'm Todd Watson." That way, you acknowledge that your prior meeting was memorable. Since you've offered your name, your partner will usually follow your cue and give his name.

▶ Ask a friend to remind you of the forgotten name: "Jerry, I know I've met that guy over there with the red tie. Remind me of his name."

▶ Don't worry about it. Hope that the person's name will occur to you as the conversation goes along. Often, as you begin talking, you'll remember the name.

Yes, Mind Your Manners

Life is more casual today, and few people can quote chapter and verse on the protocol of introductions. But it will make you feel more confident to know the rules, so here they are.

Shaking hands and standing up. Anyone who is introduced to anyone else should offer to shake hands. Gender and age used to govern who put out his hand first. Those distinctions are obsolete today. Reaching out to shake hands should be almost simultaneous. It's proper to stand when introductions are being made unless you are seated in a restaurant or are in some other environment that makes standing difficult.

To introduce peers to each other. Say either name first; it doesn't matter which one comes first. Use both first and last names, and speak distinctly. "Jackie Arnold, this is Rob Baker." Give each some additional information about the other person, if you know that person well enough. "Jackie, Rob is on the audit staff. Rob, Jackie is in human resources." Using their names several times will be helpful to them.

To introduce a superior to a subordinate. In today's workplace, we're moving away from focusing on these matters of rank. Nevertheless, to follow the rules, follow this pattern.

Say the name of the superior first. "Mr. Brown (or Don, depending on whether you call the person by his first name), I'd like you to meet Bob Davis. Bob, this is Don Brown." Again, it's helpful to all concerned if you can give some additional information—often just a title will do. "Don, Bob is in our legal department. Bob, Don has been division manager for as long as I've been with the company."

To introduce a customer. When introducing customers to people in your business, treat the customer as the superior. Say the customer's or client's name first to honor that relationship. "Mr. Smith, I'd like you to meet Mary Jones. Mary, this is Al Smith. We installed one of our XYZ systems in his business last week. Al, Mary heads our training staff."

To introduce women. It used to be proper always to introduce a man to a woman—in other words, to treat the woman as if she were the superior, saying her name first. That rule is obsolete, and rank should prevail. Since so many people are confused about the rules, you should not make any assumptions about the rank of a woman whose name is said first.

To introduce older people. It also used to be proper to introduce a younger person to an older person, saying the name of the older person first. Again, today's protocol would be to ignore age.

To introduce a person with no business status. When introducing someone who has no business status (such as your mother), say the name of the company person first if he outranks you. If the company person is a peer or of lower rank, say your mother's name first to honor her.

To sum up, say the name of the higher-ranking person or the person you wish to honor first. First is foremost is the only rule you need to know about introductions. That's all you need to remember.

CHAPTER 11

"What Do You Do?"

In New Zealand, they might ask it this way: "Wot do ye do fer a crust, mate?" In the United States, it's the inevitable second big question that always comes up in every networking encounter: "What do you do?"

How you answer this often-asked question is crucial. It's another one of those Million-Dollar Moments. You should be prepared to answer this question in a way that will move the conversation along. But all too often, as was the case with "Who are you?" the rituals of meeting and greeting that we have learned so well, and practice so effortlessly, get in the way of building relationships.

Understand What Usually Happens

When people ask, "What do you do?" do you:

▶ Give your occupation, job type, or category: "I'm an attorney." That's *cement*. The response falls like a dead weight—a block of cement. Your conversation partner is likely to say, "Oh, . . . nice." (Yep, that's the number-one comment when people tell what they do.)

▶ Give your title: "I'm assistant information systems manager with the northeast division of management information systems, a division of System Information Management, Inc." That's *fog*. Giving a title—especially a long, complicated, jargon-filled one—leaves you surrounded by a thick cloud of words. And your conversation partner is likely to say, "Oh, . . . nice."

109

▶ Give your industry: "I'm in real estate." That's the *blob*. That response puts you right in the middle of the great gray blob of the other 487 people your conversation partner knows who are also in real estate. You've missed your chance to differentiate yourself from all the other people in that industry that your contact has met. And your conversation partner will probably say, "Oh, . . . nice."

▶ Give the name of the organization you work for: "I'm with Disney." That's the *flag*. That response wraps you in the flag of the organization. You aren't going to be known for your talents and capabilities if you say that; your only identity will be Disneyite—a dangerous situation if you ever are laid off.

What's the problem? These commonplace responses to "What do you do?" aren't conversation builders; they're conversation stoppers.

The polite reply "Oh, . . . nice" means that the person you are talking to has no idea where to go with the conversation.

Your partner may have learned to deal with *cement* and the *blob* by asking questions: "What kind of law do you practice?" "Which one of the real estate companies are you with?"

However, if your conversation partner has to ask questions, she may feel as if she or he is having to pry information out of you. You won't have made it easy for your conversation partner to talk with you or to begin to know your capabilities and talents.

Make the Right Things Happen

Your conversation partner has a TV screen in his head. Most people do. When you tell your conversation partner about your work, there are two possibilities.

On the one hand, your conversation partner may see nothing but static—a blizzard—on the screen. That's what people see when you have responded to "What do you do?" with cement, fog, the blob, or the flag—nothing.

On the other hand, your conversation partner could be seeing something exciting going on—something that he will always remember.

As you reply to that "What do you do?" question, what do you want your partner to see on the TV screen in her head?

What one thing do you want your partner to know about you? When you come up with your answer to *that* question, you'll know what to say.

Give It Your Best

Using a formula called the *best/test* will help you. *Best* refers to what you do best. *Test* is short for *testimonial*—a short description of you succeeding brilliantly at what you do best and want others to remember.

Here's how to construct your best/test. The first sentence of your reply tells the one thing—of all your many talents and skills—you do best. The second sentence gives a brief example and is a testimonial to your talents. It should briefly show how you saved the day, served the client, or solved the problem. Use only ten words or so in your first sentence to tell what you do best. Keep it snappy and jargon-free. Aim to be understood by a ten-year-old. Use exciting, colorful, vivid language.

Consider this example. John used to answer the question, "What do you do?" this way: "I'm a sonographer."

When someone asked him, "Do you take shorthand?" he realized that he wasn't providing a clear answer. He worked on his best sentence and came up with this: "I tell people whether it's a boy or a girl."

The word *sonographer* created only a blizzard. His new sentence makes things happen on his conversation partner's screen. There he is, sitting down with the happy couple. He says, "It's a girl." The mother-to-be reaches out for the prospective papa's hand. They beam at each other. It's a memorable moment. John's conversation partner is able to see it clearly now.

John then worked on his test and came up with a concrete example. Again, he kept it short: "Last week, I told an astonished couple they were going to have triplets."

John is in a technical field. He needed to take a confusing word, *sonographer*, and translate it for a lay audience.

It's even more important for people with small businesses to describe what they do clearly. If the people they meet understand what they do, those people may refer clients or customers.

Terri used to describe herself as "a marketing consultant," a cement answer.

Now, she tells what she does best: "I help people get the word out about their products and services."

She updates her test constantly to provide a vivid picture of her succeeding with clients: "Last week, I wrote a news release that got one of my clients, a CPA, on the front page of Tuesday's business section. He just called to tell me he'd had seven calls from prospective clients since the article appeared!"

What do you know about Terri from this short anecdote?

> Give contacts specifi
>
> examples of projects
>
> so that they can
>
> describe to others—
>
> accurately and
>
> vividly—what you d

She writes news releases that get results for her clients. Using the best/test allows Terri to teach you about her Character and her Competence—to build the trust that is necessary to establish an effective networking relationship.

Now, imagine that you run into a CPA who says, "I want to let women entrepreneurs know about my services for small businesses." Wouldn't Terri's name and expertise pop up in your mental Rolodex? Wouldn't you mention Terri to this CPA?

That's the way it's supposed to work. That's the way it does work.

Be Interesting

Rather than eliciting the comment, "Oh, . . . nice" when you tell people what you do, aim for the comment, "Tell me more."

When people asked Buford "What do you do?" he used to give his title. It was so long that he had to stop and take a breath in the middle: "I'm director of student financial aid in the student affairs division of the University of Missouri (gasp!)Kansas City." And people said, "Oh, . . . nice."

Then he came up with another way to put it, a much more interesting way. He said, "I give away $32 million a year."

Did people want to hear more. You bet!

Try These Tips

Say the right *thing in your best/test.* Don't choose being interesting over teaching people what you *really* want them to know about you. A pharmaceutical saleswoman got people's attention when she said, "I sell drugs." But after thinking it over, she decided that that was not what she wanted to teach people. She now says, "I educate doctors about new drugs, so that they can give their patients the most up-to-date prescriptions."

Tell your talent, not your title. Titles tell what you are, not what you do. Instead, paint a picture in the other person's mind of you in action, you at your best.

Avoid acronyms and jargon. When the person you're talking with is unfamiliar with your "insider lingo," she will feel put off.

Resist the ego trip. If you work for a well-known or prestigious group, resist the urge to bask in that organization's glory. Don't say, "I'm with Hallmark" or "I'm at the Department of State."

Sure it's easy. Sure the listener says, "Oh, . . . nice!" as in "Wow!" But we guarantee that it won't start a conversation, and, worse yet, you just missed the chance to teach someone about your talents and successes.

Ask a question. A variation on the best/test is to answer the question "What do you do?" with a question.

David asks, "Has your bank ever put your money in somebody else's account?" Whether the answer is yes or no, he says, "I'm working with Federal Reserve Banks nationwide to design a system so that won't ever happen."

Read These Frequently Asked Questions

Here are some questions people ask about the best/test method.

Q: What if I wear several hats?

A: Prepare several different best/tests. Select the right one to use depending on whom you are talking to and what you want him to know about you.

For instance, when we are talking to meeting planners, one of us might say, "I get people talking at conventions" (best). "I just gave the kickoff keynote on convention networking at the Health-Care Educators annual meeting" (test).

When we are talking to people in professional services, one of us might say, "I help lawyers get the most out of their professional memberships and turn contacts into clients" (best). "I just finished a four-part seminar for attorneys at McCann, Henry, & Wisecoff" (test). When we're talking to people in the publishing industry, one of us might say, "I wrote the book on networking" (best). "A book club just bought 59,400 copies" (test).

Q: Isn't this bragging?

A: Many people in our workshops say, "Oh, I could never say something like that. I'd feel like I was bragging." But are you? That great American humorist Will Rogers said, "If you done it, it ain't braggin'!"

When you're asked what you do, the best way to start a conversation is to be enthusiastic and specific about your accomplishments. How else will people learn what to count on you for, what you're good at, whom they should refer to you, what opportunities to send your way?

Q: How will I know when I have a good answer to the question, 'What do you do?'

A: Ask yourself these three questions:

Does my answer give a specific, positive picture of me succeeding, me doing what I want to be known for?

Does my answer encourage people to say, "Tell me more"? Does it invite questions and conversation without being maddeningly mysterious? The real estate agent who merely says, "I'm a miracle worker" is being too cagey. She needs to add "for home buyers." Her test can further clarify her claim: "I just found a house for a newly married couple who both use wheelchairs at a price they can afford in a neighborhood they love."

Do I deliver my answer in an excited, upbeat way, in a tone of voice that expresses my delight in serving my customers or solving the problems, rather than tooting my own horn?

Q: What should I do if the person I'm talking with gives me cement (her job type), fog (her title), the blob (her industry), or the flag (her organization)?

A: Ask questions designed to draw out specific examples, learn about special expertise, or hear about unique projects. Ask:

"What's a typical day like in your work?"

"Tell me about a recent project you've been working on."

Q: I'm in a technical field. I have a Ph.D. I can't imagine being so folksy—especially when I'm with my peers and everyone is trying to one-up the other person.

A: It's okay to use your title or the jargon of your profession if you are speaking to other people in the same specialty. But be sure to supplement that with a vivid testimonial, so that people have a clear idea of your expertise.

Q: I hate what I do. I'm just an office manager. It's so boring. I'm trying to change careers. What should I say?

A: If you don't like what you are doing, don't talk about it. Instead, talk about the 5 percent of your job you do like or what you have done in the past or what you want to do in the future. Say, "I'm an expert scheduler and organizer (best). Last year, when my company relocated, I played a key role in the move. It was so exciting to help an organization go from an up-and-running office into thousands of boxes and out again in record time and with a minimum of trauma" (test).

Q: I go to networking events, but nothing much happens. What am I not doing? I need new clients.

A: Put a provocative question on your name tag. At a travel association meeting, a bank acquisitions manager wrote on her name tag: "How can a banker help a travel expert?" She got two appointments with people at the event.

CHAPTER 12

"What Are We Going to Talk About?"

There's one conversation that everybody knows, word for word. You can hear it at networking events all across the United States, from Tacoma, Washington, to Tampa, Florida. It goes like this:

"Hi, how are you?"

"Not bad. How are you?"

"Not bad. What's new?"

"Not much. What's new with you?"

"Not much. Been real busy."

"Me too. Good to see you."

"You too. We'll have to get together sometime."

"Great idea. I'll give you a call."

"Well, bye. See you later."

This is a conversation in search of a topic! Without a topic—or several—that *you* want to talk about, you'll waste your time in purposeless chit-chat like that one-size-fits-all conversation.

It pays to be prepared to talk about topics you care about. Having an Agenda—a plan for your networking conversations—is vital.

Listen for Your Cue

There are two cues that should trigger in you the thought, *Time to use my Agenda.*

One cue is that question that someone you already know will ask: "What's new?"

The other cue is the pause as you and a person you're meeting for the first time search for something to talk about. Often that pause comes just after you've finished talking about what you both do—and just before the conversation about the weather or the ball scores!

Do you wonder, *How can I direct the conversation to my business?* Here's how to manage the third Million-Dollar Moment.

Use Success Stories to Tell What's New

When somebody asks, "What's new?" Ilsa says, "I tell them I'm training for a marathon. If I tell people that, then the next time we meet, they'll ask me, 'How's the marathon training going?' That keeps me motivated—and committed to my goal." The reason she gives for electing to talk about the marathon is that she wants pledges for the charity run.

When somebody asks, "What's new?" Sam says, "I've moved my business. My new location is right next to the Metro—and the rent is actually lower!" The reason he gives for choosing that topic is that he wants to show how easy it is to get to his graphic design business.

Both Ilsa and Sam have good answers to "What's new?" and good reasons for their answers.

But all too often, people reply, "Not much. What's new with you?" and sink into another one of those superficial conversations like the one at the beginning of this chapter.

The best reply to "What's new?" is to tell a Success Story. A Success Story is a short, punchy anecdote in which you tell about a specific success.

Sharing one of your successes allows you to teach your conversation partner what you do, what you're interested in (like Ilsa), how you serve

> When someone asks "What's new?" tell a Success Story that shows you saving the day, solving the problem, or serving the customer.

customers or clients, something important about your business (like Sam), or what you or your firm have to offer.

Before you go to your next networking event, where you're sure to be asked the inevitable question, "What's new?" plan your Success Story. As you construct your story, use the letters in the word *success* as your guide:

S = Strategic. Make sure your story fits your Agenda. Think about what you want people to know about you or your business, then build your story around that point.

U = Unique. Point out what makes you stand out from the crowd. If you're in real estate, for example, don't just say, "I've been selling lots of houses." That's expected. Say, "Last week, I found a home for a couple who both needed home offices. Each of them wanted a first-floor office with outside access, lots of light, and great views. I found just the house, one that had two sunny rooms with French doors opening onto a patio just off the driveway." This story teaches your conversation partner that you can find the unusual home.

C = Clear. Be sure you eliminate all the jargon of your profession.

C = Concrete. Give a couple of specific details to help your partner see a vivid picture. Use specific words; they will stick in the other person's mind more easily than generalities will. Notice that you almost can "see" the house the Realtor was describing.

E = Exciting. Let your enthusiasm shine through. Use vivid language, an upbeat tone of voice, and a speedy, not "draggy," delivery. Make it memorable.

S = Short and Succinct. Edit your story to a maximum of three sentences.

S = Service-Oriented. Be sure that your story teaches how well you served the client, solved the problem, or saved the day.

Plan Success Stories on several different topics, then use the one that seems most appropriate to the person you are talking with.

If you construct your Success Story carefully, it can do a lot for you. It can teach people to trust you, give a vivid example of your expertise, enhance your credibility, and make people want to do business with you.

When someone at a networking event asked Carrie, who has her own PR business, "What's new?" here's what she said: "I was really scrambling last week. I was in the middle of creating a brochure for Oak Tree Mall, and my office was flooded after the big rain. So, I rented a computer and got the layout to the client on deadline, as I had promised. Boy, was he happy!"

What do you know about Carrie after hearing her Success Story? Here's what some of our workshop participants have said Carrie taught them:

▶ "She won't let anything make her miss a deadline."

▶ "She's reliable."

▶ "She'll do whatever it takes to get the job done on time."

▶ "She's resourceful."

▶ "She doesn't give up."

▶ "She handles crises well."

▶ "She's doing work for a prestigious client, so she must be good."

▶ "You can trust her; she'll come through."

As you can see, you can get a lot of mileage out of a good Success Story: a reputation for going to heroic lengths to meet your deadlines, a reputation for delighting clients, the reflected glory of having top businesses in town as clients. Best of all, a good Success Story gives your contact a concrete picture of exactly what you do.

When Louis asked Cathleen, a CPA, "What's new with you?" she said, "One of my clients was upset about a tax penalty for something that happened a couple of years ago. I wrote the Department of Revenue the most persuasive letter I could devise about the situation.

When they backed down and removed the penalty, my client was so relieved."

After you tell your story, ask your conversation partner a question that will elicit his Success Story. Our favorite question comes from Ann who asks, "And what are you excited about these days?"

Figure Out Your Agenda

More than 85 percent of the people we surveyed as they arrived at networking events hadn't figured out exactly why they'd come. They knew they wanted something, but they hadn't figured out what! They hadn't thought about whom they wanted to meet, what they wanted to find out, or how they were going to achieve their goals. They didn't know what they wanted to share, to tell people about, to pass along. Predictably, about the same percentage of people surveyed on their way out said they wished they'd gotten more out of the event.

To be an effective networker, you need to have a clear purpose in mind before you begin talking with people. That purpose comes from knowing what's on your ever-changing Agenda. As you focus on your Agenda, you'll feel eager and excited about connecting with people.

Your networking Agenda is a mental or written list of what you have to give and what you want to get.

Since each of us has unique goals, each of us has a unique Agenda.

Bill, a teacher, has a small real estate business on the side. He was elated when he finally found an accountant that he trusted and enjoyed working with. In the weeks that followed, he enthusiastically recommended her to anyone he met who was looking for competent accounting services. At the same time, Bill was looking for someone to work for him part time, doing mailings and keeping his database up to date. He had something to *give* in his conversations—his recommendation of an accountant—and he had something he was trying to *get* in his conversations—the name of a qualified person who might like to work part time. He had an Agenda.

In this chapter, you'll learn how to construct your personal Agenda so that it focuses on the things you want to get and, equally important, the things you can give as you make connections with other people. Having an Agenda will energize and empower you so that you'll benefit from your networking. You'll feel comfortable and capable of enjoying yourself, making contact, gathering information, and seeking out opportunities.

You may have dreaded networking situations in the past because you felt you didn't have anything to talk about. Actually, when it comes to topics, the problem is *not* that there's *nothing* to talk about; the problem is that there's *too much* to talk about! Hundreds of topics a day come crashing in on you via newspapers, TV, radio, e-mail, junk mail, and the Internet. No one topic looks that much more interesting than any other. It's hard, perhaps even impossible, to select from all of the ideas racing around in your head. An Agenda simplifies the situation. And you automatically care about— and have energy for—the topics on your Agenda list.

> There are two sides to networking: giving and getting. You are only in control of one side—guess which one. It only makes sense to work on the side you control 100 percent.

Begin with the Right Side

There are two sides to your Agenda: what you want to get and what you have to give. Most people, as they think about networking, focus on "what's in it for me." That's not the right place to begin. In fact, the biggest mistake people make about networking is to think it's about getting. It's not about getting. It's about giving.

Giving, not taking, is the way to build your network. It's not just a nice thing to do. It's the smart thing to do.

Psychologists have discovered a quirk of human nature that we call the Reciprocity Principle. It goes like this: If you give somebody something, he will try to give you something back. It gets even better: If you give somebody something, he will insist on giving you more than you gave him.

Doesn't that sound like exactly what you want to happen when you're networking? So, to plug into the Reciprocity Principle, give first and give freely.

You're actually in control of only half of the networking process—the giving part. Does it make sense to focus on the getting part, something you have little control over?

> The Reciprocity Principle: When you give people something, they'll insist on giving you even more back.

Have lots to give, and give generously. Be helpful to others. Often, you'll benefit from contact with someone whom you can't immediately (or perhaps ever) pay back. Believe in the great network in the sky: If you give, you will get—somehow, somewhere, some day.

Five years ago, Ellen received career advice from an executive. This year, when she received the "Member of the Year" award from her professional association, she mentioned the executive in her acceptance speech, thanked him, and told how she felt inspired to mentor others because of his help early in her career.

At first, it may seem that you are giving more than you are getting from your networking relationships. If so, you are networking the right way.

What Do You Have to Give?

People often scratch their heads and say, "Give? I don't know what I have to give." To create your have to give list, think about your accomplishments, skills, enthusiasms, and resources.

Most of us really do have plenty to give: ideas, expertise, phone numbers, introductions to other people. The possibilities are endless. But if you have a hard time figuring out exactly what you can offer, try using this formula.

Think to yourself, "Give *more*."

M = Methods. Can you make life easier for your contacts?

> ▶ My expertise on how—and how not—to build a brick patio.

> ▶ Information about the pitfalls of computerizing a business. (Nobody should have to go through the chaos I did!)

> ▶ How to negotiate the best deal on severance if you've been laid off.

O = Opportunities. Can you can alert people to an opportunity?

> ▶ An apartment to sublet for six months.

> ▶ Rex kittens (extremely short-haired cats for people with allergies).

> ▶ A job opening at Allied Sciences.

R = Resources. Can you offer someone or something?

> ▶ The name and phone number of a great band for weddings and parties.

> ▶ The name of my veterinarian who makes house calls.

> ▶ A great article I just read on how people react to Web site design.

> ▶ A place—my conference room—to hold meetings.

E = Enthusiasms. Are you excited about something?

> ▶ My professional association. Our programs for professional development are terrific!

Get ready to give. Before an event, list three resources, tips, or opportunities to tell people about.

▶Taking jazz singing lessons from one of the best singers in Washington, D.C.

E = Expertise. Do you know something that would be useful to your contacts?

▶Ideas for weekend jaunts with kids in the Seattle area.

▶Techniques for using your newsletter to generate new and repeat business.

As you become more aware of what you have to give to others, you'll always be able to narrow down the universe of topics to a list of things you want to talk about. The things you have to give automatically become topics. These topics connect you with the people you meet. They also let people know what to count on you for.

Being prepared to give means taking stock of your accomplishments, resources, skills, and enthusiasms. It means acknowledging that you are a unique and special human being with a contribution to make. If you wish you had more to give others, this may be a sign that you need to stock up. Do more. Experience more. Learn more. Risk more. Take a negotiation skills class. Learn Thai cooking. Take that vacation you've been talking about. Go ahead with the catering business you've dabbled in for so long. Anything you become enthusiastic about becomes something to share. Your enthusiasms are things you're so excited about that you'd talk to anybody, anywhere, anytime about them. When you live to the fullest, you'll just naturally have lots of resources, experiences, and opinions to give to others.

Having things to give makes it easy for you to go from just associating with people to interacting and exchanging with them. When you Listen Generously and find resources and ideas to give, you automatically move from the Associate stage into the Actor stage with your contact (see Chapter 8). As you give, you provide evidence of your Character and Competence. You create trust so that your contacts want to send opportunities your way.

What Do You Want to Get?

After you've thought through what you have to give, it's time to think about getting. The list of things you want to find, connect with, create, understand, learn, and know about is also endless. Look at your desk; look at your life. What problems are you trying to solve? What opportunities do you want to investigate? What are your upcoming challenges?

To help you jog your memory, think, "Get *real.*" Notice the examples.

R = *Results*. What outcome do you want?

▶ Office furniture I can afford.

▶ Training so that I can get up to speed on my computer graphics software.

▶ Tips on growing *big* tomatoes.

E = *Expertise*. What do you want to know about?

▶ A good, convenient day camp for my nine-year-old.

▶ Tips on appearing on a TV talk show.

▶ The best way to find good employees for my start-up.

A = *Access*. Who do you need to link up with?

▶ Someone who knows about careers in training and development.

▶ A part-time secretary with a background in the health field.

▶ A publisher for my book.

▶ People who are thinking of selling their homes and moving to retirement complexes.

L = *Leads*. Who or what do you need a link to?

▶ A veterinarian to join my business referral group.

▶ A good Mexican restaurant that delivers.

▶ An experienced emcee for the chamber of commerce Trade Show.

Give and Get with Ease

In our workshops, we ask people to make lists of things they would like to give and get. When they realize that they actually do have a lot to offer, they immediately feel more comfortable about networking. When they bring what they really need to the surface of their minds, they immediately feel more eager to network. People choose one item from each list—one thing they have to give and one thing they'd like to get—and write both items on stick-on name tags.

The people in the room become a living bulletin board, a human swap meet. They talk with one another about the things they've written on their name tags. As they begin to discover one another, the energy level in the room heats up, the excitement builds, and the noise level rises.

Figure 12-1 lists some of the things people in one workshop wanted to give and get.

You'll notice that there are no exact matches between the have to give and want to get items on this list. If you don't know of a classy restaurant in New York City, introduce your conversation partner to Phil, who used to live there. Don't worry. If you have an Agenda, you'll be able to find common interests with your conversation partners. What counts is that the talk on any of these topics will be meaningful and useful—and therefore valuable for someone. As in the rest of life, sometimes you'll give and sometimes you'll get. Clarify your Agenda and talk with people about the topics on it. Zig Ziglar, author and seminar leader, says, "You can have everything in life you want, if you help enough other people get what they want."

When you "go public" with your Agenda in this way, networking becomes an exciting process of search and connection.

Now, you probably aren't actually going to write an item from your Agenda on your name tag the next time you go to a business or social event. But you can prepare for any such occasion by making a

FIGURE 12-1. Sample Agenda items.

Have to Give	Want to Get
Information on owning your own business.	Someone to buy my Boston condo.
How to start a job strategy and support group.	The best antique mall in Nashville.
Recipes for big crowds.	Tips on using my new Palm Pilot.
Good restaurants in Toronto.	Speakers for our state conference.
Fund-raising ideas for nonprofits.	Help with an association chapter history project.
What it's like to be a corporate trainer.	An apartment for my mother to sublet.
My car! It's for sale!	Tips on buying a house at the Lake of the Ozarks.
Where to ski out West.	A place in New York City to take clients out to dinner next week.

written list of items you have to give and want to get. Put the list in your pocket. You won't need to refer to it; you'll simply feel the confidence that comes from being prepared.

You can assume that everybody else in the room—even if they don't realize it—also has an Agenda. Discovering other people's Agendas and following your own Agenda will give you a whole new approach to networking. "Chance," it is said, "favors the prepared mind." Preparing your Agenda will prepare your mind for making great connections.

Stan is vice president of sales for a burglar alarm company. He has twenty-four salespeople spread over a four-state area. Figure 12-2 is a sample Agenda he used at a networking event.

Did Stan find what he was looking for? At the end of the meeting, he had the names of two chiropractors, three businesses that agreed to donate items for the auction, and a Boston contact.

When someone asked him, "What's new?" he started talking about Cajun cooking. His conversation partner told Stan about a spice store that he's going to investigate.

With an Agenda, you'll see results from your networking every time.

FIGURE 12-2. Stan's Agenda.

Have to Give	Want to Get
Information on the new video-based sales training package he uses.	Magazine articles or books for his salespeople on how to start referral groups.
Ideas on how to do a trade show booth that gets attention.	Job leads for his brother-in-law.
The name of an excellent chiropractor.	Businesses that will donate items for the hospital auction.
How to cook Cajun.	Contacts who can recommend people he might hire in Boston.

Practice Agenda Making

Think of an upcoming networking situation. Take a moment and list some things you'd like to get, find, connect with, know more about, and create in your life. Then list what you have to give in your conversations with others—resources, ideas, skills, experiences, talents, and enthusiasms, for example. Be as specific as possible. If you put "happiness" on your want to get list, for example, you'll be disappointed because no one can give that to you.

Go Public with Your Agenda

The cardinal rule about anyone's networking Agenda is, "If there's no mystery, there's no manipulation." Managing conversations is quite different from manipulating other people. Managing is okay; manipulating is not. Effective networking is based on telling people what you want and making sure that you take every opportunity to contribute to the success of others by giving them anything you can.

Were you brought up to believe that coming right out and saying what you want is pushy, self-centered, and overbearing? Were you taught that you should not see people as opportunities? Many people were. As a kid, you might sometimes have had to toss out subtle clues or be indirect in order to get what you wanted. As an adult, however, you can avoid the feeling that you are using people. Tell them, straight out, what's on your Agenda. Your honesty about your purposes will increase your sense of competence and profession-alism. With these new ground rules for networking, the people you meet become opportunities for you, and you become an opportunity for them. Here's a surefire test to determine if your Agenda is manipulative. Ask yourself, "How would I feel if my Agenda were the headline on the front page of tomorrow morning's newspaper: *Joe Jackson Hunts Job in Health Care*? What if everybody knew what I wanted? What if they could see right through the subtle clues to what I actually have in mind? Would they feel good about me and my purpose? Would I?" If the answer is yes, your Agenda item is a good one to talk about.

> In networking, be up front, be honest. If there's no mystery, there's no manipulation.

Avoid asking for information that people normally are paid to provide. If you meet a lawyer at a networking event, don't describe a legal problem you're having and ask for advice. If you meet a computer consultant at a party, don't describe a problem you're having with your computer and ask for advice. On the other hand, it makes sense to find out what kinds of cases a lawyer handles. Asking for that kind of information would be acceptable, and the information might be valuable in the future, both to you and to the lawyer, whose name and specialty would then be on file in your mental Rolodex™.

Get comfortable telling people how they might be useful to you in the future. Imagine that you're in a networking situation and complete the following sentence: "I'd like to know you better because . . ."

You could say, "I'd like to know you better because I'd like to know more about what you do as a marketing manager." Or, "I'd like to stay in touch so that we can share strategies about how to make our home-based businesses grow."

How would you feel about "going public" with your reason? Perhaps you'd like to know this person better because he could be in a position to hire you some day. Is there any benefit in keeping that part of your Agenda hidden? What could be the benefits of sharing that reason with the person? Perhaps you'd like to know this person better because she can probably refer potential clients to you. Is there any reason you can think of that you shouldn't tell her that?

Sally, who owns a tutoring business that employs forty-two tutors, said to the principal of a private school, "I'd like to become known to you because I imagine people often ask you to recommend tutors for their kids."

Corrine, who has her own training company, had lunch with Diana, who is in the marketing department of a greeting card company. Corrine was aboveboard about her Agenda. She said, "I hope that, when you need training, you'll think of me. I'd love to work with you on a project." A few days later, Corrine saw a column by humorist Dave Barry making fun of an ad he'd seen for a service that would send cards to your friends and family for you after you were dead. She knew Diana would get a kick out of it, so she sent her a copy of the column. It's little things that build relationships.

Exchange Something

If you still have negative feelings about accepting help from others or being beholden to others, focus your energy on making an exchange. The way to make a fair exchange is to offer something equally valuable. Give something back in the conversation. If you're job hunting or you're new in town, you may feel that you have nothing to give. That may be true today, but you can promise yourself that you will help someone else once you're established.

One thing you *can* give at any time is appreciation. Take the time to say "thank you" to people who help you. Make your thanks prompt. Write a note that same day. In the note, be specific about what Jack did for you: "Thank you for giving me Bob Johnson's phone number." Tell Jack what you did with the information. That lets Jack know that you thought it was important. "I have called Bob and set up an appointment for next Tuesday." Being specific does something else. It could be that Jack will see Bob between now and next Tuesday. Your note may help Jack to remember to mention you. Now, that's networking!

If you are uncomfortable with the idea of going after what you want, remind yourself that people are free to choose. You will certainly say no when someone asks for information you aren't willing to give or offers a service or product you don't want. Trust your conversation partner to say no if you offer something he doesn't want or ask for something he isn't comfortable giving.

Be prepared to be spontaneous.

If you are uncomfortable with the idea of "selling yourself," think of it as giving others the opportunity to take advantage (in a positive way) of your expertise, your talent, your training. You're a resource to other people. Believe in yourself and promote yourself. If you offer a service or resource that no one wants right then, what have you lost? Nothing. What have you gained? Others may tuck that information away and use it later.

Build every relationship for the long term. Never assume that you can use and discard people.

"I ran into a woman at the swimming pool. We'd taught first grade together years ago," Harriet remembers. "We hadn't kept in touch, but we hadn't burned any bridges either. When I was looking for new clients, I remembered seeing her at the pool and sent her a brochure about my consulting services. A few weeks later, her husband, who is a lawyer, called me and wanted coaching on management skills."

The idea of the Agenda is a powerful one. It will help your networking be more pleasurable, purposeful, and profitable. Share it. Teach others about the idea of the Agenda, and you will increase your chances of getting what you want, but not at anyone else's expense.

A light bulb went on for one of our workshop participants. She said, "Oh I get it. You've got to be prepared to be spontaneous!"

CHAPTER 13

End with the Future in Mind

If someone asked you, "What's the most difficult moment in networking?" what would be your answer? Would you say, "Ending"? Most people do. Introductions and meeting people are stressful, they'll tell you, but at least there's a routine: You shake hands and exchange names. On the other hand, there is no protocol for ending conversations. As a result, the end almost always seems awkward.

Prepare for the Next Time

Your Critic may move into high gear when someone—even someone you've made a good connection with—ends a conversation with you. If you are the one doing the leaving, you may feel guilty because it seems as if you are rejecting or abandoning the other person. As a result of these feelings, people say, "I believe I'll freshen my drink," and walk away, not even bothering to head in the direction of the bar. Or they may simply say, with no intention of doing so, "I'll see you later." Or they may drift away when a third person enters the conversation.

To change your mindset about the final moments of a conversation, imagine that you'll continue your dialog at some time in the future. Always assume that you will see your partner again. Think, "I'm just beginning this relationship. It will be exciting to see it develop." Always prepare for the next time. Making a conscious closing will set the tone for your next meeting.

Listen for the Bell

Tune in to the timetable. There's a bell that goes off in people's minds after a conversation has been going on for about five minutes. At networking events and at many quasi-business gatherings, such as cocktail parties or receptions, people have a vague notion that they should speak with as many people as possible. Trust your powers of observation. You will be able to tell from your partner's body language when he is ready to move on. Your partner will look away, gather up possessions, and perhaps even move farther away from you. Trust the bell in your head—your intuitive sense of when it's time to say good-bye.

Honesty is rare in the final moments of a conversation, but that's what works best. Be totally honest. Here's how to leave a conversation gracefully and competently with your own integrity (and your partner's) intact.

Center on Your Agenda

Your Agenda will serve you well as you make conscious closings. Saying, "I want . . . , I must . . . , I need . . ." eliminates the feeling that you are abandoning your partner. Shift the attention to where you are going and the purpose that is motivating you.

Here are some suggestions for closing a conversation by referring to your Agenda:

▶ "I want to wander around and say hello to everyone at this meeting."

▶ "I vowed when I came today that I'd find *someone* who is working with this new software I just got."

▶ "I'm going to circulate and welcome some of the new people."

▶ "I need to see three more people before I leave tonight."

▶ "I want to go talk to the speaker."

▶ "I must speak to the membership chairman before he leaves."

▶ "I want to see if there are any other engineers (or people from my company, or home-based businesspeople) here."

▶ "I want to meet some other entrepreneurs this evening."

Ask Your Partner for a Referral

To change conversation partners, ask your current partner for a referral to someone else in the room. Say:

▶ "I want to find other people who are working at home. Do you know anyone like that?"

▶ "Do you know anyone here who is involved with management training?"

▶ "Is there anyone else here that you recommend I talk with about the public relations committee?"

▶ "I'm going to the annual meeting next month. Do you know anybody who went last year?"

▶ "Do you know of anyone who is thinking about moving to a new office this year? My company is expanding its office design services."

Take Your Partner Along with You

If you feel uncomfortable ending a conversation and walking away from someone, invite that person to go with you:

▶ "Let's see if we can find the registration booth."

▶ "Want a drink? I'm thirsty."

▶ "Would you like to come with me to talk with the new president? I want to ask her about next month's program."

Introduce Your Partner

Often, as you look around the room, you'll see someone you want to introduce your partner to. Don't think of this as a way to get rid of your partner. Instead, always be thinking, "Who is there here that I know and that my partner might need to meet?"

Say, "Lenora, you mentioned that you're going to Vancouver next month. I want to introduce you to Sam. He grew up there and could tell you all about the sights."

Or, "Tom, as soon as Bill arrives, I want to get you two together. Last month you said you were thinking of franchising your stores, and he's a franchise lawyer. I'll bet you two would have a lot to talk about."

Play Concentration

Remember that kid's game where you lay all the cards face down on the table? You turn over a ten of hearts, but you can't have it until you find a match. Your challenge is to remember, after a few turns, where that ten of hearts is.

You can play Concentration in a room full of people. You meet Marjory, an interior designer, who specializes in helping seniors downsize and move to smaller quarters. A few minutes later, you talk with Cynthia, who says she's writing a book entitled *Moving Mother*. You think to yourself, "I must introduce Cynthia to Marjory. What a match!" You go out of your way to bring them together. Whether you stay with that conversation or not, they will remember you as a person who knows everybody.

Sum Up and Appreciate

One of the most memorable ways to close is to sum up the conversation and show appreciation for your partner. To do that, shake hands and acknowledge the conversation and its importance to you. You could even acknowledge the importance in your life of the relationship you have with your partner, which perhaps goes way beyond this encounter. Find a specific quality in the other person or a moment in the conversation that you can genuinely express appreciation for:

- ▶ "If the other members of ASID are as enthusiastic as you are, I'm going to be very glad I joined."

- ▶ "It's been interesting talking with you about your new business."

- ▶ "I'm so glad to know more about your department."

- ▶ "I enjoyed hearing about how you got involved in interior design."

- ▶ "Thanks for telling me about your new marketing tactics. I'm looking forward to hearing next month how they are working out."

Explain the Next Steps

Finally, say what you will do next, or what you would like your partner to do next, to continue the relationship. Many of these suggestions are reassuring to your partner because, rather than just melting away, you are being very specific. We call these magnet statements because they are designed to pull you and your partner back together at some point in the future. They provide you with the energy to continue the conversation and build the relationship. They signal interest. Let your sincerity shine through. Look the person in the eye. Ask the person for his card so that you'll have the necessary information to follow up. Jot a note to yourself on the back of the card while you are still with the person or soon after you part. Verbalize what you will do or what the next step in your relationship will be:

- ▶ "I'm going to send you that article we talked about."

- ▶ "I'll ask Jim to call you."

- ▶ "I'll see you at the next meeting."

- ▶ "I don't want to monopolize you this evening. Can we arrange to meet later?"

▶ "I'll get back to you next week."

▶ "I hope we can do business after the holidays."

Or ask your partner to follow up:

▶ "Give me a call next week and we'll set up a time for me to tell you about my publishing experiences. I'm glad you asked me for advice. I'm always eager to help a fellow author. Here's my card."

Shake Hands and Leave

After making these final statements, shake hands and leave quickly. No dilly-dallying. Use your body language to emphasize your purposeful leave taking.

Remember watching a wonderful miniseries? Remember the good feelings of expectation you had when you saw the words "To Be Continued . . ." on the TV screen? That's how you want to leave your partner, with those words hanging in the air, setting the stage for the next episode in your relationship.

A Ritual for Leave Taking

To close a conversation easily, remember this *LEAVE NOW Formula*:

L = *Let go* of your partner after five minutes.

E = *Explain* what you must do. Be honest.

A = *Act* on your Agenda.

V = *Veer off* to talk with a referral.

E = *Exit* easily to another conversation by taking your partner with you.

N = *Note* what's gone on between you and your partner. Sum up the conversation and appreciate something that your partner said or did.

O = *Outline* the next step for your partner.

W = *Walk*. Shake hands and leave, purposefully.

Do You Have Questions?

Here are some of the questions people have about endings.

Q: What if we're interrupted?

A: Sometimes you are interrupted before you can close a conversation. Mark was listening intently to Susan as she talked about her expanding business when two other people joined their group and the conversation got sidetracked to another topic. Soon, the chair called the meeting to order. Susan and Mark ended up at different tables. Mark wanted to finish their conversation and find a way to reconnect after the meeting because he figured she would need his office design services sometime in the next year as she added more office space. Before he left the luncheon, he made a point of approaching Susan again, asking for her card, and offering to send her an article he'd written on office lighting.

Q: What if you really want to keep on talking?

A: Occasionally, you will find yourself in a conversation that's too good to leave. You want to keep talking with your contact even though the unwritten rule says, "Circulate."

Hal began to talk with Marilyn, the speaker. After five minutes or so, he began to feel uncomfortable because she wasn't having an opportunity to visit with anyone else. Even though they both clearly wanted to continue their conversation, it seemed rude to do so. Finally Hal said, "I don't want to monopolize you. Let's plan to get together sometime in the next month. Do you have your calendar with you, or would it be better for us to talk on the phone to set a date?"

Do Something with Those Cards

After a networking event, you go back to your office with a pocket full of business cards. What can you do with them?

First, sort through these cards to find any on which you've written a note to yourself about something you promised to do. Lay those cards aside and follow up quickly, within three business days.

Develop a system that allows you to retrieve names, phone numbers, addresses, and other information easily.

You can:

▶ Use a Rolodex™.

▶ Use a notebook with plastic pages into which you can insert your cards.

▶ Invest in contact management software for your computer.

▶ Buy a Palm Pilot™ so that you can take your addresses wherever you go.

Contact management software is a must for the serious networker. Since there are many brands on the market and a variety of special applications are available, you'll want to research this software on the Web and ask your friends and colleagues to find the best package for you. Best-selling products include Act!™, Telemagic™, and SalesLogix™.

Ideally, you'll be able to fit many kinds of information into your database. Here's a partial list of the kinds of information to include: last name, first name, middle initial, nickname, business address (include space for country), business phone, 800 number, business fax, mobile phone or pager, source (referral from whom or organization at which you met your contact), secretary's name, contact's birthday, contact's spouse, home address, home fax, home phone, and e-mail address.

The software should also allow you to make notes when you contact someone so that you'll have a record of your interactions and should "tickle" you to remind you to call at a certain time.

You'll want a system that allows you to find people by sorting on various items, such as zip codes, states, trade show contacts, past clients, prospects, etc.

The beauty of this software is that it makes it easy to stay in touch with and be visible to people in your network. Code your contacts according to whatever items you choose: people who work for associations, media contacts, people who bought products from you this year, etc. You'll be able to print labels or envelopes for small or large groups of people. For instance, if you're traveling to see clients in Atlanta, you might print out a list of names, addresses, phone numbers, and "contact history" of all your business contacts in Georgia, Florida, and South Carolina.

Most software systems can be customized to fit your needs exactly.

Sam sent a fax to everybody he had met in the last three months.

Georgina sent her company newsletter to all the people who had been her clients in the past three years, as well as to prospects.

Juliette sent a thank-you note to all sixty-one people who had helped her in her job search—along with her new business card so that they could update their files.

The key to using any system is to enter the information regularly. Don't allow those cards to pile up. Use them.

Take the Time to Keep in Touch

When people think about creating an active network of 50 to 250 or more contacts, they worry about how much time it will take. It takes less time than you might think.

To keep in touch, make a phone call. Send a note or postcard. Marla has postcards printed with her company logo and her picture. She keeps a few in her briefcase, so if she's caught waiting somewhere, she can write a few and send them off. Karl, a chiropractor, put a questionnaire about office stress and muscle pain on the back of his postcard and sends one to new contacts to remind them of his services.

If you work for a company, don't expect to do all your networking on company time. You must invest your own time as well. Take every opportunity to give valuable information to your contacts or to direct business their way. Mail someone an article that you think she might be interested in. Meet for lunch. Check in at professional meetings. Exercise together. Travel to a conference together. (See Chapter 14 for additional ingenious methods for maintaining contact.)

Dean and Marta met at a luncheon meeting of their professional group. As entrepreneurs, they were always looking for work. They shared many common interests and friends. They were very clear with each other about their career focus. He said, "I'm a career coach for lawyers who want to reassess their career options." She said, "I teach executives how to give speeches." Their networking is practically effortless because each of them knows what the other has to give and wants to find. As you look at their interactions over a period of one year, you can see that Dean and Marta spent only about three hours networking with each other during that time.

February: Marta sent Dean a news article telling about a one-week course for lawyers on career-changing issues. Dean followed up and was invited to be a guest speaker.

April: Dean called Marta with the name of a law firm that was looking for a motivational speaker. Marta passed the lead on to a speaker who had referred an executive client to her.

May: Marta and Dean had lunch, updated each other on recent successes and challenges, and enjoyed each other's company.

September: Marta referred her lawyer cousin to Dean for career counseling.

December: Dean and Marta chatted at a holiday party. Marta told Dean that she was looking for clients in Europe. Dean told Marta to contact a lawyer he knew who had recently returned after spending a year in London.

It's not the amount of time, it's the quality of the interaction that counts in networking.

CHAPTER 14

Follow Up Effectively

Next time you go to a networking event, stand back and watch people do the business card bump. People stand there, clutching their cards in their hands, looking out over the crowd, picking their prey, striding over, shaking, smiling, schmoozing, and heading off again to repeat the process.

That's not the way to network. When you do the card thing, you make only a cardboard connection, not a real connection.

And then, what happens when one of those folks you've "carded" goes back to his office? Imagine this.

> **Handing out your business card makes only a "cardboard connection."**

He pats his pocket, which is bulging with cards. He takes them out and counts them. He says, in a self-congratulatory tone, "Twenty-seven cards," and puts them in a stack on a corner of his desk, where they proceed to haunt him. Every time he goes past his desk, he hears their little voices:

"Hey, over here."

"Who am I?"

"Yoo-hoo, what are you going to do with me?"

"Would you even know me if you saw me?"

"Hurry up. I'm getting too old, sitting here."

Finally, the haunting gets so bad that on one of his trips past the desk, he just reaches out, ever so casually, and with the side of his hand, he shoves that stack of cards off the desk into the round file.

It's so sad. All that time and effort, and all those people end up in his wastebasket.

And the really awful thing is that all over town, in twenty-seven other offices, at that very same, exact moment, his card is probably falling into twenty-seven other people's wastebaskets.

If your networking isn't paying off, give more attention to following through.

> Instead of doing the "business card bump," go for the long-term, mutually beneficial relationship.

The Problem with Follow-Up

"To me, the problem is that I go to a networking event and meet a lot of people, and then—nothing happens. What am I doing wrong?" asks Mike, a CPA.

"I talked to her at last month's meeting, but I can't figure out what to do next. If I don't do something pretty soon, she'll forget who I am and what we talked about," says Nancy, a middle manager in a *Fortune* 100 company.

"I know I should stay in touch with past clients, but I don't know what to say when I call," says Roger, a freelance designer.

"Bob's company is similar to mine, and I'm sure I could learn a lot from him. Come to think of it, we're doing some advertising that he'd probably like to know about, but I'm not sure what the next step is in getting to know him," says Susan, a sales rep.

Mike, Nancy, Roger, and Susan are typical of networkers every-

> Reconnecting and staying in touch are the keys to networking success.

where. They're trying to figure out how to stay connected, and how to fit this relationship building into their already overloaded lives.

All too often, networkers, even rather savvy ones, don't follow up systematically. They spend lots of energy making initial contacts, and then don't know how to cultivate them so that the relationships pay dividends down the road.

Pave the Way

Effective follow-up begins with a good conversation, one in which you Listen Generously to find out what's on your conversation partner's Agenda. A meaty conversation will give you ideas about how to follow up. The best follow-up is based on your conversation partner's Agenda, not yours.

Ideally, during that first conversation with someone, you'll suggest another meeting. You might say, "I'd like to talk with you more about that. May I give you a call next week to set up a time to get together?"

Networking events are places to make plans to get together later.

It usually takes six to eight meetings to establish a networking relationship, so every time you meet, set up your next meeting. Say, for example, "I'll give you a call next month so that we can get together for lunch."

If you do not pave the way for reconnecting like that when you meet, you may never see that person again.

Pay Your Way

By the way, always pay your fair share of the cost of networking. It's better to go dutch treat than to pay for a networking contact's meals, for example. Remember, you're trying to establish a mutually beneficial relationship. Ignore titles and work on developing peer relationships, not superior-subordinate relationships. If one person always pays, the relationship also will become unequal. You can't buy a networking contact. Most relationships work best when each person pays his way, not only with money, but with valuable information or referrals or resources.

Reasons to Reconnect

Many networkers feel uncomfortable about taking the first step to reestablish a dialogue.

If you are afraid that the person you'd like to reconnect with won't remember you, ask a colleague or friend to reintroduce you.

You have a good reason to reconnect—you'd like to build a relationship with this person because you think that the person would be useful to you and that perhaps you could help her, too. But that probably feels like way too much to ask for initially. People tell us that they would feel more comfortable if they had an excuse for calling or setting up another encounter.

We call these excuses reopeners because they reopen a conversation by reminding your contact of something you have in common.

Refer back to when and how you met. "We met in that computer course a couple of weeks ago. I started using one of the software packages they suggested. How about lunch sometime next week? I'll tell you about it."

Refer to a common need. "Since we are both starting businesses, I was interested in what you said about looking for office space. I'm working on that, too. How about getting together to talk about strategy?"

Refer to proximity. "We work near each other; let's get together for lunch." Or, "We live in the same neighborhood; let's meet at the deli for supper next week." Or, "We sat at the same table at the chamber of commerce dinner. I'd like to know more about the sales training program you mentioned." Or, "I enjoyed talking with you when we sat next to each other at the committee meeting last week. I'd like to know more about your business. How about if I pick you up for this week's meeting, and we can talk on the way?"

Refer to a common background. "I noticed that we both went to the University of Florida. I got a flyer saying that there's going to be an alumni get-together to watch the game next week. How about meeting me there?" Or, "Don't you have a degree in English, too? I'd be very interested to know how you made the transition to PR. How about coffee later this week?"

Appreciate your contact's contributions. "I thought your newsletter article was very interesting. I'd like to hear more about the volunteer work you're involved in. How about lunch?" Or, "You're going a great job heading up the program committee. I did that for the Des Moines chapter, and I know what a big job it is. We developed a great checklist for planning any event. If you think your committee members could use it, I'll drop it by your office."

Refer to a common acquaintance. "You know Burt, don't you? When I talked with him, he suggested that we get together. I'm heading up the fund-raiser for the hospital. Burt said you did one last year and might be able to give me some pointers. How about breakfast next week?"

Refer to time or money savers. "I heard you say that you're feeling overwhelmed with paperwork. I was so overwhelmed I hired an office organizer. I'd be happy to share some of her tips with you. They helped me completely overhaul my office. Would you like to come over and see what I did? I'll be in late Tuesday afternoon."

The Five Goals of Follow-Up

What are you trying to achieve as you nurture networking relationships? Aim for these five goals as you reconnect, follow up, and stay in touch.

Teach your contacts:

1. Your name and how to reach you easily

2. Exactly what you do

3. To have faith in your ability to serve or supply them—or people they refer to you—expertly

4. What kinds of clients, customers, or job opportunities you are seeking and what you can refer to them

5. What kind of information you need

As you reach these goals with your contacts, you will begin (and continue) to reap the benefits of networking. If your contact is a client or a customer, staying in touch will encourage repeat business and referrals.

Tactical Trade-Offs

As you decide how you will follow up, here are some of the things you'll need to consider: Do you want face-to-face time, or can you use the written word or electronic communication? Do you want to contact only one person, or do you want to contact many people at the same time? How much time can you afford to spend? What's your budget? Follow-up ideas come in all flavors. As you choose your method, take these kinds of trade-offs into account. Balance the time or money each method takes with its potential for building the relationship. Then decide which ways are right for you with a particular contact in a particular situation.

> **Tickle yourself. Jot reminders on the backs of cards you collect so that you can follow up and follow through.**

Getting Face-to-Face

Whenever you can, arrange to see people face-to-face. Sure, you can call or drop someone an e-mail, but face-to-face encounters are the fastest way to develop the trust that's so essential to a developing relationship.

Turner wrote a letter to his franchise training director recommending Gloria, a speaker, for the next training conference and sent her a copy. Rather than calling to say thanks, Gloria dropped by Turner's store. She said, "Your letter was wonderful. I appreciated it so much. I will follow up with the training director. Do you have time to give me the grand tour of your store and to tell me about your products and services? I want to understand exactly what you and your fellow franchisees do before I make a proposal to the training director. And I want to be able to recommend you to anyone I run into who needs printing."

Lend a book. Deliver a book or audiotape that you have enjoyed to a contact. As you visit, ask about projects that person is working on and be ready to tell about your latest successes and challenges.

When Mike met Charles at a Rotary International luncheon, Charles said he'd like to read the latest Tom Peters book, but that he was number 238 on the library's waiting list. Mike asked for his business card and said, "I have a copy. I'll give you a call and bring it over to you as soon as I finish it."

Face it. When face-to-face contact isn't feasible, send your face. Have a notecard that fits into a business envelope printed up with your photo on it. Sending your photo card when you need to communicate puts your face in front of your contact.

Using the Media

Are you out of town on business or vacation? Take some addresses with you. Buy a handful of postcards or, before you go, have postcards printed with your picture, your logo, a saying that makes people think of your service or product, or some interesting facts about your industry. Write notes telling about something you saw or did that your contacts would be interested in or use the note to confirm a future meeting with your contact.

On vacation in Fort Myers, Florida, Lewis, a graphic designer, sent postcards showing a photograph of Thomas Edison's home to a dozen contacts. He wrote: "Enjoying my vacation. I just toured Edison's home. Isn't it interesting that we use the light bulb as a symbol for a great idea? I hope you'll think of me when you need a (sketch of a light bulb) for graphic design!"

Contacting One Person

Take a guest. Invite your contact to a sports event, museum activity, or speech. Use your social activities to explore business possibilities in a relaxed setting.

Barbara, who has her own training business, noticed that season tickets to the university theater were only $60 for six plays. She bought two tickets and enjoys inviting someone to join her. "I'm able to catch up with six different contacts during the theater season. It's a way to fit networking into my life," she points out.

Travel together. Going to a convention? Call a contact well in advance and suggest that you take the same plane.

Pull up a chair. Plan to sit next to each other at a meeting or event. Call your contact before the event to arrange to spend time together.

Notice publicity. As you peruse the newspaper, watch for publicity about any of your contacts. Clip articles and send them with sticky notes. Or cut out your contact's advertisements and send them to your contact with a note telling what made the ad leap off the page and grab your attention.

Share a cab. Split the cab fare as you go to a meeting or event.

Park and walk. Park your car in a new spot in the company parking lot every day and walk into the building with a different person.

Get feedback. Ask your contact to review something you've written—brochure copy, your résumé, a newsletter article, a contest entry. Then call or visit your contact to discuss her comments. If you change anything about your materials as a result of the feedback, give a copy of the revised piece to your contact, pointing out how the comments helped you. Offer to review something your contact has written.

Tom asked people attending his professional association, "Who should I talk to in my job search?" Several people mentioned Margo, a past president of the association and a person who was well respected in the profession. Tom talked with her and asked if he could send her a copy of his résumé. She said, "Sure, but I don't know of any openings anywhere right now." Along with his résumé, Tom sent Margo a self-addressed, stamped postcard and asked her to comment on his résumé. Because it was so easy to do, Margo returned the postcard with a couple of suggestions. Tom called to thank her and then sent her the new version. Later, he followed up with a phone call. By that time, he had much more of a relationship with Margo. She had begun to trust his Character and Competence and eventually provided two job leads.

Get fit. Invite a contact to go for a walk or a workout. Use your fitness time for networking.

Reaching Many

Send the news. If your business involves providing information—and whose doesn't?—produce a print or electronic newsletter. Highlight your successes and new products and services. Show how clients or customers benefit. Help your contacts see how they could use your expertise. Quoting or featuring customers also enhances your credibility and testifies to your Character and Competence.

Provide a calendar. Send your contact a calendar of events you'll be involved in or clients you'll be working with. This idea works well for musicians, artists, trainers, consultants, craftspeople, speakers, and freelancers, for example.

Have a bunch to lunch. Ask a few people you'd like to know better to lunch. Pick your lunch bunch carefully so that the benefits of their becoming better acquainted with you and with each other are obvious. Marcella, who owns a small advertising agency, frequently invites a mix of clients and potential clients to a catered lunch in her conference room. "They seem to enjoy meeting each other. Often, the stories my current clients tell to my potential clients sell them on using my services."

Announce your news. Get the word out about an achievement, a move, a promotion. Send a news release, postcard, or note. This is a good way to teach contacts about your Competence.

Read all about it. Send your contacts an article that mentions you as an expert. If you haven't been in the news recently, send an article that gives information on the kind of service or product you provide. That way, you can "piggyback" on an article in the news media, positioning yourself as an expert.

Jim's firm analyzed overhead costs for small and midsized businesses. When the *Wall Street Journal* featured an article on rising overhead costs for small businesses, he sent copies, with a personal note and his brochure, to twenty potential clients he'd met recently at networking events.

Tip the talkers. Before a meeting begins, chat with the speaker or emcee. Let that person know what interests you about the topic and your experience with it. Presenters appreciate knowing more about their audiences. A mention of you from the podium will act almost like an endorsement and will certainly give you more visibility and credibility,

Fred, the owner of a franchise sign shop, showed up early at a workshop on marketing and talked to the speaker. When she asked about his work, he said, "I make all kinds of signs and banners for all kinds of businesses. I also do a complete range of signs that comply with Americans With Disabilities Act regulations." When workshop participants moaned about how difficult it was to bring their business signage into compliance with ADA, the speaker said, "Fred's company has done a lot of that. Fred, stand up, so people will be able to find you during our coffee break."

Wish 'em a happy. Send a card on an unusual holiday (Fourth of July, your birthday, Labor Day) to avoid having your message become just one of many at the end of the year. Or send birthday cards to contacts on their birthdays.

Spending Time

Set a goal for the number of networking calls and meetings you want to engage in every week. When you are planning your week, pull out your calendar and schedule your networking—just as you schedule everything else that's important.

Be a winner. Entering awards programs takes time and effort, but if you win, it's worth it. Publicize your achievement.

Robert, the president of a quality assurance consulting firm, encourages his consulting team to enter the Quality Assurance Association's awards program. At the awards banquet, every consultant was recognized and other members of the association were encouraged to ask them about their projects. "Winning gave us the Good Housekeeping Seal of Approval, not only with our peers in the association, but also with our clients and potential clients," Robert said. "The credibility and expertise of each person on the team was enhanced."

Saving Time

You can do networking on the run. Use bits and pieces of time effectively. You can even multitask: If you are going to be doing something anyway—eating lunch, attending a play, exercising—save time by turning that occasion into an opportunity to network.

Let your secretary do it. Make a list of people you want to stay in touch with and have your secretary send them a short personal message every couple of months.

> Schedule your networking just as you do everything else in your life that's important.

Extend an invitation. Want to see someone more frequently? Encourage your contact to visit and perhaps to join an organization you already belong to.

Pass it on. When you discover a service or product you really like, promote it to others. People will thank you for providing a shortcut to a great "find."

Offer a ride. What events are you going to soon? Is there a contact you'd like to know better to whom you could offer a lift to a meeting?

Give a goodie. Send your contact a bagel and cream cheese or a couple of doughnuts—or even a single specialty tea or coffee bag—along with some information you'd like that person to take the time to look at. Notice that this technique "creates" time in your contact's day for him to focus on your information.

Sign up a volunteer. Many people say that they'd like to volunteer a little time to a good cause, but they don't know what to do. Invite your contact to volunteer with you.

Wendie's final project for her graduate degree introduced eleven-year-old girls to women with careers in scientific fields. Her project was designed to encourage young girls to think about careers in science and to provide role models for them. She invited her contacts to take part in the project and enlisted their help to find additional mentors for the girls. After the project was over, she invited the women to a dutch treat "celebration brunch" at a local restaurant to become better acquainted with them and to allow them to meet each other.

Create a quiz. Design a quiz to teach people about your product or service. Put the quiz on a wallet-sized card to give out to potential clients or distribute it by fax, mail, or e-mail.

Jeff, who owns a carpet store, created a quiz: Do You Know How to Buy Carpet? When he meets someone who is thinking about buying carpet, he says, "Give me your business card, and I'll send you my quiz. It will help you know what to look for as you make your decision. Of course, I hope you'll come by my store as you are shopping."

Spending Money

These techniques do cost money, but they may be worth it.

Give a prize. Become known for what you give away. Provide your product or service as a door prize at a meeting you are attending. Write out what you want the emcee to say about the prize—and about you! That way, your donation will teach people what your business is all about and help them feel more comfortable striking up a conversation with you after the meeting. You also could provide products to be sold at a charity auction or to be used for a public television membership campaign gift.

Throw a party. Invite contacts to your place of business to give them a better idea of what you do. If you work at home, team up to find an interesting place for your open house. Select your cohost carefully. Look for someone with whom you might have customers in common.

Carol, an artist, works at home, so she joined forces with a frame shop owner, Kari, to showcase both businesses with an after-hours wine and cheese party. She and Kari invited both past and potential customers to view Carol's drawings and to see Kari's frames.

Connect with a card. Make your business card special—a conversation piece as well as a source of information.

Lucia's card is bright blue and cut in the shape of a big, floppy shoe. Anyone who sees her card knows that Lucia is a clown. She gives her cards to contacts and asks them to pass the cards along to people who are having birthday parties or special events and might like to hire a clown to entertain.

Lucia could also make a refrigerator magnet featuring her blue shoe with her name and phone number on it.

Add to the library. Give contacts a copy of a book you have written or a book that relates to the product or service you provide. One key idea in following up is to provide contacts with something that they will keep a long, long time, so that your name and phone number are available and visible for a long, long time. Giving a book accomplishes just that.

Saving Money

These techniques have little or no cost.

Pass the perks. Provide access to events, people, and resources—dinner with a visiting author, your library of training videos, a sneak preview of a movie, free tickets to an event.

Host a meeting. Do you want to show some influential people where your business is located and give them a clear image of what you do? Offer your business as a meeting place for a committee or board. To make your business real to attendees, give a quick guided tour. Be ready to talk informally about awards on the wall, new equipment, new capabilities, and various services that you provide.

Speak out. Speak to the local chapter of an association. Provide a news release for the program planner to send to the business calendar in your local newspaper.

Making Money

Your follow-up technique can even be lucrative!

Teach a course. Teach at a community college or open university. Publicize the course to your contacts. Even if they don't take the course, letting them know that you are teaching establishes your expertise and competence.

PART 5

Score with the Super Skills

Now, how about applying what you've learned about networking? In the next chapter, you'll find out how to create a Strategic Positioning Project that will help you achieve your highest aspirations. It will make you the natural and only choice when opportunity comes knocking. Then, in the following chapters, you'll find tips and techniques galore to help you make the most of your memberships and the conventions you attend. What about technology? You'll get the inside information on why technology is making networking easier—and more complicated—and how you can use all those gadgets to the fullest.

CHAPTER 15

Think Big

How would you like to be the natural and only choice when the opportunity of your dreams comes along? Whether you are self-employed or work inside an organization, the time and money you spend building your circle of contacts will yield the biggest return when you design a big-time, long-term project that will put you in the right place at the right time with the right people.

Take a few moments and add up the money and time you're currently spending. Then, you'll know your budget for developing your project. You may decide that you need to carve out more time and drum up more money so that you can reach your goal.

Ask yourself: "How much money will I spend this year on networking activities?" Whether you are paying for these items or your organization is footing the bill, add up what the investment will be. See if you can come up with an actual dollar estimate of what you'll spend on professional memberships and dues, receptions, trade shows, conferences (include travel and lodging), business luncheons and breakfasts, seminars for clients, client entertainment, golf outings, and any other event you or your company pays for where the intent is to make career and business contacts, and you have the opportunity to do so.

These expenditures often appear in several different budget categories, so be tenacious in tracking them down. Look under categories such as entertainment, client development, holiday party for clients, memberships, and new business development. If you prefer to think of the figure as a percentage of your annual operating budget, that's fine, too. The important thing is to come up with a way to measure your investment against the return you're getting.

In our seminars, people have reported spending amounts that ranged from a measly $75 to a grandiose $75,000 on memberships. And when they add in all the other events and venues, that top figure can rise as high as $150,000. Of course, our audiences span a wide variety of industries, professions, and job types, from lawyers to interior designers to entrepreneurs to nurses.

People whose numbers fall at the lower end of the range say, "Gosh, I'd better get going on this if I'm to be competitive!" People whose numbers are at the higher end of the spectrum say, "Wow! I never realized how much I'm spending. I'd better make sure I'm getting a good return on my investment."

Your next task is to tally the amount of time you're currently planning to spend this year on contact-building activities. Again, include professional meetings, conferences, trade shows, meals, and any other event where the purpose is to network and you have the opportunity to do so. We've heard numbers from a low of twenty hours a year to a high of six hundred hours a year, or about twelve hours a week. Time is money, so make strategic choices about how much time you want to devote to networking and use the techniques you've learned as you've read this book to ensure that you reap the benefits in return.

> **Invest time and energy to build the net worth of your network.**

Finally, ask yourself this bottom-line question: "Given the time and money I'm spending on networking, am I getting my money's worth?" The main mistake we see people making is that they race around to activities and events without a clue as to what position they are trying to attain in the marketplace, in their industry, or in their corporation.

If that's what you've been doing, *stop*! To maximize your investments, design a Strategic Positioning Project for yourself. Create a project that will mature in three to five years (or sooner) and that will give you the visibility and credibility to achieve your highest aspirations.

Set Your Sights High

Throughout this book, we've provided examples of mini-projects and midi-projects. A mini-project can usually be accomplished in less than six months. It will take only a limited amount of money, time, and effort. If you want to learn more about careers in a related department, for example, you might volunteer for the task force that's providing employee input on what aspects of the current performance evaluation

Design a big-time, long-term project.

form need to be updated. That way, you can spend time with a person from the department you want to know more about.

A midi-project can usually be accomplished in a year. It will take more money, time, and effort. You might want to take on a substantial community activity to fulfill your departmental objective of raising the visibility of the bank you work for among small business owners, for example. So, you join the chamber of commerce and immediately volunteer for a high-visibility committee position. That way, you'll have many opportunities to meet members who own small businesses.

But this chapter is about developing a mega-project. Mega-projects are multiyear projects that require intensity, commitment, and perhaps even self-sacrifice, not to mention money, time, and effort. Some people ask, "How can I plan a project in such detail? Life is full of surprises, twists, turns, opportunities, and changes. I can't see three years out—or even three weeks out!" That's a good question. Remember the old saying, "Luck is being ready to move when the universe says, 'Now!'" Of course you'll roll with the punches, keep your options open, and take advantage of plums that fall in your lap. But if you start with a plan, you'll be in a much better position to use all the unforeseen resources and opportunities that are just around the corner.

Set Your Goal

As you design your unique and strategic project, ask yourself, "What opportunities do I want to position myself for?"

Mega-projects have big, life-changing goals:

▶ "I want to move into management."

▶ "I want to work in Europe."

▶ "I want to change career fields from computer sales to counseling."

▶ "I want to prepare to do something completely different from my current job when I retire."

▶ "I want to leave the firm and go out on my own, so I must build my practice very quickly."

▶ "I must prepare to be laid off. The government agency I work for is downsizing, and I've been told that my job will go away in less than two years."

▶ "I want to relocate from Big City to Small Town, U.S.A., and I don't even know which small town in which corner of the country!"

▶ "I want to adopt two children and stay home with them for four or five years, while staying up-to-date and visible in my career field."

Plan Your Project

Brainstorm. Go for quantity as you come up with options for your ideal project. Read provocative publications, from the *Wall Street Journal* to *Fast Company*. Ask colleagues for ideas; borrow models from what others have done; adapt ideas to your organization. Narrow your choices to a few.

Research two or three projects. Use your network within your organization, your community, your profession, and your industry to do some preliminary research. Then pick your project.

Test your project. As we interviewed hundreds of networkers, we noticed that their projects had similar characteristics. Most of their big-time, long-term networking efforts could pass at least four of the following five tests.

The Doorway Test

Does your project position you where the people who can help you achieve your goal are streaming through? Create or find a "doorway." Position yourself in that doorway so that you meet those people and they begin to know you.

Whom do you need to know? Who are your ideal customers, clients, or employers? What do you need to learn about these people? How do you want them to perceive you? What do you need to teach them about your Character and Competence? Where will you find them? Where do they spend time? How can you participate in those Arenas?

Mitch is a twenty-eight-year-old attorney who specializes in wills and trusts. When he moved to Chicago to join a firm there, he knew no one. He'd be the first to tell you that he found his project (and his doorway) by accident. He loved ballroom dancing, and he noticed a newspaper article about a tea dance at a downtown hotel. He went to the dance and enjoyed himself hugely. The second time he attended, it hit him: The senior citizens at the dance were potential clients. Sure enough, as he got acquainted with his dancing partners, they naturally asked about his work. Enough of them eventually became clients that the partners sat up and took notice.

Melinda, a partner in a CPA firm, had to look to find the doorway that would lead to her goal: a constant stream of women business owners as clients. She offered to be on the board of directors of the Women's Business Center, whose mission was to guide and support women business owners. The board position gave her credibility and visibility. Melinda also taught classes at the center on financial matters for growing businesses—whether they were start-ups or pulling in revenues of a million dollars or more. As women business owners became familiar with Melinda's expertise through the professional work she did at the center, they just naturally became clients.

To pass the doorway test, make sure that your project puts you in your targets' doors—or brings them to yours.

The All or Nothing Test

If people see you doing one thing well, they will assume that you are good at everything. If people see you doing one thing poorly, they will assume that you do nothing well. That's the All or Nothing Principle. Is your project a vehicle for demonstrating Character and Competence? Even if your project has nothing to do with your exact area of expertise, if you are competent, people will just naturally make the leap and assume that you must be good at what you do.

Brian works for a large hotel chain but expects to start his own event planning business in a few years. He wanted to start early to develop a reputation that would assure that he had clients when he opened his doors. He decided that the best way to become visible to the largest number of people in his industry was to manage the creation of his association's Web site. He had the technical expertise, so he was confident that the project would be a good way to show his Character and Competence. And it would give him access to people in the meeting planning business at the local and national level as he solicited ads for the site from vendors, worked with members to develop content, and coordinated the overall project. He believed that with this feather in his cap, plenty of potential clients would know who he was, trust in his Character and Competence, and he hoped, be eager to secure his services.

Lee, a tax attorney, was looking for something to do when he retired. During his career, he had developed a reputation for being able to explain hard-to-understand concepts. He was asked to teach a class in an MBA program that targeted executives. Teaching was a natural for him. In the classroom, in story after story, example after example, his extraordinary expertise and track record shone through. Of course, many of his students became clients, but Lee also began to plan a retirement career as a storyteller. He decided to hire a speech coach and to attend storytelling festivals and workshops to nurture his new-found dream.

To pass the all or nothing test, be sure that your project puts you in positions that allow you to showcase your abilities. Then perform brilliantly. That way, you'll get a reputation for doing everything well.

The Bottom-Line Test

Can you arrange to have the time in your schedule and the money in your budget to support your project? Will your project yield a significant return? Is the outcome of your project measurable? Will your project contribute to your or your organization's bottom line?

Cerene is a financial planner whose long-term goal is to be invited to give a two-minute "financial tip" for women every day on CNN. To prepare for that opportunity, she proposed a monthly show for women to her local cable TV station. She's learning everything she needs to know to be comfortable in the world of TV. She interviews guests and reviews new books. Cerene estimates that the project will cost her about $2,000 this year and will take about three days a month. That's a huge investment, but she's confident that the experience she's gaining with her show will lead to a syndicated show and ultimately to that call from CNN. In the meantime, just four months into the project, the show has already netted her a client, and she says she loves calling experts in the field and saying, "Hello, this is Cerene Irving, host of Channel 32's *Money Magnet Show*. I'd like you to be my guest in November. Can we talk?"

Dan's goal, as a human resources manager, is to make an extraordinary contribution at work. Dan is in charge of the corporation's Employee Satisfaction Survey. After talking with peers in his professional association, he decided that he should try to join the Horizon Group. To receive an invitation to join this exclusive group, he networked with current members, folks from other *Fortune* 500 companies who also handle employee satisfaction surveys. They convinced him that membership would help him (and his company) stay up-to-date on state-of-the-art survey strategies, and after a year, sent him an invitation to join. Dan then had to convince his boss that the week away from the office every year and the $5,000 membership would be worth it. He made a detailed proposal that was accepted, even in a tight budget year. Three months after Dan attended his first meeting, he proved to his boss that the Horizon Group was valuable. He'd learned time-saving techniques, he was able to use questions that had been tested carefully, he knew what to do when the company acquired a German subsidiary, and he had new ideas about using the results of the survey. Dan was nominated for an employee-of-the-year award and was satisfied that he was making, and would be able to continue to make, a major contribution to his organization's success.

To pass the bottom-line test, make sure the way you are spending your time and money is best for reaching your goal. Choose a project with a big impact.

The Five-Year Test

Does your project point you toward your goal? Will you have the clients? Will headhunters call to see if you would be interested in jobs in London or Paris? Will you make partner? Will your business succeed? Will you be promoted? Does your project set the stage for the phone call you want to receive in three to five years?

Maggie, an author, wants the manager of a beautiful resort or spa to call. She can just hear that person asking her to become the "writer in residence" at the spa for two months during the winter. She wants to give readings from her numerous and delightful books and lead writing workshops for the residents and guests. With this vivid picture in mind, Maggie has no trouble deciding where to market her speaking and writing services now. When associations and other groups invite her to speak, it's easy for her to decide which ones to accept. International Association of Spas and Resorts? Yes! American Association of Automobile Manufacturers? Probably not. She's researching spas. She's writing articles about spas for magazines. She's looking forward to that call.

Deirdre has had jobs of increasing responsibility in the high-tech industry. She accepted a new job that was a lateral move for her, but was with a company she really wanted to work for. Not content to languish too long in this mid-level marketing position, she designed a strategic project. Her goal? To become known to people in the corporate hierarchy who might tap her unused talents and advocate for her when openings come up. She made a list of the people whom she especially wanted to know and to have know her. As program chair for her professional development association, Deirdre had to find speakers for the monthly meetings. When her committee decided to do a program on employee retention strategies, Deirdre invited one of the people on her list, her second-level manager, to be on the panel. Deirdre had several opportunities to talk with the manager about the program and to show her Character and Competence. She even offered to drive her manager to and from the event because parking was difficult and because, of course, she knew that they would have more time to talk. Now she's moved on to person number two on her list.

Your project will make you the natural and only choice.

To pass the five-year test, be sure every activity in your project targets the outcome you want down the road.

The Pig in Mud Test

Does your project represent a magnificent blend of your unique personal and professional interests? Does it represent who you are, what you value, what you like to do, where you want to go, and what you do best? Will your project make you "as happy as a pig in mud"? We are from Kansas, and we have seen pigs in mud. They wallow. They roll. They close their eyes in ecstasy. They are happy, content, and comfortable, and they want to be right where they are and no place else.

Bill, the owner of a mortgage company, graduated from the university fifteen years ago. An active alumnus and avid supporter of the university's basketball team, he had a strong network of contacts there. He created a project that helped his alma mater, allowed him to expand his business in a very natural way, and made him very happy. Here's how it happened. It came to his attention that the president of the university didn't have any discretionary funds to use for worthy projects that came up from time to time. So Bill offered to start the President's Club. It was a group of generous donors who created a fund for the president to use on innovative projects that would improve the university's visibility and attract talented students. When some students wanted to enter a robotics contest in Japan, they were able to buy the supplies to build the robots and their airline tickets with money from the fund. Imagine how the president bragged about his students when they won the contest! Imagine how grateful he was to Bill for creating the fund. In his nationwide fund-raising campaign, Bill found that alumni often asked him about his business, and some of them wanted him to handle their mortgages. Bill expanded his business so that he could do mortgages in many states and took his business to a whole new level.

To pass the pig in mud test, be sure your project makes you happy!

CHAPTER 16

Make the Most of Memberships

Joining organizations is the best way to come in contact with a multitude of people and build your personal and professional network. Whatever your profession or interest, you can find a group of like-minded people. In fact, for any given job type, industry, or business, you'll have many possible groups to choose from.

Jon is an architect in Easton, Maryland. He specializes in designing hospitals and has a personal and professional interest in landscaping. He could join the American Institute of Architects, the chamber of commerce, the American Institute of Landscape Architects, the local Rotary Club, the American Association of Hospital Administrators, the Chesapeake Healthcare Association. Then there's the group that's restoring plant life along the Chesapeake Bay. Or how about the Lion's Club? Or he could join the alumni group for his alma mater, Boston University. Jon's list of possibilities is endless. Yours probably is too.

So, how can you strategically make the most of your memberships? First, decide the amount of time and money you'd like to invest in networking during the next year. Then, with your career and business goals in mind, choose your organizations carefully. Third, when you participate, act in ways that teach people to trust in your Character and Competence.

Tally Your Time and Money

If you haven't already done so, grab a piece of paper and a calculator, and tally up the time you are devoting to networking. Can you document how much time you are spending? Is it too much, given the results? Is it too little, given your and your organization's needs and goals?

Now, if you haven't already done so, calculate how much money you spent on memberships last year. Include dues and other expenses for activities at associations, professional groups, referral groups, and clubs. Include money out of your own pocket as well as dues and expenses your organization paid for. What's the grand total of your investment?

> After you become a member, the important work of creating relationship begins.

Are you surprised to see how *little* you actually spend, given how important meeting new people and reconnecting with long-time contacts is to your organization's bottom line and to your long-term career goals? Or are you shocked to realize how *much* you spend and want a better return on your (or your company's) investment?

Do you need to increase the effectiveness of your networking to get your money's worth?

How much time and money should you ideally spend?

Choose Organizations Wisely

To find the right organizations for you, check your library. The reference librarian will show you how to find lists of local organizations and nationwide or worldwide associations. To find groups that will extend your circle of contacts and offer programs of interest, check the Internet, look in the phone book, or read the business pages of your newspaper.

Ask other people in your profession what organizations they benefit from the most and check out those groups. Ask customers and clients what groups they belong to. There may be an associate member category for people who provide services.

Once you've targeted a few organizations, do your homework. Don't leap before you look. Attend a couple of meetings as a guest. Talk to new members and old members. Read several issues of the newsletter. Scan the membership directory. Before you write your check and commit your time, remember that you are about to place a very talented person—you—in a key position. Assess the organization's value to you by answering these questions.

1. How many members are there? (The bigger the better for networking, but it may be easier to move into a leadership position in smaller groups.)

2. Can I get excited about the group's mission? Does it connect with my networking goals?

3. Are people in the group likely to need my product or service or to refer business to me? Are people in the group likely to provide valuable resources or information?

4. What do people say about the group? What's its reputation in the profession or community?

5. What opportunities to associate with my peers will the group offer me? What opportunities to associate with stars in the field?

6. Does the group provide a good networking culture by encouraging people to introduce themselves and talk to each other about important business and career agendas?

7. Does the group have special activities to help newcomers feel welcome and meet people?

8. How easy is it to participate? How quickly could I move into a leadership role that would give me visibility and career experience?

9. Do the leaders seem genuinely excited about their participation, or are they playing "somebody has to do it"?

10. Are the programs interesting? Do the topics and speakers provide valuable professional growth?

11. What would my time commitment be? Can I make that commitment for at least one year?

12. What exactly could I contribute to this group?

Make the Most of the Meetings

Just say "hi!" What's the most successful opener for starting a conversation with somebody? There's nothing complicated about the answer. The word is, "hi!" Just "hi!"

It's a "hi!" that flashes a message in neon lights: "I feel great about meeting you, and I'd like to talk with you." That "hi!" says, "I'm happy to be here, and I'm looking forward to getting to know you." It's inviting and energizing and relaxing, all at the same time. It's inviting and energizing because it signals that you're a person who is committed to helping this conversation move along. It's relaxing because it signals that you're a person who can take care of himself in a conversation. It's not the kind of "hi" that sends the message, "I'm just saying this to be polite, and I hope you won't take this as a signal that we have to talk." What a difference! And the difference comes from the tone of voice and the body language.

Practice the two kinds of "hi." Feel the difference between the two.

Joan remembers learning about the power of just saying "hi!"

"Shortly after I was married, I went downtown for lunch with a neighbor, whose name was Sue Jones," she says. "We went to the department store cafeteria. You could sit anywhere. We went over to a table and put our trays down. Sue looked at the two strangers sitting there and said, 'Hi, I'm Sue Jones.' I never would have introduced myself to strangers. I was so stunned, so impressed. So, I made a button in my brain and labeled it Sue Jones. After that, when I would go to various events, I would push my button and say, 'Hi, I'm Joan Martinson.' That helped me to begin talking, just pretending I was Sue. I still do it. I still, ten years later, have my Sue Jones button. When I'm uncomfortable being myself or when I'm feeling shy, I push the button and become Sue Jones, and I'm immediately comfortable reaching out to people."

Finding a role model—a Sue or Sam Jones—may help you feel more comfortable as you open conversations. Be on the lookout for people who handle situations in a way that appeals to you. Observe how they do it. It's all right to copy someone else's manner. If you do it consistently, it will become part of your own style.

> **Volunteer for an activity or job that shows off your best skills and spotlights your business capabilities.**

Give yourself a job. You don't have to wait to be elected to the board. You don't even have to sign up with a committee. Just look around and be helpful. Pitch in at the registration desk. Greet newcomers. Doing something will make you comfortable and give you a reason for starting conversations.

Check in with acquaintances. Meeting new people may actually be easier than beginning a conversation with a person you see only rarely and know only slightly. Don't berate yourself for not remembering all the details of that person's life or work. And it's easy to put your foot in your mouth inadvertently when you begin a conversation with someone you haven't talked with recently. Assume that the person's life has changed. It probably has.

"A man whom I'd worked with several years ago had transferred to another division of the company," says Jerry. "Seeing him again, I asked about his wife. He said, 'Oh, we've been divorced for two years.'"

To avoid that kind of slip-up, ask general questions rather than specific ones:

▶ "We haven't talked for a while. Catch me up on what you've been doing."

▶ "How's your year been?"

▶ "What's changed for you since we last talked?"

▶ "What's new in your life?"

These kinds of questions allow the other person to bring you up to date, revealing as much as he wishes. The answers will guide your conversation.

Talk about what you're thinking. Notice what you are thinking, and then talk about it. Make a statement about what's on your mind. Opening a conversation that way is much more likely to create a connection than commenting on something that has nothing to do with you or the occasion, like the weather or the ball scores.

At a convention of your professional group, say, "This is my first conference. Got any suggestions about good speakers or sessions? I really want to get my money's worth."

At an annual awards banquet for people in your professional organization, say, "Have you looked at the display of entries that won awards? I was impressed by the publicity for the preemployment drug testing program."

At a reception to welcome the new head of your division, say, "I know there was a news release put out about the new boss, but do you know any more about him? Do you know anyone who worked with him in his earlier jobs?"

If you're new, say, "I've never been here before. What happens next?"

Notice how each of these openers tells a little about what you're interested in and gives the other person something to go on, a lead to follow up on. The openers also ask your partner for an opinion. In that way, they encourage a more personal and interesting conversation than if both of you are spouting generalities about things you care little about.

Say what you see. Another way to begin is to look around and be interested and inventive as you react to your surroundings. React to the past-president's ribbon hanging from Walt's name tag. In an office, look for awards or posters on the wall or personal items on the desk about which you can comment.

"Before a business meeting got underway," Meg remembers, "I joined a group of three or four people who were chatting. One of them, John, had his arm in a cast. I figured the rest of the group had already asked him, 'What happened?' So I decided not to ask again. As the meeting started, I asked Betty what had happened to John's arm. She said, 'Oh, I don't know. Nobody asked him about that.'"

You may think, "Don't ask about his cast, her tan, that beautiful necklace; twenty other people have probably already asked." Or, "That's not proper." Why not? When we were children, we may have asked embarrassing questions about the obvious ("Why is Aunt Betty's tummy so fat?") and been shushed rather than told she was pregnant. Or perhaps we've heard that it's not polite to comment on someone else's possessions. That's ridiculous!

Comedian Lenny Bruce once said, "When you are eight years old, nothing is any of your business." Some of the rules were taught as children no longer apply.

As children, we may have gotten another message—a far deeper one: "Don't notice other people." In school, teachers said, "Keep your eyes on your own paper." Other adults may have told us, "Keep quiet" or "Don't make personal remarks." As children in our crowded and sometimes frightening world, we are taught, "Don't talk to strangers." We learn not to make eye contact. Those restrictions may make sense on a subway; they don't at a professional meeting or a networking event.

Reflect on the occasion. Ask questions about the event or activity. Or ask about people's interest in it. If you're at a conference or a business meeting, ask:

▶ "What do you hope to get out of this?"

▶ "Is this the first time you've come to this?"

▶ "What looks interesting to you on the meeting's agenda?"

▶ "What do you think is the most important issue on the meeting's agenda?"

Notice that you are moving quickly into asking for opinions and evaluations.

Another option is to find out why the other person is present. You might ask:

▶ "How did you first find out about this organization?"

▶ "Is today's program particularly interesting to you?"

▶ "What makes you keep coming back to this organization's meetings?"

Link up with your competitors. Often people avoid talking with other people who are in the same business or profession. But such people can be excellent contacts, and they may even eventually refer business to you. Always be ready to offer some information to your competitor first. That way, it won't appear that you are trying to get something for nothing.

Introduce yourself to the leaders. You can spot the leaders. They're the ones rushing around. Don't be intimidated; walk right up and say, "Hello." If you're considering joining the organization, make an appointment to talk with a leader after the meeting. At that time, be ready to ask some questions about the organization. If you have joined, begin to contribute. Taking an active role will bring you into contact with the leaders naturally.

Talk and sit with people you don't know. Nearly 75 percent of people in our workshops admit that they end up sitting next to the people they came with at networking events. If you are attending the event with people from your own office, agree beforehand that you won't sit together. Your job at a networking meeting is to make contact with people you do not know or do not know well.

Come with a purpose. Nearly 85 percent of people in our workshops confess that when they attend networking events, they have no specific purpose in mind, nothing they want to find or connect with or learn, no one they particularly want to meet. Know what you want—and ask for it. What can you do before a networking event to make sure you meet the people you want or need to meet? Here are some ideas.

> Before an event, set goals. Plan to talk with four people you don't know, refresh your relationships with three people you do know, and sit with somebody new.

- ▶ Call someone and offer to give her a ride to the event, so that you can have some uninterrupted time together.

- ▶ Call someone and suggest that you sit together so that you will have a chance to talk.

- ▶ Call someone else and say, "I hope you are going to the meeting this Thursday. How about grabbing a cup of coffee afterwards?"

- ▶ Call the administrator and ask for a list of attendees, so that you can plan whom you want to talk to or meet.

- ▶ When you are talking to someone about a specific topic, ask, "Who else do you know that you think I should talk to about this?" then ask your original contact to introduce you.

The Biggest Mistakes Members Make

- ▶ They join, but they don't go. They show up so sporadically that they can't reap many benefits from their membership.

- ▶ They appear, but they don't interact. They eat another olive, listen to the speaker, and leave.

- ▶ They skip the networking portion of the meeting, arrive just in time for the meal, and duck out just as the speaker is winding down. Then they wonder why networking doesn't work for them.

▶ They talk and sit with people they already know.

▶ They make no effort to be visible; instead, they try to blend into the crowd.

▶ They wait for others to make the first move.

> When you join an organization, put at least three-fourths of its events on your calendar.

▶ They think handing out business cards is networking.

▶ They give up too soon and hop from one organization to another, never giving themselves or others time to establish relationships.

▶ They have "nonconversations," rather than productive conversations, with other members. ("Hi, how are you?" "Not bad. How are you?" "Not bad. What's new?" "Not much. What's new with you?")

▶ They arrive without any idea of what they have to give or what they want to get.

▶ They violate good networking protocols or are unaware of Netiquette within the group.

▶ They forget that the best way to show Character and Competence is to contribute time and energy.

Plan Network-Friendly Meetings

If you are in a leadership role in an organization, it's your job to make meetings network-friendly. Take this quiz to your next board meeting and discuss the questions. Use the information in this book to encourage great networking opportunities at your meetings.

1. During the networking portion of the meeting, do group leaders introduce newcomers and help them feel welcome? Do leaders plan and facilitate activities to help people connect?

2. What are the ground rules in your group for separating good networking from undesirable marketing or hard sells? Are guidelines explained in the newsletter and reviewed at meetings from time to time?

> **Make an Agenda of things to talk about and don't leave home without it.**

3. If a meal is served, are tables small enough to encourage conversation across the table? Request tables for four or six people. Tables for eight or ten people reduce networking opportunities by 75 percent, as people are reduced to conversing primarily with the people on their left and right.

4. Are there members who serve as "ambassadors" to help visitors and members strike up conversations? Do greeters have special name tags or some way to be identified?

5. Does the group have any way to measure the effectiveness of the networking at meetings? How many contacts/introductions/conversations would constitute a successful meeting for your members or guests? How many people does an average member or guest interact with at a meeting? What are the results of that interaction? What percentage of guests eventually join? Why?

6. Does the group conduct follow-up interviews or quick phone or fax surveys with members to find out how events could be made more network-friendly?

7. Are committee jobs and leadership responsibilities described as benefits or burdens? Do you point out the value of getting involved?

8. How many networking subgroups does your group have? What makes them work?

9. If members could get everything they came for at a meeting, what would that be? What would have to happen?

10. Do members tell success stories that showcase how they have made valuable contacts? How, when, and where are these stories told? How are stories like these incorporated into the group's history so that everybody can learn how networking, at its best, really works?

Don't Try to Buy a Network

Whether you choose to be active in your alumni association, the chamber of commerce, a trade or professional association, a service club, or an organization for people who own Irish setters, you'll find that groups are your route to knowing and becoming known to a large number of people. But remember, joining a group doesn't mean that you join anybody's network—or that they join yours. Often, people think they have a network because they belong to a lot of organizations. Not so. You can fill out the membership forms, pay your dues, receive the newsletter, and even go to events, and still not have a network.

The only way to create a network for yourself is to invest your time and energy in the success of others. It takes personal contact and individual

You can't buy a network. Networks are built conversation by conversation, not by writing a check for your dues.

effort to forge long-lasting, valuable networking relationships. Most of the best opportunities and resources in life will come from people, not print. Memberships are one of the best investments you can make in creating a circle of contacts that count.

CHAPTER 17

Connect at Conventions

What's so hard about going to a convention? You send in your registration, buy your plane ticket, pack your suitcase, and go. Right?

Wrong. That's the way *most* people go to conventions. However, what you actually get from a conference depends on the tactics you use to get the most out of the experience. You could read a book or current professional journal and receive virtually the same information you'll receive from attending a convention. The difference, though, is obvious. A conference brings people face-to-face. If you don't make effective contact with the other people at the convention, you'll go home feeling vaguely dissatisfied.

If you think about it, you'll realize that you—and your organization—have expectations about how the experience will benefit you. You probably assume that you'll gain valuable knowledge. Your organization assumes that it is paying for you to bring something back from that week in Miami besides a suntan.

How to Go to a Convention

Is a convention on your calendar? If your how-to-succeed-in-business plan includes a conference, follow these ten tips to get the most out of the event.

1. Before you go, show people at work the brochure and trade show exhibitor list. Ask your colleagues if there's anything

you can do for them at the conference: Attend a particular session? Introduce yourself to a potential customer?

2. Pack a cell phone. If you have to wait in line at a pay phone or go to your room to make calls, you lose valuable networking time.

3. Use a laptop to take notes (quotes, announcements, insights, and statistics) and zap them back to colleagues via e-mail.

4. If you are having a great conversation with someone in the hallway, skip a session. You can always buy the tape.

5. Set goals. What questions do you want answered? Whom do you need to meet?

6. Put together an impromptu discussion. As you meet people you want to know better, invite them to meet you at 6 P.M. in the lobby to go out to dinner.

7. Be visible. When you ask a question, give your name, your company, and what you do. Introduce yourself to the speakers and tell them why you are interested in their topics. They may mention you from the podium.

8. Avoid hanging out with people from your own company.

9. Make appointments for breakfast, lunch, or dinner with people you want to know or know better.

10. Be sure you are creating lots of reasons to follow up with people. Send them notes or e-mails. Stay in touch. Create that circle of contacts for your company and for your career.

Don't Wait for the Convention to Come to You

"I was standing in line at the coffee shop waiting to be seated for lunch," Phyllis remembers. "All around me were people who were attending the same convention. I could tell, because we all were wearing the same kind of name tags. But we weren't talking to each other! We might as well have been sitting back at our desks in our own offices hundreds of miles from each other.

"I waited for somebody *else* to say something. Then I realized how I was feeling—just like a wallflower at the prom. I didn't like it. And what's more, I knew that I wasn't getting as much out of the conference as I could."

What Phyllis was experiencing isn't unusual. Instead of feeling like a professional, she felt like an awkward teenager again. Instead of being able to use the conference to gain helpful hints and solve problems, she felt uncomfortable and frustrated.

There are shelves and shelves of books in the library devoted to *planning* meetings and conventions. But, amazingly, there are no books on how to be an effective participant. Using the ideas in this book, you can make conventions a valuable business experience, one that's worth your time and effort.

Expand Your Expectations

Bringing people together face-to-face is expensive. There's lots of talk in the business community about replacing meetings with video teleconferencing. On the other hand, there are strong arguments for convening in person. Your organization isn't going to continue paying the price for you to attend conventions, however, unless you can bring back bottom-line benefits. There are ways to sell your organization on footing the bill. The ideas in this chapter will help you justify the expense.

Our surveys show that conference attendees—and their bosses—expect three things from the experience: information, inspiration, and interaction.

The meeting planner designs the program to accomplish the first two.

People go to conventions for inspiration, information, and interaction.

Even if you don't take the initiative, you'll soak up information and inspiration as you attend the sessions and listen to the speakers. But generating the one-on-one connections that enrich and expand that knowledge and motivation is, for the most part, up to you. It's your responsibility to create the individual interactions that make the time and money spent worthwhile.

Take Advantage of the Meetings in the Hallway

If you want to carry back more than souvenirs and stuff from exhibitors, plan ahead to make the most of all the informal and unstructured moments, "the meetings in the hallway." You make them happen when you introduce yourself to someone sitting near you before the keynoter begins to speak, when you strike up a conversation with someone in the hotel lobby or at a luncheon, when you welcome a newcomer, or when you congratulate a new board member at the opening reception.

The hotel can be awful, the weather can be lousy, the speakers can be mediocre, but if you meet just one person who can help you boost your sales, advance your career, land a new job, or solve a problem that's festering back on your desk, you'll call the convention a success.

Use the tips in the rest of this chapter for planning ahead, connecting at the conference, and following up when you're back at work.

Get Ready, Get Set: Before You Go

Take these steps to get ready.

Set your Agenda. Make a written list of your *gives* and *gets*. By constructing an Agenda, you customize the conference so that it exactly meets your needs. (See Chapter 12 for specific instructions on constructing Agendas.)

On the *give* side, jot down things to share with the people you meet:

►New resources you've discovered

►Special expertise you've developed

►Problems you've solved

►Successes you've had

If you are a newcomer, list some insights you might offer from other arenas.

If you are a veteran, make a note of information you can provide to those just coming into the field.

On the *get* side, go for the gold and make your list as long as possible. Jot down what you want to find:

►Answers to challenges you're facing

►Solutions to problems you're dealing with

►Resources you need to succeed

►People you'd like to meet

Martina is an independent consultant in human resources who focuses on pharmaceutical companies. Her convention Agenda included the items in Figure 17-1.

Martina is ready for meaty conversations. When someone asks her, "How are you?" or "What's new?" she can turn to her Agenda for a topic. And if the person she's chatting with doesn't know about marketing "soft skills" training, for example, Martina can ask, "Do you know anyone here that I could talk to about that?" She'll probably be passed along to someone with that expertise.

Take along other people's Agendas. Not everyone will be able to

Pack your networking Agenda and come home with valuable tips, ideas, solutions to problems, new opportunities, and insights.

FIGURE 17-1. Agenda items.

To Give	To Get
Experience with contact management software for keeping track of vendors, clients, and associates.	A woodsy conference center with a relaxed atmosphere for a group of two hundred managers.
The best training films on diversity from a vendor film festival she attended.	Information on retirement options in the Southwest.
Information on bidding and contracting with companies overseas.	How to find and apply for scholarships for college-age kids. (She has twins!)
Ideas for streamlining her proposal writing.	How to market "soft skills" training to bottom-line companies.
Ideas on providing "train the trainer" programs and how to price them.	Access to several people who have recently published books to find out about their experiences and get their recommendations.

spend the time and money to go to the convention. A great way to get more bang for your buck and build your relationships with colleagues, your boss, your salespeople, or your business partner is to collect their concerns and hunt for answers to those concerns at the meeting.

After you are clear about your Agenda, tell people. Businesspeople often see conventions as "just a joy junket." Sell your attendance. Send a memo to key people in your organization telling them that you're going to the conference. Attach a copy of the program. Ask if there's anything you can do for the organization while you are in Convention City. It may be as simple as picking up some literature at the exhibits or asking a question of the speaker after a session. Your colleagues may know some of the speakers and may be able to tell you, "Dr. Dud is a waste of time, but be sure to hear Ms. Up-and-Coming." Your memo also lets others in your company know that you are serious about your professional development. Emphasize that your attendance is not just your annual trip to the Sunbelt, but an educational experience. Then report on the results when you return to work.

Choose your sessions in advance. Select your sessions before you arrive at your hotel room. Advance planning while you're still in the office will allow you to shape your experience to your goals.

Pick your sessions carefully. Focus on the knowledge you need and the skills you want to develop. Look for the right sessions that will force you to reevaluate, plan for the future, and expand your horizons.

Carefully pick a wild-card session on a topic you think you may never have a use for. (Invariably, that's the one that will open new doors for you or shine new light on old problems.)

Divvy up sessions among several people from your organization who are attending, or decide to attend one key session as a group and plan a "How-are-we-going-to-apply-this?" session immediately afterward.

Begin to think about some topics that particularly interest you and to formulate the questions you'd like to ask at the session before you go.

Design your own sessions. Recognize that some of the best sessions are not listed in the conference brochure—they're set up by you! Arrange them *before* you leave for the conference.

Here are some ideas:

Visit a branch office or corporate headquarters to increase your knowledge of the business or to visit an internal customer.

Meet with a key prospect or customer in the city where your conference is being held.

Contact a speaker before the conference begins and suggest getting together for breakfast or lunch.

Set up a meeting with a board member, a guru, an expert, a counterpart from a similar organization, or a colleague you've lost touch with. If a twosome seems intimidating, invite several people (they don't have to know one another!) to go out to dinner. Before the meeting, Arnetta called a couple of long-distance acquaintances and invited them to dinner on the third night of the conference. At the conference, when she met someone new or saw a colleague, she said, "I'm getting together a bunch of people to eat dinner at a great Italian restaurant. If you'd like to come, meet in the lobby at 6:30."

Arnetta's sense of adventure was contagious. Nine people showed up and enjoyed a leisurely dinner exploring connections and common challenges.

Plan an out-of-the-ordinary experience to stimulate your creativity. It might have a business payoff.

At a convention in New Orleans, Don took a guided tour of jazz spots. Six months later, he was producing a video program for his company and searching for appropriate music. A blues tune he'd heard in one of the jazz joints popped into his mind. His video later won an award.

In Orlando, while other conventioneers were doing the expected tour of Disney World, Jenna visited a shelter for homeless women. She got excited about a program that encourages employees to donate clothes so that the women from the shelter can dress appropriately for job interviews. When she started a similar program back home, she improved life for others and gained positive PR for her image-consulting business.

Build in time to relax, unwind, exercise, and see the sights. Seek out information about the city before you go. A request to the chamber of commerce will bring you lots of information in the mail. Search the Internet for that city's Web home page. Also browse though travel magazines. How can you take advantage of the location of the conference? If you don't find ways to take advantage of the site, you might as well be staying at home. What new things do you want to see? Plan ahead to use recreation—or even regional cuisine—to stimulate your creativity. Use the wild-card technique: Plan to see something or do something that is totally outside the realm of anything you've previously experienced. Your wild-card experience can be selected from among the tourist attractions of the city or might simply be something you would not have a chance to experience at home.

Volunteer for a job at the conference. Call ahead and offer to help out. Find the name of the chairperson of a committee on which you'd like to serve, and volunteer your talents. It's a rare group that can't use an extra pair of hands. You'll find it easy to make contact with people that way. You'll also gain professional visibility, mingle with the leaders, and build a nationwide network.

Or give *yourself* a job to do at the conference. Before you leave home, arrange to bring back a report on some aspect of the conference to a person in your organization, to your company newspaper, to your city newspaper, or to your local professional group. Having a job to do will strengthen your Agenda, and you'll feel as if you have an even better reason to meet people, ask questions, and take notes.

Show Up at the Conference

Be there! Set aside thoughts of the work stacking up back on your desk and the messages piling up in your voice mail. Use these ten tips for making great convention connections.

1. *Arrive at the convention early.* The important people—speakers, conference organizers, association leaders—are likely to arrive early for "pre-meeting meetings." Rub shoulders with the successful people. They are the ones with the knowledge. Find a mentor or a role model.

2. *Wear a smile.* Make your body language say, "I'd be easy to talk to." React to visual clues. Comment on jewelry, a necktie, a T-shirt, a name tag listing a state you've traveled in. If you're in line to pick up theater tickets with someone who is wearing the same kind of convention badge you are, go with the obvious. Say, "Hi, I'm Jack . . . Jack Armstrong. I'm at the NCAC convention, too."

3. *Volunteer (again!) to help.* Give out name tags, fill in for a panelist whose plane got fogged in, distribute handouts for the speaker. Participation leads to relationships.

4. *Introduce yourself to speakers or panelists.* Welcome them before the program, and let them know why you chose their

session. Often they are eager for more information on who's in the audience, so, if they aren't busy getting ready, talk to them. They may mention you in their presentation—instant visibility! Or talk to the speaker afterwards. Ask if he is free for coffee or lunch to continue the discussion. It's rare to be turned down. If people can't do what you ask, they may offer something even better in return. One speaker said to Robert, "I can't go to lunch right now, but why don't you join Walter and me for supper." Walter turned out to be anchorman Walter Cronkite! If you feel shy about issuing an invitation to a speaker, ask two or three other people with similar interests to lunch and then ask the speaker to join the group.

5. *Participate in the sessions.* Ask a question. This does several things. It forces you to think actively rather than just sitting passively and taking it all in. When you ask your question, stand up and talk loud enough to be heard. Introduce yourself and tell where you're from or what organization you're with. You'll be remembered because you have been seen. Your visibility makes it easier for people to come up to you after the session and start a conversation. If there is time, you might even announce that you'd like to talk to people who "have successfully used an executive search firm" or "have solved the problem of doing long-distance sales training when field offices are spread out"—whatever is on your Agenda. Your question may attract others who have the same interests. "Every time I have asked a question, someone interesting has come up to me afterwards and started a conversation," says Rhonda. Also listen carefully to other people's questions. Follow up after the session by getting together with those people and

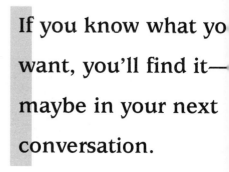

If you know what you want, you'll find it—maybe in your next conversation.

commenting on their questions or asking more about their point of view. Those are instant conversation starters.

6. *Sit with strangers.* At sessions and meals, don't sit with people you already know. Use that time to meet someone new. Tell yourself that there are no accidental meetings, and try to figure out what you and the other person have in common. Find out what others are looking for and help them connect with resources and contacts.

7. *Look for excuses to introduce people to each other.* Listen for commonalities, then be a great connector. "Fred, I've got to introduce you to Sam over there. You both grew up in Chicago." "Mary, I want you to meet Sunita. You are both program chairs for your chapters. I know you'll have lots to talk about!"

8. *Consult the list.* You may receive a list of attendees in your registration packet. Use it and the conference registration materials to see who's there. Look for people you'd like to meet. Make it a game. Take every opportunity to start conversations. Welcome first-timers. Thank an association leader for his hard work. Say hello in the elevators. Meet people who have the kind of job you have now. Meet others who have the kind of job you think you'd like to have next. Meet people from your own geographical area. Discuss regional or state activities. You might find out about new activities you'd like to take part in, or, if you're already active, you might enlist an enthusiastic new member for your regional, state, or local organization. Your Agenda will give you ready-made topics. Plan to talk with people about trends in your field, about what's going on in your industry, or about career paths.

9. *Give feedback.* Offer suggestions to the meeting planner and conference committee about how the convention could be made more network-friendly. Complaining is strictly off-limits. Make positive suggestions. Offer to help so you'll stand out as a creative contributor.

10. *Be prepared to job hunt—even if you don't think you're looking for a job.* Update your résumé and take a dozen copies with you. Make sure your business cards are up to date also. Put together a few samples of your work. Throw in a U.S. map. If you are interviewing for a job, you may want to be able to locate Bigville on the map. Find out what you're worth. If there is a placement service, sign up and set up interviews with prospective employers. This lets you practice your interviewing skills. It also gives you an idea of your marketability and the going rate in other parts of the country for the kind of work you do. If you are in the process of hiring, interview people for your job opening. Even if you don't fill the job with a person you interviewed at the conference, you'll have an idea of what kinds of people would be interested in your job opening. You'll have a benchmark against which to measure the people you interview when you return home. You also may be able to pick up a job description for a job you are creating. Then you won't have to write the job description yourself from scratch.

Follow Up After You Get Home

Sit down at your computer with your notes, and compile a list of major ideas, resources, and contacts. Turn sketchy notes into action steps. Make a list of people to follow up with. Do it within a week. Did you promise to send your counterpart, a franchisee in Albuquerque, that interesting article on selling to baby boomers? Do it! Did you say you'd review someone's résumé and send it back? Do it!

Tell your boss about the conference. Then follow up with a memo. Pass along all the exciting ideas you heard. Tell the boss whom you talked to, what sessions you attended, what you learned, and why the conference was valuable both to you and to the organization.

Don't forget to send memos to the people in your company whom you asked for advice or who gave you a job to do. Translate what you learned into positive observations, suggestions, or plans for your company or organization.

Go ahead and write that article for your company newspaper. Your fellow employees might be fascinated to hear what keynote speaker Colin Powell said about leadership. Of course, if you're really gutsy, you will have gone up to Colin and asked him for any experiences he's had that would especially apply to your industry.

Take a tip from Beth. As she was sorting through all the cards she received at the national convention, she reread the notes she'd made on the backs. Then she hit on another idea. She pulled out her association directory and highlighted in yellow all the folks she'd met. She tagged them with sticky notes—yellow for members and blue for vendors. She copied the notes from the backs of the business cards into the directory and refreshed the name/face connection. Next year, when she goes to the convention, she'll pack the book or tear out the highlighted pages and take them with her.

Later On, Get Reinspired

Finally, six months later, take out your notes and reread them. Choose a rotten, rainy Monday morning for this exercise. You'll find that all the ideas and enthusiasm and inspiration you felt while you were at the convention will come flooding back. That's what a convention is for: to give you ideas and to stimulate you. William James, the psychologist, was talking once about the time it takes for the unconscious to incubate ideas. He said, "We learn to swim in the winter and skate in the summer." You may find that ideas from the conference have now incubated and are ready to be hatched.

Also at this six-month point, send notes to some of the people you talked with at the convention. Ask them if they are going to be attending the next one. Keep in touch with your contacts. Put them on your holiday card list. That will make going to the next conference much easier: You'll be looking forward to seeing valuable business contacts, not strangers.

Assess how well you did at focusing on your Agenda. Did you answer your questions? Did you solve the problems you took with you to the conference? Did you meet many of the people you wanted

to meet? If you can say yes then you have succeeded at the art of con-
ventioneering.

Plan Meetings That Get People Talking

Chances are that sometime, somewhere, you'll be involved in planning a convention, a sales kickoff, a regional conference, or a meeting
for your local chapter. The sessions may be fantastic, the food may be
delicious, the hotel may rate five stars, but what brings people back
next year are the connections they make this year.

Here are twelve ideas to increase the interaction. Some further
ideas are given in Figure 17-2.

FIGURE 17-2. How to plan network-friendly meetings.

No-Nos	Know-Hows
Hope that people are comfortable connecting.	Teach the "rules and tools" of networking with special preconference materials.
Assume that everyone has an Agenda.	Give preconference and on-site aid and encouragement so that people create new Agendas every day.
Print too much on name tags or print the names too small.	Print bold and colorful first names.
Leave newcomers on their own.	Get great greeters.
Think people want polite chitchat at meals.	Suggest table talk topics at some meals.
Expect speakers to know how to get people talking.	Show speakers how to encourage small groups and "in the hallway" follow-ups.
Assume that people will find each other.	Offer many small "meetings within the meeting."
Hope that people will stay in touch.	Give them reasons and tools for getting together.
Wonder how it went.	Do focus groups and fax-back surveys to find out.

1. *Prepare attendees before the conference.* Put articles and tip sheets on "networking know-how" in your magazine, newsletter, and convention publicity/registration packets. Clear how-tos on the "netiquette" of making contact in this organization give attendees the confidence to go from casual conversations to great connections.

2. *Make name tags novel.* Print first names *big*. As conversation starters, add special ribbons or colored stickers designating interests to help people find each other.

3. *Give out several blank name tags.* Tell people to wear a new one each day and write on it something they're eager to talk with others about. Or preprint name tags that say, "To make a great connection with me, talk to me about . . ." and ask attendees to write in a topic they want or need to talk about. Agenda-based name tags make it easier to open conversations.

4. *Maximize the mix and mingle.* Include some short, structured, one-on-ones or threesomes to encourage mixing and meeting. Choose an energetic, well-known person to lead the session. Plan the questions carefully to fit the group's interests and culture.

5. *Manage the music.* Use music to energize or entertain, but keep the volume low and don't let it compete with conversation. People will leave your expensive reception in droves if they can't hear one another!

6. *Give a hand for hospitality.* Train leaders, staff, and volunteers how to introduce people to each other. Teach them how to encourage conversations at mixers and sessions. Invite people to go out to dinner or attend special events.

7. *Give people a way to begin conversations.* As people come into a session, pose a provocative question or topic on the overhead screen and invite people to chat about it until the session starts.

8. *Spark up your speakers.* Remind your speakers that attendees want to talk with one another as well as listen to experts. Suggest ways for speakers to include some interaction in their sessions. Also invent ways for speakers to meet attendees. Encourage speakers to attend receptions and meals where attendees can talk informally with them.

9. *Make the most of meals.* Table talk isn't easy when the room is noisy and the tables are set for eight to ten. Work with the hotel on noise control and request smaller tables of four to six whenever possible. Using a table talk host or simply a bold sign at each table, suggest a topic or issue that people can discuss over lunch. Topics that generate a lot of energy are ethical issues, future trends, or what's going on in local chapters. On "free" nights, invite people to sign up to go out to dinner in small groups. Designate a restaurant, host/hostess, and meeting place. Announce a "lunch bunch" for first-timers, people interested in certification, people who want to swap tips on doing research on the Internet, etc.

10. *Schedule small success groups.* Create small group meetings or rap sessions on topics of interest. Give the groups time to meet on two or three occasions during the conference, then by e-mail during the year. Offer a "meet the pros" session. Attendees sign up in advance for thirty-minute round table discussions with a "pro," who will talk about a preannounced issue or topic.

11. *Foster follow-up.* Be bold about suggesting how people can follow up and stay in touch after the meeting—on the Internet, with conference calls, at regional or special interest group meetings.

12. *Find out with a focus group.* Ask attendees, "How could we make this a more network-friendly event?" Interview them at a breakfast focus group or with a fax poll. Trust them to tell you what helps them get the interaction they came for.

CHAPTER 18

Plug In to Technology

Suddenly, it's everywhere. A dazzling array of communication technologies is multiplying at a dizzying speed. Imagine, for example, a badge that swaps contact information with other badges. When you meet someone who shares your interests, your badges "recognize" each other and the devices' LEDs glow green. E-networking is likely to blow your socks off.

What will the future bring?

More convergence. Buy one device; it multitasks. How about wireless e-mail, a Web browser, a music player, a notepad, a personal datebook, and a digital camera all in one? It's here. How about instant messaging with voice recognition, language translation, and text-speech conversion? How about a unified messaging system? It will retrieve your e-mail, fax, or voice message right on the Internet, give you a phone number for receiving voice mail and fax, and read your e-mail to you over the phone. You can speak your reply; the system will attach it as an audio file to an e-mailed reply.

More miniaturization. Your information appliances will be smaller and smaller. They'll reside on your belt, or on your wrist, or in your eyeglasses.

More speed. How fast can we go? New communication vehicles will carry messages at speeds two hundred times faster.

More in your face. Instant messaging is spreading like wildfire. It's much faster than e-mail; it also demands your attention *now*.

197

More compatibility. Technologies will finally talk to each other. Interoperability is the name of the game.

More coverage. Planning on scaling Mount Everest? You'll be able to take your technology with you and any other place in the world you might go.

This technological proliferation is both good and bad for networkers. Wherever you are, you can plug in. But, the fact that communication is now instantaneous, portable, worldwide, and 24/7/365 means that managing the technology has become an issue. How can you make the most of your e-networking? Here are oodles of tips. Of course, with technology aging—or developing—in what seems like dog years, we can't guarantee that all these tips will still be useful when you are reading this chapter. If some of them are old hat, we apologize. For the latest, visit our Web site (*www.ContactsCount.com*) and sign up for our newsletter.

Know "E-Netiquette"

First and foremost, observe the protocols.

1. When you leave a voice message, say your name distinctly. Take a tiny breath between your first and last names to separate them. Spell your name if people have trouble understanding it.

2. When you leave a voice message in response to a voice message, let the person know when you'll be available to have a conversation, so that the phone tag won't continue.

3. When you sign up with a list discussion group, look for a frequently asked questions file. It will contain the rules for that discussion group.

4. E-mail programs allow you to attach sound, picture, and word files to e-mail messages or to insert them into messages. Be aware, however, that these files require extra download time and thus may irritate your recipient.

5. Don't list dozens of names in the To or Cc box.

6. Give each e-mail a specific subject. Don't just title it, "Message from Eleanor." That makes it hard for your recipient to find the specific e-mail in which you gave directions to the meeting.

7. Use words in your subject line that signal the message's level of importance, for example, urgent.

8. If you wouldn't stick a smiley face on a letter to this person, don't use emoticons (smileys).

9. When you're out of the office, use an auto reply to respond to every incoming message.

10. If your message doesn't require a reply, say so.

11. Don't leave the full text of a long message on your reply.

12. Copy as few people as possible. Don't automatically hit Reply to All.

13. Check out your organization's e-mail policies. Such policies may cover legal and security matters, the number of messages that you may send each day, and the style and tone you should be using.

Know Your Technology

Act as if you know what you're doing. Yes, even read the software manual, if necessary.

1. Don't double up on your communications. Don't send a letter, a fax, a voice mail, and an e-mail.

2. The way your messages look may be lost when you send them through the Internet to people who are using a different e-mail program to read them.

3. You can't use italics or bold in e-mail. You can use other characters, such as asterisks, to dress up a message.

4. Limit your line length to sixty-five or seventy characters across, or some recipients may receive the message with text wrapped at the wrong places or not wrapped at all.

5. Compose offline. If you are copying a document to your message area, save your document as a plain-text file, then copy it into the message area.

6. To clear out an overcrowded address box, assign group names.

7. Use filters and folders. Most e-mail programs let you route messages with identifiers, such as the name of the sender, to folders. You also can have messages automatically forwarded to an e-mail name in your address book.

8. You can make e-mail from clients, for example, turn red in your inbox. You also can sort by any category, subject, sender, or date you wish.

9. If you delay sending a message but don't change the date on it before you send it, your recipient may not see it, because it will hide back among already-read mail and won't be at the bottom of his inbox.

10. When a sender of unsolicited e-mail offers to remove you from a list, don't fall for the ruse. Replying just confirms that your e-mail account is active.

Up Your Visibility

Use the communication vehicles to present yourself and make yourself known.

1. Are all your contact numbers on your business card? Include your office address, phone number, 800 number, fax number, pager number, mobile phone number, e-mail address and Web site. You may also need to add your home e-mail. To squeeze all this on your card, you may have to print on

the back or have a fold-over card. Please do make your contact numbers big enough to read!

2. Create an e-mail address for yourself that reveals your name instantly. Don't use something inscrutable like lb3077x.com.

3. Do you want people to go to your or your company's Web site? Insert a live link.

4. The crafting of the message you have on your voice mail is as important as the design of your business card: Both should reflect your professionalism.

5. Compose an e-mail that contains information from your business brochure. That way, you have a prewritten follow-up "form letter" with your company information that you can quickly send to people.

> Create an e-mail "brochure" that you can zap out when someone asks about your business.

6. Use a signature line (it's like a letterhead) on your e-mail. It's automatically stamped at the bottom (or top) of every e-mail you send. If your e-mail program doesn't have a way to make a SIG file, type the information in a text file on your computer and copy and paste it to every e-mail you send. Include everything that's on your business card—and more. Add a slogan that will help people remember you.

7. Use a signature block to promote yourself in an acceptable way when you send a message in a list discussion group. Usually such groups frown on selling in any form.

8. Any time you send your Web address or any Web address, type it with http:// . . . . Most programs will let the recipient click on the address and go there instantly.

Demonstrate Your Character

Slow down and be careful as you use instant technologies. Take time to think first.

1. Make sure you know where the "uh-oh" or "oops" button is. It will take back messages you shouldn't have sent. (That's a joke, folks. No e-mail program has such a button, so *think* before you send.)

2. Take plenty of time to review every message, especially a sensitive or important one. Click on "send later" to give yourself time to reflect on what you've written.

3. Never send anything by *any* medium that is bigoted, racist, sexist, or sexy.

4. Always acknowledge and respond to personal e-mail, and do it in a timely way. You'll have to decide what timely means. An ignored e-mail conveys a poor image of you or your organization.

5. Be careful when you forward messages. It's as if you wrote them yourself.

6. If your company e-mail has a signature line and you insert your name above it, recipients (or the company's lawyers) may assume that you are speaking for the company. Be careful.

7. Courts have upheld a company's right to treat employee e-mail as its own property. Use your office e-mail for personal communications cautiously. Beware! E-mail gossip is dangerous. Don't send anything that you'd mind seeing posted on your company's bulletin board. There is no such thing as a private e-mail.

8. E-mail is not the best medium for working out negative incidents or for handling emotional disputes or hurt feelings. If you can't meet face-to-face with the person, at least call her

on the phone. In person or electronically, make this your goal: to disagree without being disagreeable.

Get Your Point Across—Efficiently

Do you think logically and clearly? Do you write well? Do you speak succinctly? These skills have become more and more necessary as you communicate via today's information devices.

1. What's people's number one complaint about the messages on their voice mail? Rambling. Know exactly what you're going to say. Write it down, if necessary. Put the most important issues up front. Limit the message to less than a minute. (You can speak about 150 words per minute.)

2. When you leave a message on voice mail, begin and end your message with your phone number. Make it easy and efficient for the person to call you back immediately

3. Use the subject line to deliver the entire message: Mtg. chgd to 9/16/02. All else same. EOM (end of message).

4. Include all vital information in your e-mail on the first screen. For long documents, put the contents or an executive summary on the first page. If a message is more than three screens long, send it as an attachment.

5. If you answer the questions Who? What? Where? When? Why? in your e-mail, you won't leave out essential information, like the time of a meeting. Check yourself using the five Ws.

6. Think before formatting. Simplify. Use headlines and subheads in your e-mail to direct attention to key issues or actions: Action Requested, Person to Contact, Deadline, How To, or Next Step. Use bullets. Write in short paragraphs and insert a blank line after each paragraph for readability.

7. When you reply, mention the topic. Don't send content-free replies, such as "Thanks" or "I agree!"

8. Spell check before you send.

9. Remember your ABCs. Before you send your message, check its accuracy, brevity, and clarity.

Make Contact

Building your network just got easier.

1. Do you want to find a list discussion group (or listserv, from the name of a software program used to run them)? With a little searching, you'll be able to find thousands of forums where you can share ideas, ask questions, and learn from others with common interests.

Hang on to that old school tie. Many universities offer online databases that help you find other alumni who can offer guidance and assistance.

2. If you are job hunting or changing careers, learn about a career field by joining a list discussion group.

3. Do you have a stack of business cards that you've not yet entered into your contact management system? Now you can buy a device that electronically scans and saves business cards. It also allows you to retrieve information using the name, title, company name, address, phone or fax number, or a memo you've added with the attached keyboard. The device also includes a notebook, a calendar with a reminder alarm, a calculator, and a built-in world time clock.

4. Want to do some e-networking? Visit a Web site and send a

short introductory e-mail to the creator or manager of the site to start a dialog.

5. To get acquainted with a regular correspondent, e-mail a photograph of yourself.

6. In face-to-face communication, we rely on gestures and non-verbal cues to supply part of the meaning. Be aware that e-mail lacks these meaning enhancers. That means that the words you use must be crystal clear and must also convey the emotional tone you want your message to have. When you communicate on the telephone or face-to-face, you know immediately whether your message has been received, understood, and mutually agreed to. You don't with e-mail.

7. *Fast Company* magazine has a global network of Friends of FC—leading businesspeople, provocative writers, out-of-the box thinkers, and cutting-edge educators—that it can contact to stay up-to-date on trends or to get feedback on an idea. Do you have a list like that?

8. Start a support group on your company intranet. Ask your human resources department about intranet policies in your workplace. Suggest a survey to discover what people are interested in. Your special-interest network can focus on a variety of topics: It might link people who are dealing with a family member who has Alzheimer's with community resources or link people in different departments who all deal with customer service issues.

9. You can post a question on a bulletin board where 3 or 4,003 people might see it. You may receive a far richer answer than if you called three or four people in your network.

10. Use instant messaging to spot who's online and hold a virtual meeting. This hybrid of e-mail and chat allows "live," one-on-one conversations or group conversations on line. We predict that new "netiquette" will be needed to deal with this intrusive, pop-up technology.

11. Use e-mail to send a colleague or coworker a pat on the back. If you want to make his eyes light up, type "Great job!" in the Subject line.

12. It's great to e-mail someone in Paris and not have to worry about the time difference. But if you are mailing to someone who has learned English as a second language, be especially careful. Be even more careful if you know your message will be translated.

13. Use message boards to share or get tips.

14. Do you put out a newsletter to promote your business? Be sure to provide valuable information along with ads. Don't sign up people automatically. Ask them. Be scrupulous about removing people who say, "Unsubscribe me!" from your mailing list.

15. E-mail doesn't cut it when you're trying to cultivate camaraderie and trust. And don't e-mail if you want to brainstorm. E-mail is not the place to rev up the energy, excitement, and chemistry you need for idea generation. Get face time. Have periodic meetings or retreats to bring people together, if possible.

16. Two randomly chosen documents on the Web are, on average, only nineteen clicks away from each other, reports *Science News*, kind of a nineteen (rather than six) degrees of separation.

PART 6

Win in Your Workplace

Are you cultivating a career in a corporation, or seeking success in sales, or pursuing professional services, or working at home in sweats, or pounding the streets job hunting? Networking can help you get the job done and advance your career.

If you're an employee, what's the number one way to hang on to your job, climb the ladder, and succeed? Network! If you're a salesperson, what's the best way to prospect for leads who quickly become customers? Network! If you're a professional, what's the classy and comfortable way to grow your client list? Network! If you're a home-based businessperson, what's the best way to stay in touch and access the resources you need to prosper? Network! Whatever your workplace, you'll find out how networking can take you to the top.

What if you're a worker without a workplace? Whether you're a brand new college grad, a former military officer looking for a second career, or someone who just wants to make the next move, you'll be able to use special networking skills most job hunters don't know about to find the perfect job faster or to leap from one career field to another.

CHAPTER 19

Network Inside

No matter where you work—a corporation, a government agency, a nonprofit, or an institution—networking at work has never been more important. Why?

With traditional corporate hierarchies and career paths rapidly becoming obsolete, people must increasingly rely on their own ability to build and mobilize informal networks at work.

Bonnie Nardi, design anthropologist at the AT&T Labs in Menlo Park, California, and her research team say that networks have emerged as the main form of social organization in the workplace. "Social networks," they say, "are key sources of labor and information in a rapidly transforming economy characterized by less institutional stability and fewer reliable corporate resources. The personal social network is fast becoming the only sensible alternative to the traditional 'org chart' for many everyday transactions in today's economy."

With the new communications technologies, we estimate that the typical businessperson now experiences several hundred interactions a day (phone calls, hallway conversations, e-mails). If you know what to say and do, you can use these encounters to get things done at work and to enhance your career.

Exec-U-Net, a Norwalk, Connecticut, firm that helps execs find new jobs, says that setting up a network of contacts, both inside and outside a company, is *the most important thing* an aspiring executive can do. The firm's research indicated that, to get a promotion, you are better off spending time networking than putting in long hours.

As we've worked with various organizations, we've discovered that some employees resist the idea of networking at work for several reasons.

Do you wonder how networking is perceived in your organization? Do you wonder if networking violates the corporate culture? Do you say to yourself, "Oh, I couldn't possibly do that here!"?

Do you worry that networking is not professional? Do you feel that's it's only for the salespeople? Do you say to yourself, "Oh, networking, that's sort of a smarmy, self-serving, sales thing, isn't it?"

Do you want your good work to stand on its own? Do you wish that people would automatically notice, reward, and promote you based on your work? Do you say to yourself, "Oh, I wouldn't feel comfortable tooting my own horn"?

In this chapter, you'll find lots of information and techniques for networking at work.

Why Network at Work?

Do you need to be convinced that the benefits of networking outweigh the efforts? Do you need to convince the powers that be that networking is working? Do you need to clarify networking's benefits for your organization and for you?

You need to network at work to:

Keep getting the big picture. Things change fast. Use your network to keep up with what's going on. We're told that at Corning Incorporated in 1999, 78 percent of sales were from products less than four years old. Employees there have to stay on their toes just to know what products their company makes. To check out changes in your workplace, take a look at the last few issues of your company's annual report.

Bolster the bottom line. Understand that your job depends on the success of the organization. Promote your organization's products and services—even if you're not in sales!

At a cocktail party at a conference of her professional association, Maggie met Patty, the association's vice president of finance and administration. "What exactly do you do on a typical day like today as VP of finance and administration?" she asked. Patty explained that she had been trying to get an 800 number that ended with the initials of the association from her current long-distance supplier. Maggie, who was director of public relations for another major long-distance company, offered to help, and when she got back to her office, she passed Patty's name along to a sales rep. He called Maggie a few days later to report that he had gotten Patty the 800 number she wanted and that she had switched the association's long-distance business to their company. The account was worth more than $9,000 a month in revenues.

Venture into the white spaces. Look at your company's organization chart. What do you see? Boxes linked by some vertical lines that indicate the chain of command? Now look between the boxes. What do you see? White space? In most organizations, that white space is unexplored territory for networking. That's where you'll find the unmet

The answer probably isn't in your office.

needs, the undiscovered problems, the opportunities, the connections that will enhance your career and allow you to contribute more to the organization's success.

Futurist Faith Popcorn says, "Whatever problem you're trying to solve, the answer is probably not in your office!"

"The organization chart is not the business," caution authors Geary Rummler and Alan Brache in their book *Performance: How to Manage the White Space on the Organization Chart.* "The greatest opportunities for improvement often lie in the white spaces between the boxes on the chart—in the functional and interpersonal interface—those points where the baton is being passed from one department to another or from one individual to another."

An enterprising Fairfax County, Virginia, government employee made a list of all the languages spoken by employees in various departments so that customers could be served. Her willingness to venture out helped her get a better job. It was a win for the county, a win for the citizens, and a win for her.

"At Corning, not only is there no wall between R&D and the business units, there is a constant tidal flow of unmanaged communication about problems and opportunities. This communication takes place between factories and researchers, and between individual scientists and individual business managers," reports *Fast Company* magazine.

Uncork bureaucratic bottlenecks. If you create temporary project teams to tackle problems and launch initiatives, you'll make a name for yourself. Increase collaboration with other departments.

When the corporate communications department at a major telecommunications firm invited the human resources department to lunch, it was the beginning of a rich collaboration. As people got to know one another, they integrated their strategic planning so that a human resources request for the production of a training calendar was on the corporate communications department's schedule. If you collaborate, you can negotiate to even out workload so that all the projects don't hit at the same time.

Patricia used her internal network to change an operational policy. As she was developing an amendment to the policy, she talked with a key contact in the operations department to find out the history and exact intent of the current policy. She was up front about her goal of changing the policy. Her contact suggested that she talk with two managers who had strong feelings about the policy. She interviewed those managers to determine their concerns. She researched and drafted her policy amendment. Then, she consulted with two of her peers to see if they had any additional information that she should consider. She also wanted to gain their support for her proposal. One of them told her about some recent legal developments that she was unaware of.

Without her network, Patricia might have created an unacceptable proposal. With her network, she was able to get the information and feedback she needed and to build support for the amendment among key people. Her policy change was accepted.

Any time you are working on something that will affect people outside your own department, take the time to "field-test" your idea. That way, you'll build support for the idea because you've included others in the process. "No surprises" is a cardinal rule of corporate life. Pretesting ideas prevents surprises.

Expand your knowledge base. Figure out what resources you need and put together a network made up of people representing many different interests and areas of expertise. If you introduce your contacts to one another, you can encourage information and skill sharing among all the members of the group. Your network can be a kind of informal, highly customized, personal business Yellow Pages.

Robert E. Kelley, author of *How to Be a Star at Work*, says, "Networks are the high-speed infrastructure upon which knowledge is sent and received by those who need it. Without these networks, professionals cannot do their jobs, and companies might just as well shut their doors."

Get out of that rut. If you network, you expose yourself to new ideas and ways of doing things. This cross-pollination almost always benefits the organization.

Create your safety net. You need to network to:

▶ Increase your visibility within the corporation, nonprofit group, or government agency so that opportunities find you!

▶ Take responsibility for the management of your career. If you network effectively, you'll create career opportunities for yourself.

▶ Explore options in case your job goes away.

In these days of rightsizing and restructuring, it's smart to keep your ears open for opportunities within your organization and to make yourself visible.

Determine what skills you have that could be used in other areas of the organization. Figure out how to showcase those skills. What can you do to make others aware of your capabilities?

Maria offered to manage the 10-K run for a local charity. Sue noticed how much the community sponsors liked working with her and how well organized she was. When a job opened up in Sue's department, she thought of Maria.

Jim wanted to move from a technical area into training. When managers were invited to teach a career management course, Jim volunteered. He was able to brush up on training skills as he took the train-the-trainer course and to showcase his teaching skills as he presented the career course. When the training department was looking for a technical trainer, Jim's name came up, and he was able to make the switch.

As you network to enhance your career mobility, figure out what you have to give in the networking relationship. If you are intent only on gaining from the relationship, you may feel uncomfortable.

Margo was editor of the company newspaper. Since she had a good background in political science as well as in journalism, she wanted to move into governmental affairs. At a reception given by the company political action committee, she met George, who was director of the company's governmental affairs department. Margo talked with him about her goal of working in the governmental affairs area. In the course of their conversation, she also found out that George was expecting his children to visit over the Christmas holiday and was wondering what activities he could provide for them. Margo, who had children of about the same age, was able to suggest several fun excursions. One way to give information and ideas to someone who outranks you is to look beyond your job expertise.

If you network in this way, you'll never have to worry about career resiliency and lifetime employability.

Assess Your Corporate Culture

Perhaps you've decided, as you've thought about the reasons to network and read about successful inside networkers, that you need to work on your network. Begin by assessing your corporate culture. Then go on to consider the current state of your network.

Is your organization network-friendly? To determine how supportive your workplace is, ask yourself these questions:

▶ Do those at the top recognize that networking is valuable?

▶ Do corporate executives ever mention networking?

▶ Is training offered? (You can suggest networking workshops.)

▶ Is networking during office hours considered *not* working?

▶ Are you encouraged to belong to professional associations and to attend both monthly meetings and conferences?

▶ Are you encouraged to volunteer in the community, serve on boards, etc.?

▶ Is it easy (and expected) for you to collaborate with people in other departments—to venture out into the white space on the organization chart?

▶ How much money does your organization spend on professional association dues and conferences? How much does it spend on collateral expenses, such as travel, lodging, etc.? Is anyone tracking whether the organization is getting its money's worth?

▶ Are networking activities or goals part of your annual performance plan?

▶ Are you rewarded when your networking contributes to the success of the organization?

Recognize that in some organizations, networking violates the cultural ground rules. If that's your assessment, talk with your boss and your colleagues about the reasons for encouraging inside networking. Use ideas from this chapter to convince them that networking at work pays off, both for the organization and for the individual.

Recognize that in some organizations, the word *networking* makes people uncomfortable. Don't be fooled. A lot of networking is probably going on, but under the alias of "relationship building" or "teamwork" or "collaboration."

Some forward-thinking organizations are deliberately working toward creating a more collaborative culture, setting up mentoring programs, sponsoring women's networks and minority networks, and providing ways for people to interview others and discuss lateral moves and opportunities for upward mobility.

Even if you've decided that your organization's culture isn't very network-friendly, you'll still find ideas in this chapter that will work for you. Don't focus on self-serving objectives; rather, focus on serving customers, streamlining internal processes, getting the job done, and having an impact on the bottom line.

How Strong Is Your Inside Network?

Use this quiz to rate the strength of your current inside network.

1. Do you know people at all levels of the organization? Do they know your name and what you do?

2. Do you know all the people whose work intersects yours in any way?

3. Do you know people who have jobs you might like to have someday?

4. Are you involved in any cross-functional efforts or interdepartmental activities (temporary assignments, committees, task forces, special projects, volunteer activities)?

5. Are you plugged into the grapevine? Do you find out quickly what's up?

6. Do you take every opportunity to meet face-to-face to define and discuss complex problems, shifting priorities, or areas of responsibility?

7. Do you know and talk with others about trends that will affect your job in the future and the tools to get the job done today?

8. Do you have effective internal channels through which to send information?

9. When you see a problem that involves people from various areas, do you take the initiative to bring people together to solve it?

10. Do you drop by to see people—even when you don't need anything?

Could you answer yes to most of those questions? If not, make building your inside network a priority.

Map Out a Plan

Draw a map of your contacts. On a big piece of paper, draw a circle and put your name inside it. Then draw circles with the names of everyone at work that you interact with. Add circles with the names of everyone you think you should interact with. If you don't know the name of one of these people, use his title or describe the type of job he has. For example, you may decide you want to know the editor of the corporate newsletter or some person in the IS department who can troubleshoot problems. You can find out those people's names later. Who else do you want or need to know in order to solve problems, contribute to the bottom line, uncork bottlenecks, or create career security? This map is your current and potential network at work.

On your map, rate each relationship:

Write + 1 next to the name of any person with whom you believe you have a positive, mutually beneficial relationship.

Write -1 next to the name of any person with whom you believe you have a negative, unpleasant, or unproductive relationship.

Write 0 next to the name of any person with whom you have no relationship or a neutral relationship.

Stop: Do Not Read Further Until You Have Made Your Map!

You may be amazed as you take a few minutes and analyze your map.

Where is your circle? At the center of the page? At the top? How big is your circle compared to the other circles? Do they vary in size?

Did you connect all the other circles to your own circle with lines? Did you arrange the other circles in any way? You may gain some insights into the distance you perceive between yourself and other people by this analysis. What else can you discover about your network? Do you have a lot of 0 ratings? What does that tell you? Are there lots of circles without names?

Next, create your strategic plan to increase the breadth of your network, the strength of your network, and the effectiveness of your network.

Using your map, make a list of everyone who has a + 1 by his name. Begin with this group.

The next time you get together with one of these people, take the opportunity to mention the way the two of you have worked together—the problems you've solved, the processes you've improved, the projects you've collaborated on. Remind the person of milestones in the history of your relationship—how you met, what you have done for each other, your successes, and even your failures. Say how much you appreciate that person. Let that person know that you want to continue your relationship and to enhance it. Verbalize your trust in that person and your reliance on that person's expertise. Ask for that person's help and offer your help. You don't have to be specific. Say, "I know I can count on you to brainstorm with me when I need a good idea. You know you can always call on me for help." Use these meetings to confirm your relationship.

Resolve to consistently be on the lookout for ways in which you can contribute to that person's success and to stay in touch on a regular basis, even when you don't need anything. You might want to suggest that you have lunch once a month, for example.

Next, make a list of everyone who has an 0 by his name. Choose someone on the list and come up with a concrete reason for getting together. You might say, for example, "I'd like to work with you to streamline this process. I'd like to explore how we could cut several days out of the processing time." Or, if you are thinking about your career, you might say, "Long-term, I'd like to make a move from my staff position to one that has more impact on the bottom line. I'd like to know how you did it."

Remember that in order to get, you must give. As you become acquainted, listen for that person's workplace goals and challenges so that you can contribute. Listen Generously so that you can give more than you receive. Take every opportunity to be helpful.

Understand that you will need to meet face-to-face with the person six to eight times in order to build a mutually trusting and beneficial relationship. Trust is built on an appreciation of the other person's Character and Competence. Learn about the other person and teach that person to trust you. Put those meetings on your calendar over a period of six months or so. Supplement those meetings with e-mail, phone, fax, etc.

Finally, ask yourself what's going on with the relationships you rated -1. If one of these relationships involves a person with whom you absolutely must work effectively, put a higher priority on repairing that situation.

"But," you may be saying to yourself, "you don't know Joe—he's impossible!" Or, "Nobody could work with Kayla!" It's true. Sometimes you must deal with difficult people. And sometimes sticky situations and shrinking resources can make even the nicest people hard to get along with. If that's the case, see the situation as an opportunity to develop your own influencing skills. Get a copy of *The Empowered Manager: Positive Political Skills at Work* by Peter Block. Learn his system for cultivating Allies and for limiting the negative impact of adversaries, opponents, bedfellows and fence-sitters. Block would suggest meeting with the problem person and saying something like this: "In the past, we've had conflicts. I'd like to change that so that when we work together, it's positive and productive. Let's talk about how we can overcome the past and start fresh."

Suggest ground rules for the way you'll work together in the future. You might say, "When you see a problem, suppose you come to me first, rather than talking to Sue and Bill and Wang." Or, "If your people are running behind by more than thirty-six hours, I'd appreciate your letting me know so that we can adjust things here."

You may or may not be able to improve the relationship or even get the project back on track, but your sense of confidence and your reputation as a relationship builder will grow.

If you have tried to change the nature of your interactions without success, give up and spend your time and energy on someone who is more amenable to working with you.

Put It in Your Planner

Whatever your job description, some percentage of your work time should be spent building this inside network. You decide. Pull out your planner or Palm Pilot and begin to schedule your networking. Just having lunch once a week with a networking contact would give you fifty opportunities to strengthen, broaden, and deepen your working relationships. Make networking a way of life, not something else on your to-do list.

Pair Up with Peers

It's valuable to exchange information with your peers, people at your own level throughout your organization. Jerry, who worked in the corporate planning department, happened to sit down at the same lunch table with Marcia, who was the corporate speechwriter. He told her about his involvement with the school district where he lived. She said she'd just written a speech on education for the chairman of the board and knew that he was very interested in finding a way to support projects like the one Jerry was working on. She suggested that Jerry talk with the chairman about corporate funding for the project. Jerry did and was tapped to head up the corporation's efforts with educational institutions.

> The networking Ta
> Take networking of
> your to-do list and
> make it a way of li

Your peers can provide support for you outside your own work group. They can give you information that is vital to your career. And they can increase your visibility in the organization. Cliff, an engineer, in a conversation with Amy, told her about his involvement in church activities. When Amy, a meeting planner, was looking for someone to give the invocation at the annual holiday luncheon, she thought of Cliff. At the luncheon, Cliff demonstrated his public speaking skills and later was tapped to handle an important executive presentation.

Also network with people who have jobs like yours, but who work in other industries. A professional association can provide those opportunities, bringing together people from a variety of companies. Be on the lookout for ideas that will help your organization succeed.

Industry-specific organizations bring you in touch with people in other companies. Home builders and their suppliers are all members of the National Association of Home Builders. They face similar problems, and they rely on each other for good ideas. Getting visibility in such groups may increase your job mobility, since there is usually a lot of opportunity for job movement among similar organizations. Within some industry-specific groups, there often are subgroups for people with various kinds of jobs—remodelers, for example.

Understand Power

At work, people with titles that are higher than yours may intimidate you. However, titles alone do not make people powerful in organizations. You may already have more power than you realize. Or you may be able to develop more power, even without getting promoted. At the very least, understanding where power comes from can help reduce your feelings of intimidation when you are dealing with people "up the ladder."

It's commonly said that the people on the front lines or the factory floor have the power to make or break the organization. In training classes throughout corporate America, there's been talk about "flipping the pyramid." In this way of looking at organizations, the people at the bottom of the organization are shown on top to make the point that executives should be supporting those people. Empowerment of employees not only is one of today's buzzwords, but also makes good business sense.

Titles and job descriptions give people one kind of power. There are other kinds of power that are available to everyone.

Respect bestows power. Natural leaders gain this kind of power because of the way they act, their charisma, and their personalities. The best way to gain this kind of power is to watch the people who have it and to model your behavior after theirs.

You've probably heard people say that information is power. It's true. Expertise and experience make people powerful. As you master your job, as you learn more, as you achieve, you can become more powerful. This kind of power comes from knowing more than most other people. You can take every opportunity to increase your knowledge and the information you have about your business and your industry.

Finally, there's the power that comes from the ability to provide rewards or punishments in organizations. Certainly, it can be intimidating to talk with the person who has the power to fire or promote you. But anyone who can influence the flow of resources can reward or punish. Punishment takes place when resources or information are withheld, rewards when they are provided freely. Secretaries who control who gets in to see the boss wield this kind of power.

So, when you feel intimidated by someone, analyze what kind of power he has. Simply understanding that person's source of power may help you to overcome your feelings.

Stay in Touch with Subordinates

When you talk with subordinates throughout the organization, use these tactics:

▶ Learn their names and use them.

▶ Ask specific questions in order to gain meaningful information.

▶ Work to create a climate in which bad news can be given to you.

People at levels below yours are excellent sources of support and information. In every interaction, introduce yourself and get to know people. Then, when you need help, you'll know whom to call. When your computer is down, do you call the Help Desk, or do you call Angie, who runs the Help Desk? There's a difference in the quality of support you will get if you make these relationships personal. Is that kind of wooing of subordinates manipulative? Not if you are sincere about your interest in them as people and in collaborating to serve your customers. Contact them frequently, not just when you need something. Remember reciprocity. Try to give as well as get. If nothing else, give appreciation for a job well done. There is never enough of that!

> **Don't let anyone tell you that talk is cheap. Conversational skills are important business assets.**

As the boss, you are responsible for initiating conversations with subordinates; it's only good manners. Even more than that, it's the way to create an environment in which your subordinates will feel free to give you bad news. Getting honest, straightforward information from the people who work for you may be vital to your success.

Much has been said in management literature about the power of "managing by walking around." Often, however, managers have no idea what to say as they walk around. They say things like "What's new?" or "What's going on." These questions put their conversation partner's mind on overload. He thinks of too many topics. The predictable answer is, "Not much." As a boss, ask specific questions—the more specific the better.

Here are some ideas for questions to ask subordinates that will provoke meatier responses:

▶ "What's the most challenging thing you're working on? Why is it challenging?"

▶ "What's the most recent thing you've learned about doing your job?"

▶ "If you could change one thing around here, what would it be? Why haven't we done it already?" (If you ask this question, be prepared to deal with the answer!)

▶ "What's your best skill? How did you develop it?"

▶ "If a problem comes up, what are a couple of strategies you use to tackle it?"

If an employee presents you with a problem, ask, "How could you handle that?" Only if the employee truly can't handle it should you ask, "How could I best help with that?"

Don't worry about having all the answers before you begin having these kinds of conversations. If something comes up that stumps you, say, "I don't know the answer to that one. I'll get back to you by the end of the week." Write the problem down and get back to the employee within the specified time period.

Score with Superiors

When you talk with people whose titles are higher than yours, use these tactics:

▶ Prepare, practice, role-play.

▶ Be aware of the difficulty of conveying bad news up the organizational hierarchy.

▶ Talk about topics on which you have equal or more expertise.

Be prepared. If you're talking "up the ladder," be sure you are well prepared. Plan, rehearse, even role-play the conversation. That way, you'll feel more sure of yourself. Watch for a tendency to chatter too much. Research indicates that the lower-ranked person will talk more than the higher-ranked person, probably out of nervousness. Curb that tendency.

Decide when to pass on bad news. In organizations, there's a prevalent notion that "they shoot the messenger around here." That explains why it's so difficult for bad news to travel upward in organizations. In your organization, is it a myth or the truth that messengers with bad news are "shot"?

Be the expert. It's one thing to be talking about work topics to someone who intimidates you. It's another thing to be talking about other topics. Usually, you'll feel less intimidated when you are talking about nonwork topics. Steer the conversation to a topic about which you both have equal amounts of information or a topic in which you are the expert. Talking about sports, for example, may create a more equitable situation. That may explain why sports conversations occur as often as they do in organizations. You may even have more expertise than the person who intimidates you has. Archie once had an interesting conversation with baseball Hall-of-Famer George Brett on the subject of baseball card collections—a topic on which Archie was the expert.

Be Aboveboard

Networking with people who are above you in your organization can be intimidating. You may feel uncomfortable and concerned that others will think you are bootlicking. You can avoid those negative feelings by getting in touch with your Agenda. Be sure it's an up-front Agenda, not a hidden Agenda. Examples of hidden Agendas are: "I want to snow this person" or "I want this person to like me better than my colleague so that I will be picked for a promotion." These are not Agendas that you would want displayed as headlines in tomorrow's newspaper. If you are only trying to curry favor, you will—and should—feel uncomfortable. People with these kinds of motives are the ones who are accused of buttering up the boss and are scorned by both their colleagues and the boss, to whom their tactics are painfully obvious.

There's a small but significant difference in an up-front Agenda that you would be comfortable showing to the world. You can legitimately work from these Agendas, for example: "In this conversation, I want to clearly demonstrate to my boss the level of my expertise on this subject." Or, "I want my fund-raising skills to be visible, so that I'm a natural candidate for the new venture." In both cases, you'd probably feel fairly comfortable communicating your up-front Agenda to your boss or subordinate.

If you sincerely and openly network with everyone in your organization—your work group, your subordinates, and your peers, not just people above you in the organization—you will feel more comfortable. That kind of openness will become your way of operating in the organizational environment.

After Organizational Earthquakes, Rebuild Your Network

Reorganizations, mergers, acquisitions, layoffs—they are still an inescapable part of the corporate scene. One thing is sure: Any corporate upheaval destroys the relationships you've carefully built within your organization.

You may feel like hunkering down and hiding. Don't. Reconstruct your network, using these ideas:

▶ Acknowledge that the "good old days" are gone forever, then (quickly) commit yourself wholeheartedly to the new enterprise.

▶ Focus up. Let your boss know that you are ready to help to create the new order.

▶ Bring your subordinates on board. Meet one-on-one for lunch. Or get together after work. Recreate the pre-upheaval camaraderie. Recommit to doing a good job. Look forward, not backward.

▶ Reach out to peers you relate with on the job—anyone whose job intersects with yours.

▶ Escape your cubicle and build new bridges with related departments, functions, and divisions.

▶ Volunteer for cross-departmental teams and activities.

▶ Spend time shoring up relationships with customers, clients, suppliers, and vendors. (If they believe your company is in chaos, they may defect. Be positive. Also remember that these networking contacts could provide your next job.)

▶Find ways to relate to competitors, perhaps through industry associations. Always be upbeat and positive about what's been going on in your organization. Boost your company's reputation every chance you get. (Remember that your next job could come from your current competitor.)

Avoid Erroneous Assumptions

Know the rules. Here are eight erroneous assumptions that you'll want to avoid as you network at work.

1. Assuming that people you work with are automatically part of your network. Not true. You must create and nurture the relationships.

2. Assuming that everyone is an equally good networking contact. Not true. Seek out the experts and people who will give back. As you talk with people in your network, agree to respond quickly to their requests.

3. Assuming that you can ask for information or help without giving first. Not true. Listen Generously to your contact. Does that person need something that you can supply? If you can't discover anything, ask, "How can I help you?"

4. Assuming that you can access anyone. Not true. The best contacts are busy people. Use referrals, references, and introductions by a third party. And become known for the people you connect.

5. Assuming that you can get by without doing your homework. Not true. Don't waste your contact's time. When you ask for something, do as much study or research as you can. That will provide you with some basic information. Jot down what you've found as you've tried to solve the problem or find the out-of-the-ordinary information. Note any blind alleys you discovered. Form your question(s) carefully. Make your quest interesting and intriguing for your contact. Link

your question or need to something of interest to your contact. That way, you're not just asking for a handout. Is there a payoff for him? Try to find one. If you can't, be sure you volunteer to help him—and follow through.

6. Assuming that your request is so important that your contact will drop everything to answer it yesterday. Not true. Make sure you give your contact enough time. If you need something, don't procrastinate. Ask early, before you are desperate.

7. Assuming that when you receive the information, the interaction is over. Not true. Get back in touch to tell your contact the rest of the story and what use you made of what he gave you.

8. Assuming that muttering "thanks" as you are talking with your contact is enough. Not true. Say thank you with panache. Send a handwritten note. Take your contact out to lunch. Send a funny card. Send flowers. Write a note to your contact's boss. Take every opportunity to give credit publicly.

CHAPTER 20

Rev Up Referrals

What if, all over town, there were people who knew your business so well and were so invested in your success that they consistently referred just the right kind of clients and resources to you? What an impact that could have on your business!

Of course, you're probably already getting some referrals from past customers and contacts. But what if you made getting referrals a major part of your overall sales strategy? If you want industrial-strength networking, join or start a referral group.

In this chapter, you'll find out how referral groups work, how to pick one or start one, how to make yours succeed, how to plan activities to help members get to know one another's businesses, and how to do the right things—and avoid the pitfalls—so that you reap the benefits.

See How They Run

It's 7 A.M. Members are gulping coffee and gobbling bagels. By 7:15, they're getting down to business. First, they take turns delivering "thirty-second commercials" designed to remind everyone of the basics of their individual enterprises. Next, three members present ten-minute briefings on their products or services. A travel agent drapes a lei around the shoulders of her business suit and tells about her new Hawaiian package tour. A handyman describes how he saved the day for a homeowner who frantically called him from work after a neighbor noticed an ominous stream of water gushing forth under the garage door. A stockbroker talks about his favorite high-tech stocks.

After the briefings, members—who have already been to the bank with the income from business referred to them *by* other members or business *from* other members—jump up to say thanks. People also give thanks for resources, business advice, and valuable contacts. By 8:15, members are heading for their offices or businesses.

We tracked the progress of one group of seventy people over a one-year period. The dollars reported ranged from a low of $3,100 worth of referred business in one week to more than $94,000. (OK, there's a Lexus dealer in the group who got the lion's share of that week's business.)

> **It's not the amount time but the quality of the interaction that counts in networking.**

"I got 25 percent of my business through the network one year," says Bob, a commercial photographer. His group is a nonprofit organization in Virginia that grew out of several local business and community groups. Participants are required to provide a total of at least twenty leads a year for others in the organization, which meets every other week. "That puts everyone in the group on your sales force," Bob says.

Many referral clubs are run as profit-making businesses: You pay an entry fee and monthly charges to participate. Look on the Internet under "Business Referral Clubs" to find out more about charges, benefits, and requirements.

In local chapters of Ali Lasen's Leads Clubs, business owners, salespeople, managers, and professionals give brief presentations and exchange leads. The clubs offer workshops on networking, a free newsletter, and ways to advertise your business.

Business Network International (BNI) provides a structured and supportive system of giving and receiving business. The founder, Ivan

Misner, claims that some participants have added as many as fifty new clients in the first two years. BNI points out that you might spend as much as $1,500 for a one-time newspaper ad. But for a small membership fee, a local BNI club can turn thirty or forty other club members into your own sales force. Their statistics assert that the average member gives about forty-five leads per year. BNI has chapters in many countries around the world, from Malaysia to Sweden.

One of the members is Vincent, a builder in Van Nuys, California. Leads from a real estate broker in his chapter who recommended him for two remodeling jobs brought him $90,000 worth of work. The added business is great, says Vincent, but more important to the long-term growth of his firm are the networking skills he has gained. "I'm a better networker now just because I spend time doing it," he says.

PowerCore, based in Atlanta, has referral clubs in many states, from North Carolina to Texas, and claims about 3,500 members nationally. Founded by Wendy Kinney, PowerCore's process gets results. A unique internal mentoring program called PowerLinks helps new members get connected. Area coordinators and coaches also are active in helping new members get up to speed fast.

Kinney's half-day InfoMercial Workshop, which is free to members, helps members develop networking skills and self-promotion tools.

Three types of businesses benefit the most from PowerCore referral groups, reports Kinney: highly competitive businesses (such as real estate, insurance, or remodeling), service or information-based businesses (such as Web design and printing), and businesses that are so new or unique that potential customers don't even know they exist.

Bill, a former naval officer turned real estate agent, attributes more than $60,000 in commissions to referrals from his PowerCore club in his second year of membership. Lucy, who sells nutritional supplements, finds that the continued contact at weekly PowerCore meetings helps her break through the negative image some people have of network marketing companies like the one she's involved with. Terry, who owns a franchise business, raves that in his first year with the club, 10.5 percent of all his business came through Power-Core. In his second year of involvement, that figure leaped to 21 percent. In 2000 he expected to add another 10 percent.

Shop Around

Shop around until you find a group that meets your needs.

To find groups, ask people in your network. Sometimes groups are sponsored by chambers of commerce or government small business development agencies. Others are the brainchildren of individual businesspeople. One very successful club in Maryland was started by a bridal consultant and a stockbroker. Watch your newspaper for meeting notices. Check with your library to see if it has a list of groups. Call the chamber of commerce. Inquire at local business support centers run by universities or community colleges, or ask the Small Business Administration.

New groups are springing up, and membership in established groups is booming. The variety of formats and systems is amazing. The cost of membership in a club varies widely. Some groups charge an initial entry fee. Others just charge per meeting. Some charge enough to fund joint advertising projects or a newsletter to help members get to know one another. Nonprofit groups may charge only for refreshments. Others include the price of breakfast or lunch in the meeting charge. Some charge only when you show up. Others require that you pay three to six months in advance. Some groups meet in a restaurant or hotel. Others find meeting space at the office or store of a member to keep costs down. Find a model that works for you.

One group in Arizona has 146 members; other groups swear that 12 to 15 is optimal. Most groups allow only one business of a particular kind to participate. That means, for instance, that one travel agent isn't competing (in the group) against another travel agent. Other groups allow anyone to join. Some groups carefully track and report on every lead given and taken. Other groups are much more informal and still get results.

The Arizona group teaches its members to say, "I'm a resource for anything you need." Members hand out one another's cards. Even though the group is very large, smaller Success Teams, made up of four to six people, get together each week for lunch. They know that learning more about how to help one another is a prerequisite for success.

Most referral groups publish some kind of membership roster, brochure, or flyer for members to give to their clients whenever appropriate. One Maryland group publishes a newsletter that introduces both members and prospects to the businesses. That group has also tried some joint advertising, using the theme "Do business with people you trust."

You sell not only what you make, but who you are.

Can your business profit from a referral group? Some types of businesses tend to achieve quicker results—read referrals—than others. Caterers, gift services, bridal consultants, travel agents, printers, and florists are examples of businesses that do well. Accountants, lawyers, architects, doctors, and financial planners must be more patient to make their memberships pay off.

The amount of trust it takes to turn over your financial future to someone is much greater than the amount of trust it takes to turn over the printing of your next business card. Remember, too, that the dollar amounts of the referrals vary greatly. Dave, a real estate agent, passed along a remodeling job to Chuck that eventually netted him $62,000. LeeAnn, a computer consultant, gave Jerry a lead for his advertising specialties business that resulted in an order for twenty T-shirts, with a $200 value.

The most effective groups recognize that three ingredients build strong referral groups:

1. The quality of members. Choose people who are known for their Character and Competence.

2. The quality of the referrals. Give leads that are qualified and preferably come with a personal introduction from you.

3. The quality of the members' networking skills. Teach members how to cultivate relationships and proactively look for business opportunities for each other.

Check It Out

Investigate groups before you join. Find out about:

1. Membership and other fees. Low-cost groups may be as effective as high-cost groups.

2. Attendance rules. Some groups ask members who miss a certain number of meetings to give up their seat to someone else in that business category.

3. Expectations about how many leads a member must provide. How much pressure is there to produce? Sometimes the quality of the leads diminishes when people are hounded for quantity.

4. Time commitments. In addition to the scheduled meetings, how much additional time is required?

5. Leadership responsibilities. Will you be expected to serve on committees?

6. Entrance requirements. Are there rules about the size of your business or how long you have been in business?

7. Categories of businesses in the group. Is the group noncompetitive, with only one member per category?

8. What members say about the group's value. What is the turnover?

9. The group's reputation in the business community. What do people think of the group?

10. The group's track record. How long has the group has been in existence? What bottom-line value do members place on their participation?

Don't Just Join, Join In

Once you sign up, take your share of responsibility for making the group an effective referral source for you. Here are some guidelines for participating:

▶Be there. If you don't attend every time, you won't reap the benefits.

▶Give it time. Referral group leaders say that it takes a year for your business to begin getting the number and kind of referrals that make a big difference in your bottom line. Advertising gurus say that prospects must hear or see your message nine times before they become customers. And, since prospects aren't really paying attention two-thirds of the time, it takes twenty-seven exposures to make nine impressions. If your group meets every other week, that's a year's worth of exposures before your message sinks in.

> Network with competitors so that you can refer business that's too small, too big, too far away—or simply something you have no interest in doing.

▶Create sound bites. As you do your "thirty-second commercial" over and over, vary it so that it focuses on the different aspects of your business and attach a one- or two-sentence Success Story to give a vivid example.

Don, the vice president of sales and marketing for a temporary agency, never introduces himself with his title. Instead, he says things like:

We screen our temporaries—screen like we're panning for gold. Last week, a customer called me and said, "We made our project deadline, thanks to the incredible people you sent us."

Do you need an extra pair of hands? My agency can send you people who are experts on any of eighteen different software packages. We're the people power people.

Don holds up a paper doll he bought at a party supply store. As he talks, he pulls that one paper doll out into a string of twenty-five. "Whatever you're short of, we have someone with that skill who can be there within twenty-four hours. Yesterday, I filled a request for a bilingual receptionist in less than three hours."

▶Help the group grow. Bring prospective members whose businesses represent unfilled categories. If your group doesn't have a photographer, find one who'd be interested in joining and whose expertise and business practices would reflect well on you and the other members. Be alert for prospective members whose customers might also need your services. If you build decks, find a landscaper. The homeowner who is interested in putting in a rock garden might also want a new deck.

> **Create customer-common alliances with other business-people. Refer your customers to your allies and get referrals in return.**

▶Demonstrate your Character and Competence. In everything you do and say, show people that they can trust you. Then they won't hesitate to refer you to one of their customers or friends.

▶Get together in ever-changing groups of three or four outside the referral group meeting to learn more about how you can help one another get business.

▶Tell people how they can help you.

▶Listen Generously so that you know what kinds of information or leads to give. The Reciprocity Principle *does* work. If you give, you will receive.

▶Ask others in the group for feedback—about how you introduce yourself, about how to describe your business. Others will help you refine what you say to make it as effective as possible.

▶Encourage the group to provide books or training programs or hire networking specialists to do workshops to enhance members' skills.

▶Practice all the networking skills in this book and teach them to others.

Start Small

To speed your success, do one-month blitzes. Put together success teams of four or five members, and use these ideas to strengthen your relationships quickly. The next month, create new teams. Here are twelve ideas for success teams:

1. Meet several times. Eat lunch or breakfast together.

2. Give each team member ten of your business cards to hand out to potential clients or customers.

3. Test each other to make sure *each one of you* can describe— accurately and vividly—exactly what your teammates have to offer.

4. Visit each other's places of business.

5. Ask each member of the team to describe his ideal customer (or an actual customer) in detail so that you know what type of customer each member of the team is looking for.

6. Ask each team member to tell you about a current business or personal challenge and do *everything in your power* to assist him in coming up with a solution.

7. Designate a spokesperson to share your team's experience with the rest of the members at a regular meeting of the referral group.

8. Talk about where you might find or run across people to refer team members to. Keep the idea of referrals at the top of your mind.

9. Ask each team member to tell stories about satisfied customers or clients. Why exactly were they so happy with the team member's product or service?

10. Provide a special incentive for team members to try your product or service and to experience how good you are.

11. Brainstorm with the other team members how else you might be able to help one another.

12. Teach these activities to others in the referral group.

Spice Up the Meetings

After several months, Jan's group was getting stale. The steering committee decided that it was time to change the meeting format and wake people up. They decided to start off every meeting with three, five-minute one-on-ones. In pairs, members were asked to discuss questions that would nudge them out of "Ho-hum" and into "No kidding?"

Here are the questions they used over several months:

▶ How did you get started doing what you do? Why are you in the business you're in?

▶ Where is your place of business? Describe how to get there from here. Is it the best place for your business to be? What are the pros and cons?

▶ What's your problem/concern/ challenge today or this week? Brainstorm possible resources or solutions with your partner.

▶ What's your unique capability? What do you do that most oth-

> **Don't allow conversations to deteriorate into clichés, comments on the weather, and chitchat about the ball scores.**

ers in your line of work don't do? If you don't have a unique capability, what could it be?

▶ Describe a recent satisfied customer. How do you know that the person was satisfied?

▶ If you had a smart person to help you all day today, what would you have that person do?

▶ What one thing gets you down? What do you do to get "up" again?

▶ What's the one reason for your success so far? What have you done right?

▶ What's the best mistake you ever made—the one that you learned the most from?

▶ What would you like to quit doing in your business?

▶ What would you like to start doing in your business?

▶ If money were no obstacle, what would you need to improve your business?

▶ What other two members' businesses are most compatible with yours? (For example, what businesses target the same customers?)

▶ What did you learn in school that is not true?

▶ What did your mom or dad tell you that is true?

▶ What's your best marketing tool?

▶ What would you like a prospective customer to hear about your business?

▶ What motivates you?

▶ What do you get the biggest kick out of?

▶ When is your slowest time of the year? What do you do about that?

Start Your Own

Some groups struggle along. Perhaps too many of the members are start-ups. Perhaps turnover is high because people have unrealistic expectations about the amount of business they'll get—and how quickly they'll get it. Some people who don't understand the need for trust expect instant referrals. Perhaps the group is *supposed* to be a referral group, but spends a lot of its time listening to programs about topics that are irrelevant to members' business growth. (One group's newsletter listed the following programs: "What's New at the Zoo," "Argentina Today," and "The Responsibility of the Media in a Democratic Society"!) Perhaps people just plain don't have the networking skills it takes to be good referrers. If you are involved with a struggling group, don't assume that the *idea* doesn't work, assume that the *group* doesn't work. One solution is to start your own.

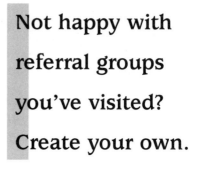

Not happy with referral groups you've visited? Create your own.

There are pros and cons to starting your own referral group. The biggest plus is that you can hand-pick members, rather than link up with an already established group of people. Another benefit of starting your own group is that you'll have lots of input to design a meeting format that gives you maximum interaction. If you put together a small steering committee, there will be several of you to handle the finances, find the meeting place, and set ground rules—all important, but time-consuming, activities.

The design of some groups shows real strategic genius. The president of a security systems company carefully teaches his salespeople, who are scattered throughout the country, how to start their own referral groups. He shows them how to select the core group, so that members are from businesses that serve customers who will probably also need burglar alarms and fire safety equipment.

Remember, whether you join a group or start your own, each group has a personality, a reputation, and a networking culture. Make yours upbeat, generous, friendly, and professional.

CHAPTER 21

Make It Rain Clients

If you're a lawyer, a CPA, or a doctor, what's the word that's most abhorrent to you? How about *sales*? When you hear it, do you grimace? Flinch? Cringe? Blanch? The word *marketing* is only slightly less upsetting. So you call it something else: *rainmaking*.

Whatever you call it, you probably have become resigned to the fact that, in today's marketplace, even professionals like yourself have to sell. You must bring clients in the door, or you will find yourself on the way out.

But, you plead, isn't there a *professional* way to do it?

Abe Reich, a former chancellor of the Philadelphia Bar Association, talked about law firms having "finders, minders, and grinders." As he defined them, finders are rainmakers, minders are people who handle clients, and grinders grind out the work. All three are valuable, but everyone must market, he believed. "Writing, speaking, and taking part in professional associations, like the Bar Association, are comfortable ways to sell," he said. He was confident that his role as chancellor would benefit his firm more than his lost billable hours.

Others who take active roles in professional associations pinpoint these benefits of their activity: credibility for their firms; visibility that enhances their firms' reputations; referrals from other professionals; access to key people in business, government, and legal circles; and, of course, rainmaking.

You can come up with other comfortable ways to sell. Successful rainmakers know how to create networks from which referrals flow. In this chapter, you'll find out what people in professional services *really* think about networking. You'll discover new ways to develop your practice. You'll learn how to strategize and set up a professional relationship management program for your firm. And you'll get advice on how to create the most powerful networking mechanism of all: the Constellation.

Networking can help you turn contacts into clients. People want to do business with people they trust.

There are three things that make networking especially hard for you: your lack of time, your ambivalence about accepting client development as part of your role, and your conviction that you shouldn't have to sell yourself. Here's how to streamline the process and get more comfortable with it.

Professionalize Your Practice Development

Take a strategic view. Set up a relationship management program to provide a structured, customized blueprint for your activities. The benefits of careful planning include:

▶ Constant referrals to qualified clients

▶ Additional business from current clients

▶ Access to inside information on business trends and resources

▶ Higher visibility in your field and in the community

To make networking part of your overall business plan, use the following four steps: assess and target, initiate and connect, track and measure, and renew and reassess.

Assess and target. Where have your current clients come from? Assess your current client base to determine how you found each other. Is there a pattern that you can build on?

Where are your potential clients? Which organizations and circles of influence will logically be your best targets? Kent's architecture firm specializes in designing churches and schools. Therefore, he and his partners should focus their networking efforts on organizations that serve school administrators and clergy. Although it makes sense to use this tactic, the number of businesspeople who actually seek out and become active in organizations that serve their clients is surprisingly small. Put your energy where your potential clients are.

Which organizations are members of your firm currently affiliated with? Can they justify their memberships, or did they just join without thinking about their targets? Can they explain exactly how those memberships put them in touch with the right people? How much time are they spending each month? What is the cost of belonging to each organization? Can they document the results of their memberships?

Does it make more sense to target individuals rather than join groups? If so, which individuals would provide the largest numbers of solid leads and referrals? How can you find these people?

What amount of time can and should people be spending on client development? If the primary goal is billable hours, how can the firm encourage and reward people for taking the time to develop networking relationships?

Initiate and connect. Once you have determined your targets and identified organizations and circles in which you should be more active, how are you going to deploy the members of your firm?

Pair up organizations and colleagues whose backgrounds or interests match. Set goals for the next six months. Use the ideas in this book to get up to speed quickly and to become active and visible.

Track and measure. Devise a system for tracking leads and quantifying your efforts. Marshall was surprised to discover that twelve of fifteen new clients of his advertising firm came from one client services team. What was this team doing? It was asking, repeatedly, for referrals.

Renew and reassess. Determine how you will stay in touch with prospects, referral sources, and past clients. How will you update them on new services and remind them of your expertise? How long will you stay active in an organization if you are not getting any referrals through your contacts there?

Consider these questions as you plan.

1. What strategic goals and plans in our organization make relationship management a priority now?

2. Which relationships have brought us the best information and referrals in the past? What has been the pattern of development in those relationships?

3. What kinds of relationships do we need in order to stay informed in our field today? Whom do we already know? Whom do we need to know? Where will we meet these people?

4. What contacts do we already have who can provide introductions that will establish maximum credibility?

5. What behaviors tend to build trust with key contacts? What is the best protocol for initiating relationships? How can we best exhibit our Competence and Character to contacts?

6. What skills do we need in order to cultivate business connections? How are we going to train people over time? Do we need a formal program? Do we need mentors?

7. What do people have to offer individually as they establish mutually beneficial business connections? Is each individual prepared to sell his own specialty and to explain why his service is superior?

8. Are people prepared to "cross-sell," that is, to pass prospects and referrals to others in the firm? What process do we have or could we develop to keep people informed about one another's areas of expertise?

9. What are the plans of each individual in our organization for making contacts in a variety of Arenas?

10. What systems are in place to support members of our firm as they go forward? Do we have effective contact management software? Do people know how to use it? Are there ways to reward people for their efforts? Are we sending a conflicting message when we emphasize billable hours and also encourage networking?

Make Conversations Count

Whether you are at a networking event or a ball game, keep these guidelines in mind in order to be comfortable and professional as you make contact.

▶ Go for the relationship, not the contract. When you meet casually and the conversation moves to a "let's do some business" level, set up a convenient time to call or place to meet to complete the transaction. As you continue to talk in the casual meeting, build your relationship with your contact. If you have a really good conversation with a new acquaintance about trout fishing at Bennett Springs and develop a strong rapport, that person is more likely to think of you when he needs an accountant than if you spend most of the conversation aggressively pushing your accounting services.

▶ On the other hand, always be up front about your desire to do business with your networking contacts. Remember, if there's no mystery, there's no manipulation.

Nora and Lee had known each other for fifteen years. Lee's job was eliminated, and she went into business for herself.

Nora, the marketing director for a law firm, called Lee and asked her to recommend a computer software trainer. More than a year later, after the two had gotten together at several professional meetings, Lee called Nora and set up a lunch meeting, saying, "I want to hear about the condo you are building and catch up with your life. I also want to tell you about a series of seminars I just finished doing for employees at Super-Bank. I think your firm might find these seminars useful."

> # Go for the relationship, not the contract.

Lee made her Agenda clear when she issued the invitation. Their lunch conversation ranged from personal items to the seminar series, and Nora asked for additional information about the seminars so that she could consider them for her employees.

These relationships that bounce back and forth from friendship to selling are tricky, no doubt about it. Being scrupulously honest about your intentions will keep the boundaries clear and avoid abusing a friend's trust.

▶ Always have interesting and valuable information to give your contacts.

Lou, an attorney with a midsized firm, is always looking for new clients. However, she is building a reputation for being a fascinating person to talk to about a lot of things. Even though adoption law isn't her specialty, she has two adopted children, so she shares what she knows and then refers prospective parents to a lawyer with years of experience in that field. She also is an avid balloonist and often tells people how to give balloon rides as birthday or anniversary gifts. Lou knows that because so many people find her easy to talk to, they feel comfortable calling her in on legal matters.

▶ Talk problem solving. Your challenge is not only to describe briefly and vividly what problems you can solve for potential clients and customers, but also, and even more important, to determine what their problems are.

Marcie learned not to define her role too narrowly. "When I used to say that I was a business analyst and management consultant, I'd often go right on and say that I specialized in setting up flextime programs. Then, if that wasn't how my contact defined the problem, that would be the end of it."

She's learned to back off a bit and ask, "What kinds of things is your company doing to enhance productivity?"

▶ Tell Success Stories (see Chapter 12). One way to memorably describe your problem-solving capabilities is to tell stories. Respecting client confidentiality, you can disguise the particulars and tell how you solved a problem, or saved someone money, or increased productivity or profits. Make your stories brief and dynamic.

When someone asked Christine, a tax attorney, "What's new?" she said, "I just won a battle with the IRS. I convinced them that my client's Christmas tree farm isn't a hobby; it's a business."

What's One Conversation Worth?

People who market their services can often determine the value of a single conversation.

Joyce, a financial consultant, met a man who asked her, "What would you do if you had $300,000 to invest?" Her answer obviously impressed him, because he did ask her to manage his portfolio. She figures she made $18,000 from that one conversation.

Patti, who has her own direct marketing firm, met Anna, who designs frames for kids' school pictures. Anna hadn't thought about doing a direct mail campaign to photographers, but when Patti suggested it, she was delighted. She said, "You're just the person I was looking for, and I didn't even know it." Patti's willingness to give away a good idea netted her an excellent contract.

When Chuck, who teaches problem solving in corporations, took his seat on the airplane, he was delighted to find himself seated next to a person who had just been promoted to head up the creativity department at a large chemical company. Unfortunately, the man was exhausted, and Chuck was able to have only a short conversation with him before he fell asleep and slept through the entire flight. However, as Chuck boarded the rental car van, another man caught up with him. "Excuse me for eavesdropping," he said, "but I was sitting behind you and I'm very interested in the kind of creativity training you were talking about." Chuck has provided $28,000 worth of seminars for that roundabout contact.

Create Constellations

Your strongest referrals can come from other professionals with whom you share customers. Put together your own referral group— your Constellation—by forming alliances with top-notch professionals in other fields who have access to your market. For example, a financial adviser invited an insurance broker, a Realtor, a CPA, and a lawyer to be part of her group. Another group is made up of a lawyer, a CPA, an interior designer who concentrates on the senior citizen market, and a person who runs estate sales. When a widow decides to move into a retirement apartment, the person who runs estate sales can refer her to the interior designer. Either the person who runs estate sales or the interior designer can refer her to the CPA, who can refer her to the lawyer. The referral cycle can begin with any member of the group, so that a client of one of the members soon becomes a client of all of the members. (See Chapter 20 for more information on referrals.)

George, a Chicago CPA, has been developing Constellations for many years. "The key to business is to obtain new clients," he says. "The problem is to do that within the ethics of a profession that outlaws advertising. Networking is the solution."

As he helps other professionals grow their practices, he reaps the benefits. He cultivates bankers, lawyers, insurance agents, and stockbrokers—all people who can refer business his way. "Once you have identified potential candidates to link up with, the hardest part of the job is spending time getting to know them," he says. He goes about it systematically, setting up a series of meetings. He meets with people over lunch or dinner, visits them in their offices, and invites them to his. "I don't go and say, 'I need you to give me new business.' I say, 'Here's what I can do for you, and, hopefully, you'll be in position to pay back the favor.'

"I do a selling job on myself and a fact-finding job on the other person," he says. He finds out exactly what the person does so that he can qualify contacts for him and refer the right clients. "I make sure that if a contact needs a banker, I send him to the right one. You need to know specialists in various areas, but I cultivate only a handful of 'partners.' I want to keep them happy. I couldn't keep eighteen bankers happy."

Actually, George doesn't *send* any clients to his 'partners.' His trademark is that he *hand-delivers* the clients. He calls the banker, makes an appointment, and personally takes his client to the banker's office.

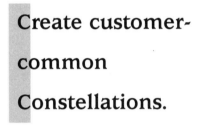

Create customer-common Constellations.

He's trained all seventy-five professionals in his firm to use the same practice development method. When he recruits on campuses for new accountants, he makes sure they are marketing-oriented. As new graduates join the firm, George trains them to build relationships with people in their own age bracket, creating networks that will grow in influence and power through the years as their careers advance.

Sandra, a marketing consultant, has created the Marketing Consortium. "Think of it as a six-leaf clover," she suggests, "with me in the middle and six related companies on the leaves." These companies do media buying, sales promotions, direct marketing, sales training, new business development, and strategic planning. Sandra's company provides creative support with ads and brochures. She always asks her clients if they need anything that her "leaves" could provide. "I don't get a percentage; I just expect business in return."

Constellations are only one way, but a very targeted way, to create your network. You don't need to know lots of people; you need to know the right people well.

Cross-Sell Your Clients

Can you sell more services to existing clients? The cost of getting new clients far exceeds the cost of getting new business from clients you already serve. That's why internal referrals are so important in professional services firms.

Conrad, a CPA, teaches the client services teams in his firm to handle their engagements in such a way that they are the first to hear about other organizational problems his firm might help to solve.

"You say the staff needs training on this new accounting software? Our training department can do that for you. I'll set up a meeting."

"You say the CEO is having a business planning retreat for all the top staff? Our management consultants can facilitate your strategic planning session. Let me call Kathryn, and we'll get our people ready to make a proposal to your CEO."

Conrad's people cross-sell the firm's capabilities constantly.

Make Asking for Referrals a Ritual

If you don't get referrals, perhaps you haven't established a routine for asking for them. Make asking for them an integral part of what you do with every client. You'd never fail to mention billing procedures, would you? Asking for referrals should be even more central.

Bill Cates, *www.ReferralCoach.com*, dubbed the "Champion of Referral Selling," suggests "foreshadowing" as a way to let the client know that you'll eventually ask for referrals. Early in the relationship, often even before someone has become a client, it's possible to "foreshadow" with comments like, "Since my business is built on referrals . . ." Or, "Sam was referred to me by Janna at Kidder, Wilson, and Smith."

Teach everyone in your firm these six steps so that they know how to ask clients—or their business contacts—for referrals.

1. Recall your track record. Encourage your client or contact to remember what you did for him. Ask, "What do you particularly appreciate about the way we worked with you, handled your project, managed your engagement, pursued your case?"

2. Remind clients that you count on referrals. Encourage them to become part of your referral system. Say, "You probably remember my saying that about 60 percent of our business comes from referrals from satisfied clients like you."

3. Review their circles. Help clients or contacts think of people who might be ready for your services. Say, "I know you're on the board of the country club. Are there others on the board who are also ready to do some serious financial planning?" Or, "I was so pleased when you said your partners complimented you about the new addition we designed for your house. Are any of them ready to look at some photos of other work we've done and talk with me about what they'd like to do to update their homes?" Or, "Which new members of the chamber of commerce do you recommend I contact to let them know about our firm's accounting services?"

Networking can help you turn contacts into clients. People want to do business with people they trust.

4. Receive specifics. Ask for any specific information that will help make your first contact successful. "Let me be sure I've got Lisa's last name spelled correctly. Does she have a car phone?" "What is a good time to reach Paul? At home or at work?" "Which of our services do you think Martin would find most interesting right now?" "Why do you think Ron would be interested at this time?"

5. Raise the possibility of success. Encourage clients and contacts to pave the way. Say, "It would be really helpful to me if you'd give Mary a call to let her know I'll be getting in touch. Naturally, I'd appreciate your telling her how satisfied you were with my work." Or, "Would you be willing to send Sacha a note telling her I'm going to call?" Or, "How about if the three of us get together for breakfast Friday? That way you can introduce us, and Fred can hear firsthand about what we've done for you."

6. Rapidly make contact. If your client gives you a referral, follow up quickly. If you don't, it could be embarrassing to both you and your client.

7. Recount the results. Get back to your client with your thanks. Show your appreciation, whether the contact resulted in business or not. Closing the loop and letting your client know what happened is just common courtesy. In some types of referral relationships, you may have agreed to pay a referral fee—a percentage of the dollar amount of the business. If you made that kind of agreement, be sure the check goes out quickly.

8. Reciprocate. Return the favor. Be on the lookout for ways you can help your client succeed. Provide resources, information, or referrals to the client or contact who gave you the referral.

Go ahead, make it rain.

CHAPTER 22

Go SOHO, but Not Solo

Are you part of the SOHO revolution? That's short for small office/home office. It means that you're part of the growing segment of the working population attracted by the thirty-second commute, the flexible hours, the tax breaks, the idea of being your own boss, and a sky's-the-limit income potential.

"SOHO is the fastest growing segment of today's business environment," says Terri Lonier, author of *Working Solo*. She estimates that by 2002, there will be 29.2 million people working in a SOHO setting. By the year 2002, about half of all home-based businesses will be owned by women, she says (see *www.workingsolo.com*).

Three trends are responsible for the surge in stay-at-home workers. First, mergers and corporate downsizing continue to "free up the futures" of many talented, experienced people. Second, the technologies necessary to set up an office at home are widely available, relatively inexpensive, and getting easier for people to use. Third, the sandwich generation has a need for more flexible schedules as they juggle child care and elder care.

According to *Success* magazine, the top ten home-based businesses are business consulting and services, computer services and programming, financial consulting and services, marketing and advertising, medical practices and services, graphics and visual arts, public relations, real estate, writing, and independent sales. And, of course, there are many franchises that work well as home-based businesses, such as Computer Tots, Decorating Den, and Molly Maid. Some types of franchises start off as home-based businesses, then later experience such growth that they move to commercial space.

Conquer the Challenges

Two challenges arise for SOHOs.

If you're someone who thrived on the camaraderie of belonging to a large organization and having lots of coworkers to kibitz with, working solo may seem lonely. You may spend too much time attending events in order to get the contact you crave. If that's you, make a plan for your networking activity. Make good decisions about which events and which groups will give you the best returns. Plan your calendar accordingly.

On the other hand, if you like working alone, you may get too comfortable "cocooning" and forget that sales success depends on networking and prospecting. Do you hate to put on that suit and head out to the luncheon meeting? Are you too busy to volunteer for the hospital fund-raiser? Are you so tied to your terminal that you're reluctant to meet new people and to reconnect with people you know?

Schedule time to network, just as you plan your other business activities. Use every social and business event as a time to explore trends that will affect your business (that new zoning law), find resources (that space to hold client focus group meetings), and tell people about your successes (that appointment to the governor's small business advisory committee). Proactively, look for and give leads and referrals.

SOHOs use networking to find customers, suppliers, distributors, lenders, investors, joint-venture partners, other kinds of partners, and mentors. In the process, people often strike up valuable business connections that will prove useful to their companies for years to come.

Be a go-giver, not a go-getter.

Many entrepreneurs find themselves networking as they go about their day-to-day tasks. Think of how often you reach out to shake hands and say hello. Now think of what would happen if a good percentage of those encounters generated sales leads or productive new ideas. Sound far-fetched? It shouldn't—not if you're as prepared to take advantage of chance meetings as you are of regular business appointments.

Lee's business was making costumes. She needed a source for unusual trimmings. She found one sitting next to her on a flight to Louisville.

Remember, you're not networking until the people you meet know your name, understand what type of customers or clients you want, trust your Character and Competence, and believe you'll reward them for their efforts on your behalf. In this chapter, you'll find tips for making networking from home work for you.

Link Up Your Life and Your Livelihood

Make linking your life. Instead of thinking of networking as something else to put on your already crowded to-do list, see it as life itself. Everywhere you go, from backyard barbecues to trade shows, you meet people. Be sure that you can answer the questions "What do you do?" and "What's new?" in ways that teach people about your service or product. Be prepared with up-to-date examples of your recent successes, projects, and clients. The more you tell, the more you sell.

Join—or start—a referral group. A referral group can bring you plenty of business. Follow the guidelines in Chapter 20. Emily, who sold Discovery Toys, started her own group of six women who lived in her neighborhood. The strength of their group was its diversity: a musician who plays for private parties, a graphic artist, a nanny finder, an image consultant, an interior designer, and Emily. They used one another's services and bought one another's products in order to get acquainted. The classical guitarist had a session with the image consultant and came up with a new look that got her noticed and added flair to her performance. The nanny finder hosted a party for all her nannies at which Emily showed her toys.

Spiff up your image. Act and appear in public as if you had an office downtown in the high-rent district. Remember, you may meet people at the grocery store or library or copy center. So wear business dress or at least business casual when you go out, not your oldest, grubbiest sweatsuit—even if that's your favorite work outfit! Always have your business cards with you, even on a run to the post office.

> **Make sure people hear about you before they hear from you.**

Choose to stand out. Select three to six Arenas and become visible in them. Pick one, such as a local home-based business association, for the business support you need from peers. Choose two populated by your clients or by people who can refer work to you. Susan, a caterer, became active in the Association of Wedding Professionals. Jaime, a remodeler, joined a real estate group, figuring that those people might provide some good referrals to homeowners who needed to have a few things done before putting their houses on the market. Use your hobbies or interests to make contact. Evan, a computer consultant, counts seven new clients this year from contacts he made at his health club. Be sure your family knows exactly what you do and what kinds of resources or clients you want to find.

Make sure people hear *about* you before they hear *from* you. Imagine meeting a prospect at a networking event who says, "Didn't I see an article by you in last month's chamber of commerce newsletter?" Or, "I heard you interviewed on the Women's Resource Network radio show several weeks ago." Getting visible in organizations and in your community allows you to make a name for yourself and enhance your credibility with people who count—even before you meet them.

Pick your not-so-prime times to network. Everybody's got high- and low-energy times and busy and not-so-busy times. Go with the flow. Mari's mornings are hectic, so she avoids breakfast meetings. Don's a slow starter, so he uses the early morning hours to network, saving his highest-energy moments for making sales calls. Many home-based businesspeople comment that they shy away from lunch events, as these can eat up three or even four hours in the middle of the day. Analyze your biorhythms, your work flow, and your family obligations and plan accordingly.

Accomplish your Agenda. Decide before you leave the house what you want to accomplish. Create your Agenda every day and focus on it. Here are some sample Agenda items:

- ▶ Meet at least two people on the board of directors and offer to be on a committee to raise my visibility in the organization.

- ▶ Find out which temporary help agency others have used and liked.

- ▶ Meet a divorce lawyer who might eventually send tax work my way.

- ▶ Identify businesses large enough to hold catered events several times a year and invite them to my tasting party.

- ▶ Meet people whose parents are considering moving into a retirement complex.

Reconnect and follow up. When you return to your office from a networking event, go through any business cards you received and decide on a follow-up plan. Do this immediately, before you get caught up in the tasks on your desk. Ideally, you'll use one of the many contact management software packages on the market to keep track of people and stay in touch.

Promote your business creatively. Since you don't have a storefront and you don't have a big sign, what can you do to draw attention to your business? Gina, a watercolorist, teamed up with Gary, who owns a frame shop in a busy mall. They hosted a Saturday "sidewalk art show" to display his frames and her paintings. Candy's stuffed animal business, Bunny Rabbit Babies, hopped in the springtime, but hibernated in the fall and winter. She donated fifteen bunnies to the playroom in the children's wing of the hospital, which led to a contract with the hospital gift shop. That exposure led to another contract with a hotel gift shop. Those two contracts tripled her business in one year.

Holler "help!"—and get it. With only the cat and the philodendron to talk to, you may feel that you are home alone. The truth is that all across town, others just like you are wondering, "Am I on the right track?" "Do I have what it takes?" "How can I grow my business?" "Whom can I talk to when I get down in the dumps?" The two best sources of support are other home-based businesspeople like yourself and hired experts.

Get the support and encouragement you need by networking with other SOHOs. Lynnette, who is in business for herself and by herself, already belonged to several networking groups of people who do training and development. But she wanted to talk over her business strategy and get support from people who were outside her own profession. So she and three other entrepreneurs started the Presidents Group. They meet once a month for an hour or so in a restaurant. Each person has a fifteen-minute turn. First, the person tells about a recent accomplishment. For people who work alone, celebrating success with others is important. "At first, we were shy about sharing our accomplishments. I guess we all grew up being told not to brag," Lynnette says. "But we found that when we took credit for our successes, it was easier to tackle the problems." Second, the person asks for help or feedback from the group on one issue or challenge. This problem can be anything from "How can I market my services so that I have more work in December?" to "How do you like this design for my new business card?" In the group, Lynnette says, "The friendships deepened as our business savvy increased." Four years later, the group is still meeting.

Use your network to hire experts. Ask around for an accountant who specializes in home-based businesses, or for a graphic artist who can give you the look you want in your next brochure. You can't do it all yourself. Often, those professionals you hire will turn out to be some of your best referral sources. After all, they know exactly what you do. And they know that when your business grows, so will theirs.

CHAPTER 23

Jump-Start Your Job Hunt

"Looking for work is the hardest job I've ever had," says Renata. When her company merged, she was told that her position was "excess." Renata is right. Job hunting is tough.

"It's hard to admit it, but I'd been in the wrong career for fourteen years," confides Roger. "The longer I stayed, the harder it was to leave. I was adding more and more accomplishments to my résumé, but I found my job satisfaction dwindling day by day. I hated Mondays . . . and Tuesdays . . . and Wednesdays . . . and the rest of the week, too!" Roger finally decided to work with a career coach to completely reassess his interests, skills, and values. Changing careers, especially while you're still in the old one, is a challenge.

Whether you choose to change, are laid off, opt for an early out and want to continue working, are reentering the job market, are moving from a military to a civilian career, or are seeking your first job, being out of work is a serious assault on your self-esteem. In our society, some people mistakenly think that what you do is who you are.

Renata and Roger made their job hunts easier by using their network of personal and professional contacts to devise search strategies, meet new career contacts, and support them through the ups and downs of change. You can too.

In this chapter, you'll learn about trends in today's workplace that make networking *the* way to job hunt. You'll get inside tips for dealing with special job-searching circumstances. You'll discover effective strategies for researching new career directions using your network. Finally, you'll find the ten top tactics for networking the right way when you're looking for work or changing careers.

Whatever is triggering your job search, you're probably already convinced that networking will help you find a new job.

But do you realize that the length of your job search is directly related to the strength of your network as you begin to job hunt?

> **The length of your job search is directly connected to the strength of your network.**

Networking know-how is by far the greatest advantage you can have in today's job market. Investing time and energy in building your circle of contacts will bring you current information on jobs and trends in your field, resources and services that you need in order to conduct your job search, and the support of friends when the going gets rough.

Unfortunately, when it comes to reaping the benefits of networking, most job hunters are "standin' in the river, dyin' of thirst," as the old saying goes. All around them are people who have information, resources, and support. Knowing how to drink from the river will allow you, the job hunter, to become a job holder—quickly and with a lot less trauma.

If You're One of the Working Worried

Begin today to strengthen your personal safety net. Most of us will have three to five distinctly different careers in our lifetimes and a dozen or more different jobs. We'll take the initiative to make half of those job changes; the rest will be the result of various kinds of organizational shake-ups. That means that your network should always be ready. Network before you need to. Start now.

In today's uncertain economic climate—with all its mergers, downsizing, and reorganizations—you never know when you are really going to need your business contacts.

"I used to call Fran every once in a while to ask her if she'd like to be my guest at the professional association I belong to," says Liz. "She was always too busy to go. Then one day she called me to say that her job had been eliminated. She was in a panic. 'I hardly know anyone in Cincinnati,' she said. 'Tell me who I need to get to know to begin looking for a new job. I'm so sorry that I didn't make time to go to the professional association meetings. I realize now how important it is to know people and to stay in touch.'"

Don't make the mistake Fran did. Fran didn't realize that you've got to dig your well before you're thirsty. Networking is a process, not an event. It takes many months to cultivate a bountiful network. Not every attempt to reach out succeeds. Yet, over time, with enough seeds planted and enough attention and patience, your crop of contacts will yield what you need: a tip about a job opening before it's advertised or an expert's insights regarding trends in your industry that make you aware of new ways to apply your expertise.

> **Your network is your safety net. Make sure it's in place before you need it.**

If You've Been Laid Off

"We're all out of work; we just haven't received the pink slip yet," says Gary. That's a healthy attitude to have in today's volatile marketplace. William Bridges, author of *JobShift,* points out that although we grew up believing in long-term jobs, to thrive in the new workplace we must give up the idea of having a job.

"Today's worker will *do* a job, not *have* a job," says Bridges. That's a tough, but true, message for most Americans who have assumed that their jobs were secure. Our interviews with people who have lost

their jobs show that 80 percent of people who are laid off are surprised—and therefore unprepared. With an "I'm here forever" mindset, no wonder they haven't created a protective network.

Bob's job was eliminated when the telecommunications company he worked for merged with a larger firm. He says, "After the
shock of losing my job wore off, I realized that I didn't have a network!
I'd been so busy at work that I'd stopped going to professional meetings and had lost touch with old friends. It took me about six months of
concentrated work to build my network. I think of it as a vast communications network that brings me ideas, leads, and support. Now it's just
a matter of time before the right job comes zinging across my 'wires.' In
the meantime, I've met some wonderful people, picked up a few consulting jobs to tide me over financially, and vowed that I'll never be
without the safety net of a strong network again."

Unfortunately, the worst time to begin networking is when you're
unemployed. But, like Bob, you can do it.

Here are some special tips to help you get going.

Beware the "information interview." When your coauthor Anne
worked for a large corporation, she frequently got calls from people
who were job hunting in Kansas City. Often, they'd say that they
didn't expect her to be hiring any new staff right then, but they just
wanted to make an appointment to come to her office to talk with
her about her job and the field of corporate communications in general. Some job-hunting books and career counselors advise this
approach, calling it "information interviewing."

The problem we have with these interviews is that you, the job
hunter, are expected to hide your Agenda. You do want to find a job,
and, at the very least, you hope that your contact can refer you to
someone who is hiring.

Anne's usual response was a tough one, but realistic. She'd say,
"My company doesn't pay me to talk to you during my work day
about my job or your job hunt." Then, to soften the blow of that much
candor (and because she did want to be helpful), she would invite the
caller to attend her professional organization's monthly luncheon.
She'd tell the caller that she'd talk with him there and also make sure

that he met other professionals. "That way, you'll have a chance to meet and gather information from several people," she would say.

Information interviewing is a great idea, but, be creative about when and where you do these interviews. You can interview people about their jobs anywhere. Talk to people at a party, in your carpool, at your kid's soccer game, at a convention, at a training session. Don't assume that they can take time away from their job duties or donate their company's time to talk with you.

Go public with your job search. "I invited four job hunters who had called me for information interviews to attend a luncheon meeting of my professional organization," Anita remembers. "As we all sat around the table, I decided to perform an experiment. I thought I'd wait to see how long it took for people to reveal what was uppermost in their minds—to mention that they were job hunting. Minutes passed. People talked about the Caesar salad, the pink tablecloths—even the weather!

"Finally, I decided to take matters into my own hands. I said, 'You are all here because you are job hunting.' After a short, uncomfortable few seconds, they owned up to their purpose in coming to the luncheon. Even then, it didn't occur to them to trade experiences or contacts or to talk about job-hunting strategy. They just plain weren't comfortable with sharing what they wanted or needed with others.

"There's a happy ending. With a bit of encouragement, they did trade information, strategies, and even leads (with some prompting from me), and I heard from two of them the following week. After following up on some ideas from their peers, those two had come up with job interviews."

The moral of this story: Often people talk about everything except what's really on their minds. They worry that if they say what they are really thinking about, they may be manipulating others or may seem to be too needy. Actually, the opposite is true. By keeping their job-hunting Agendas hidden, they make everyone uncomfortable. As you learn to see others as job-hunting resources, you'll get comfortable with making more meaningful contact—contact that can benefit both you and the person or people that you're talking with.

Network with people who care about you. Start with your family. Even people who have known you for years—your own relatives, for example—may not be aware of the details of your successes. Did you graduate with honors? Have you been recognized by your professional association? Have you achieved professional certification or accreditation? Have you been steadily promoted? Have you been recognized for specific on-the-job contributions? Provide a résumé that lists your accomplishments.

When Richard, a computer programmer, was laid off, he sat down with his mother-in-law, Jill, and showed her his résumé, answering the questions she had as she read through it. The next day, Jill had lunch with a friend who worked in a bank and mentioned Richard's success in programming customer service information. A week later, the bank called to ask Richard to apply for an opening.

Tap the experience of the experienced. As we interviewed more than two hundred people for our Fireproofing Your Career Workshops, we were astounded to hear again and again from people who had been laid off that "nobody ever asked me for my advice." Ask. Get the low-down on severance pay, benefits continuation, unemployment insurance, relationships with previous employers, interviewing tips (how are you going to answer the question, "Why did you leave Consolidated?"), tide-you-over consulting, and a host of other topics. Put the previously laid off at the top of your list of people to contact.

Go for diversity and numbers. Imagine that you want to find a job in sales. Your background is in computer technologies and medical equipment. Make a list of everybody you know.

Look at your list. At this point, everyone is a potential source of information, resources, support, and referral. Yes, include Uncle Harry, even though you only see him at Thanksgiving and he's been retired for five years. Yes, include your neighbor down the street with whom you trade tools every once in a while. Yes, include the instructor of that sales course you took recently.

No matter what her age, profession, interest, or place in the hierarchy, each person you know is important. The more diverse your network, the better. Uncle Harry might refer you to someone he mentored who has a friend in sales. Your neighbor's brother may have just been laid off, too, and you might decide to share strategies and support. The instructor of your sales course might tell you about an upcoming convention of medical equipment salespeople.

Although there is no "right" number of people for your network, as a job hunter, you need to expand and reach out much more than people who are employed do. If a network of 50 people will provide good support and protection for someone who has a job, you need to set your sights on 250 or more to speed your job hunt.

Pay attention to what you have to give. When Jim went to a professional meeting of trainers and consultants, he was hoping to learn more about the field and to meet people. But he felt that, as an unemployed person, he was at a disadvantage. When he tuned into the quiet side of networking and really listened, however, he found that he was able to contribute a lot. Talking with Sheila, he mentioned his upcoming interview for a training job with a company that helps executives learn how to operate in the global marketplace. Sheila's eyes lit up as she told him about looking for buyers for her new book on etiquette for executives who work abroad. Jim gave her the name of his contact at the company. Giving restored some of his battered self-esteem and made him feel more confident and capable about his worth in the marketplace.

Stay involved. When you are paring expenses to the bone, it's tempting to cut out membership dues to various organizations. Don't do it. Don't say, "I'm unemployed. I can't afford the money." You could be cutting off your lifeline to job information, job banks, informative programs that increase your expertise and employability, and good contacts.

Target your search. The best job searches are narrowly targeted. You may have several targets, but each one should be very specific. Deanna decided that she wanted her next job to be in one of two roles. Here's what she let people in her network know about her:

"I can design and deliver beginning and advanced word processing training."

Or:

"I can manage a word processing center—and its staff—efficiently and effectively."

Deal effectively with "overqualification." Lois had been job hunting for about seven months and was getting discouraged. When she did have an interview, she usually was told that she was overqualified. She finally figured out that the word *overqualified* meant that she expected too high a title and salary. She revised her résumé to deemphasize her previous title and play up her problem-solving abilities. In her next interview, when the question of salary came up, she said, "I'm sure we will be able to figure something out, because I am the right person to tackle this job."

Once she convinced the organization of the contribution she could make, she negotiated a one-year consulting arrangement at a higher salary than the one listed on the job description.

Ask for the right things. Saying to people, "I need a job" doesn't usually result in a good connection. Most people won't know of a specific job opening to tell you about. They'll feel embarrassed and sorry that they can't help. The conversation will hit a brick wall. Instead, think of what you can put on the "get" side of your Agenda that will naturally uncover job leads and career information.

For example, look for problems that you excel at solving. Ask all your contacts for referrals to people who have jobs like the one you're looking for. They are the people who will know about openings. Ask them how they found their jobs in order to get insights into how hiring works in that field or industry. Find suppliers and vendors. Printers, for example, often know when someone is leaving a corporate magazine editing job or when a company is starting a new publication that will require hiring a new writer.

Teach people what you have to offer. As you network, think about building what marketers call "top-of-the-mind awareness." When someone needs your specific expertise, you want to come to mind immediately. Focus on educating your contacts about you and staying in touch.

Observe the protocol. Let your contact know your plans. If someone gives you information, tell that person what you intend to do with it. Don't jump the gun. Allow your contact to determine the timing of what happens next or when you will follow through.

"I casually mentioned a job opportunity that I knew about to an unemployed acquaintance," says one executive. "I had planned, if she was interested, to phone my contact and arrange a meeting. Our telephone conversation was interrupted, and when I called her back fifteen minutes later, she already had called my contact about the position, using me as a reference. I was very embarrassed. That job had been offered to me, and I had not yet refused it."

Pay your way. When you call a contact and ask that person to meet you for breakfast or lunch or a drink, the least you can do is offer to pay. Also be sure that you schedule the meeting at a location that's as convenient as possible for your contact. Dress appropriately for the meeting. Treat every meeting with every contact as a job interview. Remember that you are teaching your contacts who you are. Help them to see you in the position to which you aspire.

If You Are Reentering the Job Market

Your biggest challenge will be to convince people that your skills are up-to-date.

Take a course or two at a community college or get an advanced degree. Education builds your credibility and puts you in touch with contacts who can help you.

Martha Lee had been out of the job market for thirteen years. She began a degree program at a university that targeted working professionals. She arranged for an internship with the organization one of her professors worked for, and later—after she'd proved herself—she was hired part-time. Networking with her classmates who had jobs provided her with additional work.

Build a bridge from your last job to your next. Dottie hadn't planned on taking time off from work. Then she had twin boys. To keep current, she worked on her master's degree while she was at home with the boys for three years. When she decided to look for a job, there was no gap on her résumé. The time she had spent at home was covered by her pursuit of the advanced degree. She also networked with professors and classmates and quickly found a job.

Explore your options. Suzanne wanted to reenter the job market part time after taking ten years off to raise a family. A decade earlier, she had successfully managed a small office, but she was unsure what she wanted to do in this phase of her career. Here's what she decided to connect with people about, conversationally speaking:

▶ Organizations that hire part-time professionals

▶ What to expect in the job interview process

▶ Organizations that would be interested in using the knowledge of the construction industry she had gained from working in her father's business

▶ Ways in which she could use her home-remodeling and interior design skills in the job market

Suzanne's conversational connections introduced her to a group called the Association of Part-Time Professionals. She's using its job bank and contacts she made there to find a position that's just right for her.

If You Have Just Graduated

To build your network from scratch, try these ideas.

Plug into your parents' network. When Traci graduated, her mother, Lynda, set up a series of lunch meetings with her networking contacts. That way, Traci, coached by her mother, was able to plug into the extensive network Lynda had developed through the years.

Begin to build your network by contacting people who know you. Talk with your professors, alumni of your school, former members of the marching band or sports team you've been involved with, fraternity or sorority alumni, your pastor or rabbi, church members, neighbors, relatives, family friends, bosses from summer or part-time jobs, your parents and their friends, and your friends' parents and their friends.

Provide these contacts with your résumé and ask them for two things: advice on how to find the job you want, and the names of people they think you should call or visit. Ask your contact to make a call to these people to introduce you. That way, you'll never have to make a cold call or send your résumé to someone who has never heard of you.

Be sure that you report back to people who have helped you, letting them know that you did contact the person they recommended and telling them what happened.

Link up with the pros. While you're still in school, join the student chapter of the professional organization in your field. If there is no student chapter, visit and eventually join the professional association. To find professional association(s) that serve the field you are interested in entering, contact your reference librarian and ask about the *Encyclopedia of Associations*. Call the national offices listed there for the phone number of the closest chapter.

You'll be welcome as a visitor. Take advantage of the organization's job bank if it has one. Get the membership directory and look for people who have the kind of job you're looking for or who work at organizations that appeal to you. Seek them out in person at a meeting or call them to set up an interview. Never ask if they have a job for you; instead, ask for advice about finding a job.

Take an active role in order to demonstrate your expertise. Lila talked with the president of the association she visited and asked if she could send him her résumé. He said, "Sure," and gave her his card. A couple of days later, he received a well-written cover letter, her résumé, and a stamped, oversized postcard addressed to Lila. In her cover letter, she asked him to return the postcard with his feedback on her résumé. That made it very easy for him to respond to her. After she received the card, she called him to thank him for his suggestions. By that time, he had developed a great deal of confidence in her abilities and had thought of a couple of people for her to contact. Lila skillfully initiated a series of contacts, designed to build a relationship, with a key person who could help her find a job.

Emphasize your marketable skills. Make sure that your résumé focuses on your job skills, not the courses you took in college. For example, rather than listing courses you took in your English major, focus on your ability to write clearly or on the columns you wrote for the college newspaper.

Volunteer. Joy, a new graduate with a degree in journalism, volunteered to produce a brochure for her church. A church member who worked for a large foundation saw the brochure, was impressed, and called Joy about a job opening he had.

Get a "career card." If you're just entering the job market and don't have a business card, take a suggestion from the National Association of Female Executives and get a "career card" or "networking card." Naturally, it will give your name, address, phone number, and e-mail address. You may also want to use a few well-chosen words or phrases that describe what you do. Jan, who has a degree in computer design, has a card that says, "Graphic design for newsletters, brochures, annual reports."

Explain what you're looking for. People will ask you, "What do you want to do?" How you answer that question determines whether you'll instantly start an interesting, productive conversation or one that just limps along. Don't say, "I'll do anything." Don't give the title you're aiming for. Don't give your major. Instead, name one skill you'd like to use (writing, Web design) and a quick example that brings your job hunt to life.

Say, for example, "I've just designed a marketing program for a law firm as a final project in one of my classes. As part of my research, I interviewed several marketing directors. I'd be very interested in any job that involved publicity for an organization."

If You've Just Been Released from the Military

Your biggest challenges will be to translate your military background into marketable skills and to expand your circle of civilian contacts in order to build a network quickly. Building your network will be especially hard if you have worked abroad for several years or have been stationed at a military installation in a remote area.

Use all of the suggestions for building and maintaining a network, as well as the tips in this chapter for people in various kinds of job-hunting situations.

Translate military jargon into English. Be sure that both your conversation and your résumé are understandable by people in the civilian world. Ask civilian contacts to review your résumé and advise you on how to best describe your accomplishments.

Focus on your skills. On your résumé, list your marketable skills, not just your military titles. And when you introduce yourself, be sure to focus on the problems you can solve, not on your past titles.

Battle the stereotypes. Talk with people about their preconceived notions about people in the military. It is common for civilians to think that military personnel are authoritarian and inflexible. If you run into that stereotype, figure out ways to overcome it and change people's mistaken ideas about your personality and approach.

Research the marketplace. Use your networking contacts to get a better idea of what job titles and salary ranges to target in your search. Some employers will be unsure about how much credit you should get for military service.

Team up. Find other ex-military people and talk with them about how they made the transition. They will be good networking contacts for you.

If You Take Early Retirement

You may find that your age makes it more difficult to get a job. But that won't be true if you've stayed active and can demonstrate your ability to solve problems.

Take part in life. Networking happens everywhere—if you participate in life.

Keith's hobby was flying radio-controlled airplanes. As a weekend flight instructor and field manager, he taught lots of people to fly.

One Saturday eight years ago, Roger stopped by the field and signed up for a class from Keith. The two became friends. One day, Keith mentioned that he'd decided to take the early retirement package offered by the large telecommunications firm he worked for, but that he would like to keep working. Roger said, "Come to work for me!" Keith's reputation was so solid that he hardly needed an interview with Roger's boss. Keith has just started his new career, working for Roger selling mobile phones.

Make your age work for you. Use the expertise you've developed over the years to teach, write, or consult. All of these activities can be lucrative second careers, can provide additional credentials on your résumé, and can lead to excellent networking contacts who may help you find a job.

If You Are Changing Careers

You have an edge over other job hunters: You're not unemployed; you can take your time.

Plan your Agenda-centered conversations carefully. About the time Matt was noticing that his travel schedule was taking its toll on his relationship with his two young sons, he also began to hear rumors about company layoffs and an early retirement buyout. He decided to plan a switch from systems analysis to teaching at a local college. His master's degree, strong technical skills, and training background made him a natural, but he lacked knowledge of the academic world. Here's what he put on the "get" side of his Agenda to ask people about:

- ▶ The names of publications in which colleges advertise for professors in the computer field

- ▶ Referrals to people who teach at the three local universities

- ▶ The name of a career counselor who specializes in career change or the academic job search

- ▶ Trends in hiring in higher education and at local colleges

▶ Referrals to corporate trainers who also teach to find out how they got their jobs

A man he met at the gym introduced Matt to one of his college professors. The two hit it off immediately. Six months later, the professor decided to take early retirement and start a business. He told Matt about his plans, and Matt applied for the job and got it.

Join the people already in the field you want to move to. Even before you make the switch, join a professional association. To become familiar with the issues and concerns of that profession, ask your contacts what books they are reading and what trade journals they find most useful. Begin to build your network of people who are active in that field. Demonstrate your skills by taking an active role in the professional group or learn some of the skills you need by attending programs and workshops.

Introduce yourself effectively. Avoid starting conversations with, "I'm in a career change." Describe your career goal. If you are looking for a job in customer service, for example, say, "I'm Lorna Emmons. I help businesses serve their customers better." That *is* what you do; you just haven't found an organization to do it for . . . yet.

Talk with job holders. Seek out people who have the job you want. Ask them how they got their jobs. You'll be amazed at the number of people who will say, "I networked." Note unusual approaches. Ask what skills, experience, certifications, or degrees they recommend. Ask their advice on how to get from where you are to where you want to be.

The Top Ten Tactics for Making Career Changes

As you plan your next move, use these tried-and-true tactics for changing careers, entering the job market, or finding a better job faster.

1. *Take care of yourself.* Being unemployed can mean wear and tear on your self-esteem. It's not fair or true, but in this society we

often get hooked into thinking that we *are* our job titles—and if you haven't got one, you're nobody. The truth is that your job is what you do, not who you are. Who you are is a human being with talents, skills, interests, and an infinite ability to learn. Since predictions tell us that at least several of our future job changes will be involuntary, the results of downsizings, mergers, or moves, it's wise to begin to separate who you are from what you do. Develop multiple identities: as a fund-raiser for the Boy Scouts, as someone who serves on the board of a professional association, as a part-time image consultant. Use your time between jobs to learn new skills, relax, build your network, and see more of your family.

Buy a spiral notebook or a gorgeous leather-bound journal. Use it to write down your hopes, challenges, frustrations, ideas, strategies, steps, and plans. It's like having a dialog with your best friend—you! You are the one person who knows the most about who you are and where you want to go. Whenever you get an idea or feel stuck or want to think something through, pull out your notebook and start writing. You'll be amazed at how this process helps you get in touch with what you want, tap into hidden energy, and map out clear plans of action

Job hunting is lonely. People who link up with others keep their spirits up and learn from one another. Join or start a job-hunting support and strategy group. Support groups are often sponsored by religious groups, adult education centers, or women's centers. One such group has the elegant name the Hunt Club.

If you can't find a group, start one. Limit membership to four or five people who are changing careers or job hunting. Give each person a turn to share the week's accomplishments: "Sent a follow-up letter to Garrett at Financial First." "Had an interview with Barker & Co." Get help strategizing about upcoming challenges. Mark's group helped him to think through his answer to the inevitable job interview question "How much are you willing to travel?" Suzanne's group gave her innovative ideas on how to become known to people in the public affairs departments at companies where she'd like to work.

   2. *Make it easy, not hard, for people to help you.* Lots of people have the erroneous idea that networking is scheduling information interviews. But networking is not an appointment. As the workplace becomes more and more streamlined, people who *have* jobs have little or no time to meet with people who are *looking* for jobs. You don't need to set up an information interview in someone's office in order to network. If you are networking effectively, life is an information interview.

Use the informal and unstructured time at association meetings, training classes, conferences, and even social events to do "mini" interviews.

3. *Target groups and teach people who you are.* Look over the hierarchy of networking opportunities in Chapter 3. Target four to six Arenas and become known in them. Teach people what skills you have and what kinds of resources and leads you're looking for. Good bets are your family (does your brother-in-law *really* know what you want to do in your next job? does Aunt Sally?), your church or synagogue, your health club, your alumni group, the parents of kids on your daughter's basketball team, the community association you belong to, the volleyball team you play on, and certainly the professional association that serves the job type or industry you've targeted.

If you're trying to expand your job options or change careers, join an organization in a nearby or adjacent field. Trainers, for example, might join the National Speakers Association; journalists might join the Public Relations Society of America. Carla, the public relations director for a hospital, is a member of the International Association of Business Communicators and also a member of Women in Communications, for example. Since she's considering a business start-up with a colleague, she also recently joined an association of home-based businesses.

Visit professional associations that serve the career you're interested in. Go to meetings. Talk with members about what they do and how they got into the field. Ask open-ended questions, such as:

▶ "How did you get started in PR?"

▶ "What do you like most about being a fund-raiser?"

▶ "What kinds of skills do you find yourself using the most in your work as a trainer?"

▶ "What are some of today's burning issues for people in the field of competitive intelligence?"

People will appreciate your genuine interest, and you never know when some little tidbit of information from one of these many conversations will make you stand out as the number one candidate in your next job interview.

4. *Be prepared to answer the question, "What do you do?"* What do you say about yourself when you go to networking events? Get ready to answer that often-asked question. When you're unemployed, avoid the mysterious, "I'm in transition." Instead, teach your talents. Give examples of past accomplishments. Talk about problems you've solved in your field. Tell about a current freelance project. Or even tell about a professional development class you're taking. Remember, answering, "What do you do?" is the perfect opportunity to teach people about your Character and Competence.

Concentrate on putting the word out, loud and clear, about what you like to do and do well. Gone are the days when you could say, "Oh, I'm a generalist" or "I'm in risk management." Those kinds of descriptions are not vivid enough to make you memorable.

Marly, a veterinarian, works for the U.S. Department of Agriculture in the animal inspection program. As she thought about her answer to "What do you do?" she knew she had something really unusual—and therefore memorable—to say: "I inspect camels and decide which ones can come into the United States."

But she realized that that answer wouldn't teach people what she wanted them to know about her that would make her next career move easier. She is hoping to parlay the negotiating skills that she's learned in bargaining about camels into a career negotiating international peace agreements. So she says, "I show people how to find common ground. Last week, after six months of patient coaching, I got eight people who speak four different languages to come to agreement." What she doesn't tell her contact is that they were talking about camels. With her answer, she is teaching her circle of contacts to appreciate her negotiating skills.

Be sure your answer focuses not just on the sensational, but on the direction in which you want to steer your career.

5. *Listen Generously and give first.* Approach social and professional events by reminding yourself that you have a lot to give. Listen carefully and think, "Who do I know? What resources am I in touch with that this person might benefit from?" When her husband's job transfer took Angela to San Antonio, she started her networking there from scratch. She met Lynn at the first American Business Women's Association meeting she attended. Lynn mentioned that she was beginning her yearly search for the perfect summer camp for her eleven-year-old. Angela remembered an article she'd read recently reviewing local camps. She promised to send it to Lynn. That was a good reason for exchanging cards. When Lynn called to say thanks, Angela told her more about the kind of job she was looking for, and Lynn gave her a lead.

Offer to help someone who's already established. Do research, organize an event, write an article, start a job bank. Mary Alice, a whiz with all kinds of graphics and presentation software packages, wanted to learn more about careers in corporate training, so she offered to do a brochure for a freelance trainer who had once been her next-door neighbor. In the process of helping out, she picked up tips and general knowledge and was able to demonstrate her Character and Competence. Her relationship with the trainer eventually led to five introductions, two interviews, and a job in a corporation designing training materials. Mary Alice is now closer to her goal: making the transition into training.

6. *Look for problems to solve.* Tom Jackson, author of *Guerrilla Tactics in the Job Market,* says, "A job is an opportunity to solve a problem—and there is no shortage of problems." Ask yourself, "What kinds of problems do I like to solve? What kinds of problems have I been most successful with?" When you describe what you do in terms of the problems you solve, you put a picture of success in people's minds.

Think of it this way: The more people there are who know precisely what you're good at, the more likely it will be that your name will come up when there's a job opening or a need for your special expertise. When you talk problem solving, you make it easier for people in your network to support you because they know what to count on you for and what to send your way.

Read Chapter 8 to get ideas about listening for problems.

Uncovering problems can give you an excuse to reconnect, as Lucy did when Tony mentioned that his company was going to do an employee attitude survey for the first time in several years, and that he'd been asked to manage the process. A couple of weeks after they talked, Lucy noticed an article entitled "How to Ensure the Success of Your Survey" and faxed it to him.

Listening for problems can give you ideas on how to describe the skills on your résumé in the exact language your prospective employer uses. When Linda heard Jake talk about his company's new initiatives in "internal customer service," that's what she called her expertise in communication skills in the cover letter and résumé she sent to him.

Listening for problems can let people know that you care about their well-being—not just in the workplace, but in life. Curt saw how distressed Lisa was about the need to care for her aging parents, who were four hundred miles away in another city. He'd collected some resources when his mother needed to enter a nursing home. He delivered a big envelope of information to Lisa's office the next day.

7. *Be clear and specific when asking for help.* Approach each situation with a list of resources and information you're looking for. Then ask directly for what you need.

> ▶ "Have you run across any information recently on negotiating salaries?"

> ▶ "I'm ready to have my résumé printed. Is it better to stick with black type on white paper, or, since I'm focusing on ad agencies that pride themselves on creativity, should I aim for something different?"

> ▶ "I'm looking for other people who are changing careers. I want to start a strategy and support group. Do you know anybody who might be interested?"

▶ "I came here hoping to meet people who work in some aspect of health research. Do you know anyone who does that?"

Don't just look for a specific title. Instead, aim to teach your contacts about your talents. Garth called Benjamin and said, "I'm job hunting in the Detroit area. I'm looking for a position as a chief financial officer." Benjamin thought for a moment and then told Garth that he didn't know of any jobs for CFOs. A few days later, Benjamin heard about a fast-growing waste-management company that wanted to raise capital for expansion. He didn't think of passing that tip along to Garth because Garth hadn't let him know that in his previous job, he'd been very successful at raising capital. Garth had made the mistake so many job hunters make: looking for a title rather than a problem to solve.

8. *Absorb the culture of the career you're investigating.* Spend time with people who have the job you'd like to have. As you volunteer for committees, go to certification classes, or attend conventions, notice what people read, how they dress, what they talk about, and who their gurus are.

Kevin was winding down his career in the Marine Corps. He had enrolled in an MBA program at a university near the base. As he got to know his classmates, he gathered information about their organizations. He asked Jonas whether there were business benefits from playing on the company softball team and Al about the appropriate garb for "dress-down" days at his company.

Look for someone who will take you under his wing, answer questions, look over your résumé, give you advice, introduce you to others. A mentor might be a friend who's already in the field, a past college professor, or someone you meet in a professional association. Many groups make getting a mentor easy by offering a formal program, complete with training for mentor and mentee.

9. *Don't make unreasonable, inappropriate requests.* Dan brought a hundred copies of his résumé to the networking meeting, left some on the display table, and gave one to everybody he talked to, saying, "If you know anyone who needs my skills, ask them to call me." This is the kind of behavior that gives networking a bad name. Why would you go out on a limb to recommend Dan to anyone you know? You'd want to be sure of Dan's Character and Competence before telling your contacts and colleagues about him. His request was presumptuous.

Don't ask people to help you find a job until you have taught them to trust you.

10. *Say thanks*. Your mother was right. Don't forget to show that you appreciate the time, information, and support that people give you. Do it immediately. Get in the habit of thanking your contacts each time they give you information. Tell them what steps you took to put the information to use or how that information led to additional resources.

Make your thanks very specific. Let your contact know exactly what she did that was so helpful to you. That's the way to encourage that kind of behavior and to assure your contact that her specific contribution made a difference.

There are many kinds of thank-yous to choose from: a handwritten note, a formal letter on office stationery, an invitation to lunch, tickets to a play, a box of chocolates or home-made cookies, a clever cartoon, a magazine subscription. After you land a job and get your new business cards, send one to each of your contacts.

Repeat your thanks. Don't just say thank you once and never mention it again. Refer to the help your contact gave you. Send a holiday card that says, "I appreciate you!" If your networking stops when you get a job, your contacts will feel used and abused. Look for ways to stay in touch and to give to them. Keep your network active.

Pass it on. As you notice what kinds of help are most important to you as a job seeker, take every opportunity to help others the same way.

Jan says, "My thank-you cards are every bit as important as my business cards. Appreciation is a rare thing in our rush, rush, gotta go society. I want people who help me move my job search along to know that I noticed and valued their efforts on my behalf."

Be creative. Mail a postcard, send a bagel and cream cheese, leave a voice mail message, send business their way, support their causes.

When Cheryl finally got that perfect job offer, the first thing she did was call her florist and have flowers sent to the offices of the four people who had helped her the most during her six-month-long job search. One manager had developed a long list of contacts as he was job hunting. When he landed a job, he called every single person on that list to share the good news.

New Job? Ace It!

What's your most important priority as you start a new job? Don't focus only on getting up to speed on the tasks you are expected to accomplish. Spend a significant amount of your time building relationships and setting up your network. That's the way to get off to a great start.

Index

About the Authors

We want to help you put more profit, purpose, and pleasure into all of your business relationships. We recognize the commitment and practice it takes to learn the skills in this book. Our solid-content, high-interaction presentations will show your attendees how to put these leading-edge networking skills to use immediately.

As nationally known experts on business networking, client development, and career management, we do keynote speeches and workshops for corporate, small business, association, franchise, non-profit, and government clients. Audiences rate them outstanding. Our client list includes:

▶ MotoPhoto

▶ Corning, Incorporated

▶ Allied Signal Aerospace

▶ Decorating Den

▶ Grant Thornton

▶ Builders Design & Leasing

▶ Executive Women International

▶ American Institute of CPAs

▶ American Society of Interior Designers

▶ The U.S. Departments of State, Agriculture, and Interior

▶ Midwest Association of Colleges and Employers

▶ American Society of Women Accountants

▶ U.S. Cellular

▶ Telcordia

▶ Booz-Allen Hamilton

▶ Sir Speedy

▶ Marriott

▶ Verizon

▶ Blue Cross/Blue Shield

▶ Rhone Mireaux

▶ Paradigm Mortgage

▶ Federal Laboratory Consortium

▶ American Bar Association

For information on our workshops and keynotes, visit us at *www.ContactsCount.com* or contact us.

Anne Baber
Baber & Associates
13433 W. 80th Terrace
Lenexa, KS 66215
Phone: 1-913-894-4212
        1-800-352-2939
Fax: 1-913-492-6575
E-mail: *ABaber@ContactsCount.com*

Lynne Waymon
Waymon & Associates
622 Ritchie Ave.
Silver Spring, MD 20910
Phone: 1-301-589-8633
        1-800-352-2939
Fax: 1-301-589-8639
E-mail: *LWaymon@ContactsCount.cor*